T0114312

THE
RISE
& FALL OF
ECW

THE

RISE

& FALL OF

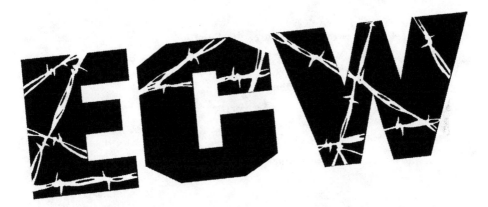

EXTREME CHAMPIONSHIP WRESTLING

THOM LOVERRO

WITH PAUL HEYMAN, TAZZ & TOMMY DREAMER

POCKET BOOKS

World
Wrestling
Entertainment®
BOOKS

New York London Toronto Sydney

POCKET BOOKS, a division of Simon & Schuster, Inc.
1230 Avenue of the Americas, New York, NY 10020

The Library of Congress has cataloged the hardcover edition as follows:

Loverro, Thom.
  The rise & fall of ECW: Extreme Championship Wrestling / Thom Loverro with Paul Heyman, Tazz, Tommy Dreamer.
    p. cm.
  1. Extreme Championship Wrestling—History. 2. Wrestling—History.
3. Wrestlers—History. I. Title: Rise and fall of Extreme Championship Wrestling.
II. Heyman, Paul. III. Tazz. IV. Tommy Dreamer. V. Title.

GV1195.L68 2006
796.81209—dc22
2006041619

ISBN-13: 978-1-4165-1312-4 (Pbk)
ISBN-10:   1-4165-1312-4 (Pbk)

This Pocket Books trade paperback edition May 2007

10 9 8 7 6 5 4 3 2 1

Designed by Jan Pisciotta

Visit us on the World Wide Web
http://www.simonsays.com
http://www.wwe.com

Manufactured in the United States of America

For information regarding special discounts for bulk purchases, please contact Simon & Schuster Special Sales at 1-800-456-6798 or business@simonandschuster.com.

To Paul.
Thanks.

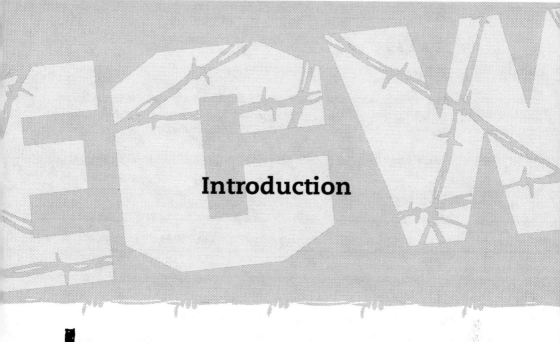

Introduction

If you had to select one word to describe what Extreme Championship Wrestling—ECW—was, it would have to be passion.

Long-lasting passion, if you happened to be at the Hammerstein Ballroom in New York on June 12, 2005.

What happened that night was a remarkable tribute to everything that made ECW such a passionate entertainment experience for everyone involved—the wrestlers, the support staff, and the fans alike.

It was *ECW One Night Stand,* a Pay-Per-View that paid tribute to ECW, and it was as if the year was 1995 again and we were back at the old bingo hall that served as the ECW Arena in South Philadelphia.

It had been four years since ECW had its last event, a show in Pine Bluff, Arkansas. Yet a sold-out crowd paying top dollar packed the ballroom on this June night to welcome back an old friend, and many more paid to watch it on Pay-Per-View.

From the moment Joey Styles came out to the ring to kick off the festivities, it was "Oh, my God!"—Styles's signature call as the ECW television announcer—from the first bell to the end of the final match. Fans were in the throes of what was basically a three-hour passion play, screaming at the top of their lungs, "ECW! ECW!" as if it was the response in a gospel mass.

They welcomed back many of their old friends—The Blue Meanie, Lance Storm, Justin Credible, Mikey Whipwreck, Sabu, Rob Van Dam, Francine—and many others who had given so much of their hearts and bodies to ECW, and still had something left to give to fans on this night, whether it was action in the ring—sometimes resorting to chairs, tables, ladders, and even cheese graters—or their words to the crowd. Van Dam, for example, told the crowd his time in ECW was the best of his career. Many other wrestlers who spent time in the promotion will say the same thing.

"There was no other experience like it," Francine says. "It was the best experience of my life. I would have worked there until I couldn't work anymore. I didn't care what offer came at me. I would have never left Paul and ECW. I was offered to leave a couple of times, and I would not go. I would have died working for that company."

That sort of passion was played out in the ring between wrestlers and in the crowd among the fans on a regular basis during ECW's glory days, and the fans tapped into that passion and showed their loyalty to ECW by their reaction to *One Night Stand*.

Of course, the "mad scientist" behind ECW was there as well, Paul Heyman, who gave a great shoot speech about what made ECW so special, and the fans showed their appreciation for creating this force of nature that had a huge impact on the wrestling industry.

A lot had happened since Heyman was invited in 1993 into this small Philadelphia promotion, which at the time was not much beyond a sports bar show. He had come into the right place at the right time to take his vision of wrestling and turn it into a reality. Three years later, Heyman had turned this tiny outfit into the white-hot promotion of the industry. It would eventually burn out, but not before becoming part of the cultural landscape for a generation of wrestling fans.

"If somebody got a ring and a show together, and Tommy Dreamer made a call saying, 'Guys, we're getting the band back together for a night in, let's say, Peoria,' guys would show up and wrestle like it was *WrestleMania*," observes Mike "Super Nova" Bucci, who was part of Raven's Flock and would team up with Stevie Richards and The Blue Meanie to form the Blue World Order.

ECW was just like that—it created memories to cherish for both wrestlers and fans.

Thom Loverro

chapter one

The Roots of ECW

To look at the history of ECW, it is important first to examine the history of the business itself, and the steps that led to the ECW phenomenon. It is particularly important in the context of the allure of ECW, because a good part of the attraction of the promotion was that it bucked wrestling tradition, going out of its way to distance itself from the practices of the past.

Wrestling was one of the first competitions men engaged in. They didn't need any tools or equipment, nothing except their hands to lock up with each other and start wrestling. Cave drawings of wrestling matches dating back an estimated 15,000 years were found in France, and early Babylonian and Egyptian reliefs show holds that are still used in modern times. Wrestling was one of the most popular sporting events in Greek society and was considered among the elite competitions in the early Olympics. The Romans helped maintain the tradition of wrestling, and it continued through the Middle Ages throughout Europe and the Far East, particularly as sporting entertainment for royal families.

When settlers came to America from England, they brought wrestling with them as part of their culture, but it was also already here, practiced among the Native Americans. It became part of the new American culture, and became more popular as German and Irish immigrants arrived in the new country. It began to take form as a professional spectator event at local carnivals, where a few wrestlers would fight each other and also challenge the crowd to see if any local tough guys could last, let's say, fifteen minutes in the ring with one of the professionals.

Even as professional wrestling grew to be a major urban spectator event in the twentieth century, it was still making the rounds on the carnival circuit in small towns, particularly in the Midwest. Some of the more popular wrestlers of the 1960s and 1970s even got their start in the carny shows. The legendary Sputnik Monroe tells this tale about his days wrestling at traveling carnivals and the wild and woolly situations wrestlers could find themselves in:

"One time I had a guy down with his arm up behind him, and I told him to give up. He said, 'I can't.' He didn't say it loud enough for everyone to hear, so I said again, 'Give up or I'll break your arm.' Everyone heard me, including the local sheriff, who threatened to shoot me if I broke this guy's arm. I said, 'He's gonna give up, or I'll hold him here until he starves to death.' I held him down until the sheriff counted to three."

Those carny roots are still deeply ingrained in the business, even today, as terms from those raucous days—*work, shoot, angle, mark,* and *kayfabe*—are still used today in the business.

The growth of the business, though, took place when contests started to take place in arenas and stadiums in big cities, the personalities in the business began getting acclaim and the attention of the press, and titles were created and recognized. The first generally recognized modern pro wrestling match came in Cleveland at the Central Armory in 1897, when Tom Jenkins defeated Martin "Farmer" Burns in two falls to win the United States championship. Burns would remain a major figure in the early history of wrestling, becoming a mentor for a young up-and-coming wrestling star named Frank Gotch, who excelled at the "catch-as-catch-can" wrestling style. In 1904, Gotch won the United States heavyweight title by defeating Jenkins, and four years later, perhaps the first superstar match in professional wrestling took place, between Gotch and the man who had become a European wrestling star, George Hackenschmidt, a wrestler with remarkable upper body strength who came into the bout reportedly undefeated.

The match, which took place before a large crowd at Dexter Park in Chicago, became one of the legendary contests in wrestling history, drawing national attention. According to reports, the match lasted more than two hours before Hackenschmidt finally surrendered. The *New York Times*, which covered the match, reported that Gotch "side-stepped, roughed his man's features with his knuckles, butted him under the chin, and generally worsted Hackenschmidt until the foreigner was at a loss how to proceed." Of course, since this was wrestling, there was controversy. After the match, Hackenschmidt charged that Gotch had soaked his body in oil, and that Gotch "dug his nails into my face, tried to pull my ear off, and poked his thumb into my eye."

Sounds like an ECW match, without the tables and chairs.

Gotch and Hackenschmidt met in a rematch in 1911, again in Chicago, at Comiskey Park, where another large crowd was on hand to watch Gotch win again, and again there was controversy and the sort of behind-the-scenes business that would always surround professional wrestling and eventually turn the sport into its current acknowledged status as scripted entertainment. Hackenschmidt had an injured knee and wanted to cancel the match. But it was such a highly anticipated event that promoters tried to salvage it with an agreement between the two wrestlers whereby Hackenschmidt would be allowed to win one of the three falls to save his reputation, but would go down in defeat to Gotch in the best two out of three falls match. However, Gotch is supposed to have double-crossed Hackenschmidt, winning the match in two straight falls. Gotch kept the United States title until he retired in 1913.

The next big star in professional wrestling was a Greek-born good-looking strongman named Jim Londos. He would be one of the stars to bridge the era where "shoot" matches—legitimate contests—began to disappear, and performers like Londos began to dominate the scene. He remained the business's biggest draw during the golden era of sport in this country, in the days of Babe Ruth, Jack Dempsey, and Bobby Jones. Londos was the first NWA heavyweight champion.

As football began to emerge as a popular sport, there were a number of professional players, who crossed over and wrestled, the best known being Hall of Famer Bronco Nagurski, whom Londos met in the ring. The other big star during from the 1920s and 1930s was Londos's nemesis, Ed "Strangler" Lewis, who worked for midwestern promoters and often defeated Londos, who represented the eastern promoters. Lewis, one of wrestling's biggest draws, had a public feud with Dempsey, demanding a match against the boxing champion. It never happened, but Dempsey did once referee a match at Chicago's Wrigley Field between Lewis, whose use of the headlock was so effective and controversial that the New York State Assembly tried to ban it, and Londos.

Former Dartmouth football star Gus Sonnenberg defeated Lewis for the world heavyweight championship in 1932, and Sonnenberg's style—he was known for the flying tackle—is believed to have started the trend toward more acrobatic showmanship and less use of strength and pure wrestling. Five years later, a young wrestler named Lou Thesz—whom Lewis would later train and manage—won the first of seven world heavyweight championships. Thesz, a well-known catch wrestler, or hooker, would go on to wrestle until 1990.

While all this was going on inside the ring, there was a man named Jess McMahon who was promoting a number of sporting events, including boxing at Madison Square Garden, and, among other ventures with his brother Ed, also owned several Negro League baseball teams, including the famous Lincoln Giants in New York. He would eventually branch out into promoting wrestling, and that part of the business would be nurtured by his son, Vincent Jess McMahon, who would eventually change the business and become one of the most influential promoters in the history of professional wrestling. At the same time, another wrestling promotion in North Carolina began to take shape—Jim Crockett Promotions. Other promotions popped up across the country, and eventually the most powerful ones divided the United States up into regions to conduct the business of wrestling, under the auspices of the National Wrestling Alliance (NWA), a group of independent professional wrestling promotions formed in 1948 under the direction of St. Louis promoter Sam Muchnick.

Another promoter who emerged as a force in New York was Toots Mondt, who would join forces with a young Vincent Jess McMahon to establish the dominant wrestling promotion in the northeastern United States, called Capitol Sports, in 1948, and would also join with the NWA that same pivotal year in the business.

Like most spectator events, wrestling suffered during the war years of the 1940s, but bounced back strong in the 1950s because it turned out to be the perfect show for the new medium that was sweeping the nation—television. Wrestling was made for television, and stars like Gorgeous George and Antonino Rocca emerged as TV stars. Vince McMahon, who saw the power of television, used it to syndicate wrestling shows throughout the northeastern United States, and eventually broke away from the NWA and changed the name of Capitol Sports Corporation to the World Wide Wrestling Federation (WWWF) in 1963. That same year, "Nature Boy" Buddy Rogers lost the WWWF heavyweight title to a young Italian star named Bruno Sammartino, getting pinned in less than a minute at Madison Square Garden, and a new era in wrestling was born.

While the WWWF grew in popularity under Vince McMahon, with Sammartino as his champion, wrestling flourished in other parts of the country as well. Amateur wrestling great Verne Gagne led the newly formed American Wrestling Association (AWA) in the midwest, featuring legendary wrestlers such as Dick the Bruiser and the Original Sheik (who was also a promoter in the Detroit area), while on the West Coast and in the South, various NWA-linked promotions were home to legends such as Freddie Blassie, Pat Patterson, Dory Funk, and Sputnik Monroe.

While the WWWF grew, Vincent Kennedy McMahon began working in the promotion and would eventually take it over from his father in 1982, in a move that would change the landscape of the business in ways that no one had ever seen before. Vince McMahon had a vision for his promotion that went far beyond the traditional way of doing business. He began expanding into other territories, turning the promotion into a national one, and took the use of television and the entertainment value of wrestling to a new level.

The WWWF became simply the World Wrestling Federation in 1979, and fell under the auspices of Titan Sports when Vincent K. McMahon took over. He had a plan to take wrestling into mainstream entertainment, and one vehicle for doing this was an idea for a mega wrestling show known as *WrestleMania*. On March 31, 1985, Vince McMahon put everything he had into one of the most successful ventures in the history of the business: *WrestleMania* at Madison Square Garden. The show featured matches between some of the greatest wrestlers of the era, including Andre the Giant vs. Big John Studd, and a main event consisting of Hulk Hogan and his tag-team partner, the actor Mr. T, who had played Clubber Lang in the film *Rocky III*—the same movie in which Hogan raised his profile beyond wrestling circles by playing a wrestling character named Thunderlips—against "Mr. Wonderful" Paul Orndorff and "Rowdy" Roddy Piper. McMahon added all sorts of entertainment touches that attracted new fans: baseball manager Billy Martin was the guest ring announcer, Liberace was the guest timekeeper, and Muhammad Ali was the guest referee. Pop singer Cyndi Lauper was also part of the show, helping Wendi Richter win the World Wrestling Federation Women's Championship from the Fabulous Moolah. In the main event, Hogan and Mr. T won, and Hogan was on his way to becoming one of the most well known

The first *WrestleMania:* Hulk Hogan with his tag partner, Mr. T.

and popular wrestlers in the history of the business. *WrestleMania* became an annual live Pay-Per-View event that set the standard for the new era of wrestling, and spawned numerous other wrestling Pay-Per-View events.

Two years later, *WrestleMania* had become something the likes of which the sports and entertainment business had never seen before. *WrestleMania III* drew 93, 173 people at the Pontiac Silverdome in Detroit. With Aretha Franklin singing "America the Beautiful," the show featured the historic showdown between Hogan and the great Andre the Giant, whom Hogan bodyslammed and then legdropped to win the match.

Drawing Pay-Per-View numbers that are often over one million buys, *WrestleMania* has been running now for twenty-two years. *WrestleMania XXI* was held in Los Angeles at the Staples Center, drawing more than 20,000 fans to the venue, and was seen in more than ninety countries. It is one of the most popular entertainment events in the world, and has helped turn the WWE, World Wrestling Entertainment, into a powerful media empire.

Success didn't happen without a fight, as WWE battled many entities along the way, including World Championship Wrestling (WCW), led by the powerful media honcho Ted Turner.

WCW originated from two companies operated by Jim Crockett Promotions—Georgia Championship Wrestling and Mid-Atlantic Championship Wrestling. In November 1988, Crockett sold the promotions to TBS Superstation in Atlanta and Turner, the flamboyant but visionary media mogul who created CNN. Turner had used wrestling shows as part of his programming for TBS Superstation, but he wanted to own the programming and expand it to his other network, TNT. He dropped the organization's affiliation with the NWA and created a new name for the promotion, World Championship Wrestling. With that, a new era of wrestling wars began.

WCW began raiding talent from other companies, wooing some of the biggest stars in wrestling, such as Hulk Hogan, Bret Hart, and Kevin Nash. And developed a stable of performers such as Sting and Ric Flair. Hogan turned heel while in WCW, with a storyline in which he joined a supposed invading renegade faction of WCW led by Kevin Nash and Scott Hall, called the New World Order—nWo.

WCW took on WWE head-to-head in what was known as the "Monday Night Wars," when WCW programmed a show called *Monday Night Nitro* against *Raw*. With former announcer Eric Bischoff running the WCW promotion, *Nitro* eventually passed *Raw* in the television ratings. *Monday Nitro* beat *Raw* in the ratings for eighty-four consecutive weeks. The rivalry grew so fierce that Bischoff challenged Vince McMahon to a fight on *Nitro,* and Bischoff put *Nitro* on a couple of minutes before *Raw* so he could give away the results of the taped *Raw* program, giving fans no reason to watch the competition. *Nitro* became a three-hour show, something never seen before in a live wrestling show.

But the tide turned when Vince McMahon developed a new generation of wrestlers that caught the attention of a new generation of wrestling fans, with stars like Triple H, Mankind, The Rock, and an outlaw rebel wrestler named Steve Austin, who became one of the biggest stars in the history of wrestling. WWE eventually won enough battles to win the war. Their storylines were fresher and more provocative, and WCW's proved to be stale and boring. Eventually, to the victor would go the spoils. *Nitro* went off the air in March 2001, and Vince McMahon would purchase what remained of the WCW, the last man standing in the battle of the 1990s in the business, and he remains in that position today.

In the middle of this war, another fighter rose up and lit a fire under the wrestling business, shaking both of these giants who had been battling for total control of the industry. It was lit in Scarsdale, New York, in the late 1970s, when an enterprising son of a trial lawyer, Richard Heyman, and a concentration camp survivor, Sulamita Heyman, wasn't satisfied with simply watching wrestling. Paul Heyman wanted to be near the show, around the show, part of the show.

Paul Heyman wanted to be the show.

By the age of 11, Heyman was an entrepreneur, collecting movie memorabilia and then selling them in a mail order business. "I used to collect movie posters, lobby cards, 8-by-10s and stuff like that," he said. "I opened up a mail order business with a P.O. box. I used to sell movie posters. I would go down to the city and buy them wholesale and then sell them through the mail."

By the time he was 13, wrestling had captured his heart. Shortly after midnight one night he was watching a show that competed with McMahon's; it was produced by Eddie Einhorn, one of the owners of the Chicago White Sox. "I saw Argentina Apollo and Luis Martinez, against Hartford and Reginald Love, managed by George 'Crybaby' Cannon," Heyman said. "At the end of this match, Argentina Apollo stole Crybaby Cannon's army helmet and smacked him in his big belly with it. Crybaby Cannon was crying in his corner as they went off the air. I thought it was the greatest thing I ever saw."

The next time he saw wrestling on TV, it was a McMahon show, and it featured an interview with "Superstar" Billy Graham. "I can't tell you what he said," Heyman claims. "It didn't really make any sense, but I didn't care. He was so charismatic. He came right through the television. He blew me away. It was an amazing moment. I thought he was great television, and I was hooked from that moment on.

"I sold out my inventory and bought some photo-developing equipment and a printing press, and started doing newsletters, called *The Wrestling Times*—'All the wrestling news that was fit to print.'"

Heyman kept trying to get access to wrestling shows as a journalist-photographer, and eventually hustled his way into what is now, looking back, a famous meeting between himself and the boss of the World Wide Wrestling Federation, the elder Vince McMahon. Remarkably, Heyman was only 14 years old. McMahon had little idea he was talking to the future of the business. But he must have realized Heyman was something special.

"Right after I turned 14, I called and asked for Vince McMahon," Heyman recalls. "I had a deep voice when I was 14 and sounded a lot older than I was. So I said, 'This is Paul Heyman, calling for Vince McMahon.' I guess since I had the attitude like I owned the joint, after about five people I got through to him. I was 14 and totally full of shit, with braces on my teeth and pimples on my face, and a whole lot of chutzpah."

Heyman said to McMahon, "Hi, it's Paul Heyman."

McMahon replied, "Who?"

"Paul Heyman, from *The Wrestling Times*," Heyman said.

"What can I do for you, Mr. Heyman?" McMahon asked.

"You told me to call you for a press pass for Madison Square Garden," Heyman said.

"I did?" McMahon asked, perplexed, since he didn't remember telling the young Heyman any such thing—with good reason, because he never had.

"Yes, you did," Heyman said.

So McMahon told Heyman to go to the second floor of the Holland Hotel in midtown Manhattan, where they had an office for credentials and other business, and ask for Arnold Skaaland, a former wrestler and manager and a long-time fixture at the WWWF, for a press pass.

Heyman took the train into town and went up to the second floor of the Holland Hotel. There he found Skaaland, smoking a cigar and playing cards with Gorilla Monsoon, a legendary WWWF wrestler who would go on to be an announcer. When they saw this 14-year-old kid with pimples on his face and braces on his teeth asking for a press pass, they laughed at him.

"Who told you to get a press pass?" Skaaland asked.

"Vince McMahon," Heyman answered.

"Okay, kid, I'll look for you," said Skaaland, winking at Monsoon about the joke.

But it was no joke. There was a VIP press pass there for Paul Heyman.

"Well, what do you know," Skaaland said, befuddled.

So on the night of the show, Heyman made his way into the Garden, wearing his press pass and carrying his camera. "A lot of the photographers already knew me because I had made such a pest of myself already trying to get in," he said. "They asked me, 'How did you get that press pass?' I said, 'I called Vince, Senior.'"

He began taking pictures, and took one particular shot of Andre the Giant and the elder McMahon talking in a hallway. "I knew that the McMahons had an affinity toward Andre," Heyman said. "They genuinely liked him and he genuinely liked them."

So the next time he saw McMahon, he had ready for him an 8-by-10 print of the photo.

Heyman walked over to McMahon and said, "Here, this picture is for you."

"Who are you?" McMahon asked.

"Paul Heyman," he replied, and McMahon sort of shooed him away.

A few minutes later, McMahon's public relations man, Howard Finkel, cornered this kid who had given McMahon the photo, and gave Heyman $50.

"Mr. McMahon really liked that picture," Finkel said. "Now see if you can stay out of sight and out of mind and confine yourself to the press locker room and ringside, and thank you for the picture. Do you mind if we use it in a program?"

Heyman said sure, use it. "I will send you a bunch more pictures," he told Finkel.

So the kid from Scarsdale began sending photos to the WWWF for use in their program, and he began to get to know people in the business.

"Any time I did photos for the programs, the deal was that I had to have an ad in there for my newsletters or fan clubs or whatever other businesses I was doing at the time," Heyman says. "I took ads out in wrestling magazines, and also got noticed by word of mouth."

Those around him recognized that Heyman had a style and manner well suited for the wrestling business, and started encouraging him to get on the inside of the industry. "I was always intrigued by the behind-the-scenes aspect," he said. "I loved how a show was put together. I loved the planning of it and the creation of the characters and the creation of an event and how a match was structured. I always wanted to produce and write and direct, more than performing. But I was getting noticed as someone who could talk fast and draw attention to myself, so I was getting nudged into the business."

Heyman, now 19 and a student at Westchester Community College, had a number of irons in the fire, none of them very conventional. He was working at the college radio station. He was also publishing several wrestling magazines. And he wound up doing public relations work for one of the most famous nightclubs of the eighties—Studio 54, the place where people went to see people and to be seen.

At the time, there was a promotion called Pro Wrestling USA, featuring a flamboyant wrestler named "Gorgeous" Jimmy Garvin. Garvin had the image of being this party hound, hanging out at all the hot spots from New York to Vegas and Monte Carlo to the French Alps. "I thought it would be great to take pictures of 'Gorgeous' Jimmy Garvin all around the hot spots in New York," Heyman says. "Even in 1985, the world's most famous nightclub was Studio 54. I called them up and had a messenger take over a bunch of my magazines. I said, 'Listen, this is an audience that you don't hit, and if you want to do Blue Collar Wednesdays or Friday Nights, I could promote it in the wrestling magazines. If you are interested, I could bring a wrestler. If not, we could go someplace else.'

"The general manager called me back and said, 'Yes, we would love to have you,'" Heyman remembers. "'Come by with your wrestler and take pictures, and we will do something with it.'"

He took Garvin to Studio 54 and did the photo spread, and the nightclub operators offered him a chance to take some photos for them, since their own house photographer was away for the weekend. While Heyman was there that weekend, Boy George came to town and hit Studio 54 with his lover, a cross dresser named Marilyn. Heyman could see that Boy George was under the influence of some substance, and alerted club management of a potential public relations disaster. The press got wind that Boy George was at Studio 54, and the paparazzi were on their way over.

"George was a mess," Heyman recalls. "He was barely conscious. I pulled the guy aside who gave me the job and said, 'If the media comes in here and sees this, you're going to look terrible. This guy is all messed up.' So we took George up to the VIP lounge upstairs and kept the media away from him.

"I told George when the night was over, I wanted two pictures of him and Marilyn, by the back door, which you can't tell is different from the front door because it has the same Studio 54 sign on it. 'I just want to take two pictures, and then no one will bother you all night long.'"

Heyman took the photos, developed them, and dropped them off at offices of the *New York Daily News* and the *New York Post*. He told photo editors at both papers that he wasn't looking for money or credit if they used the photos, which they did. He quickly got a call from Studio 54 managers who wondered how Heyman managed to get the publicity shot in the tabloids. "I told them I'm a hustler," he said. "I can do that for you all the time."

It was at Studio 54 that Heyman developed some of his promotional skills and his ability to connect with pop culture—something that would later serve him well in the wrestling business. He went from taking pictures to producing Friday night shows at the nightclub—concerts, record releases, parties, and the like. Heyman eventually worked his wrestling connections into club promotions, and created an event called the Wrestling Press International Man of the Year Award. Running about five magazines at the same time, Heyman made a deal with Jim Crockett Promotions and the NWA that if they could deliver Ric Flair, Dusty Rhodes, and Magnum T.A. to Studio 54 for this ceremony, he guaranteed he would get coverage in *USA Today*, in addition to the wrestling magazines he was running. So on Friday night, August 23, 1985, the marriage of Studio 54 and pro wrestling, with Paul Heyman presiding, took place. They had Ric Flair get the WPI Man of the Year award, and actually set up a ring in the nightclub for a match featuring a newcomer named Bam Bam Bigelow. It made a number of papers, and Heyman got the promotional itch. "I kind of got a taste for running a wrestling event and really enjoyed it," Heyman said. "I knew that to have any credibility in the business, I needed to be more than a magazine guy. Otherwise I am just a press guy trying to see the other side of the coin, instead of being an inside guy who knows how to do media."

One year later, though, Studio 54 closed down, and Heyman decided to get into the wrestling business full-time. So he became a manager, and Paul E. Dangerously was created. Heyman started out as the manager of the Motor City Madmen, a tag team on the independent circuit in the northeastern United States. He soon moved down to Florida and managed some wrestlers there, and quickly moved on to one of the hotbeds of wrestling and the home of the NWA—Memphis, Tennessee. And it wasn't very long before Memphis got a glimpse of the future of professional wrestling.

"I kind of got fired my first day," Heyman recalls. "They were kind of conservative, and I'm from New York and I'm not very conservative. I'm pretty liberal and extreme. Jerry Lawler pulled me aside and said, 'I want you to go out there and have that real New York attitude and tell people how you are going to take over everything.' I did it in a kind of crass manner, I guess. I told the story about Hotaling's News Agency, a famous newsstand in New York on 42nd Street. It has newspapers from all over the world. I talked about how I would go there and buy the Memphis *Commercial Appeal* and how Jerry Lawler is always written up as the big man in Memphis. Now that I have been down here for a day, and now that I have seen what this place is about and what Jerry Lawler is about, if Jerry Lawler is the big man in Memphis, no wonder I have encountered so many lesbians in the state of Tennessee."

In the Tennessee of 1986, that was just not done. "To me, it was nothing, a cheap joke, but to Jerry Lawler and Jerry Jarrett, I might as well have gone on there and talked in tongues," Heyman says. "They pretty much told me I was finished up the next day. I was advised, finish up tomorrow, go home Monday. I figured my last thing better be a bang, and I was sent out to the ring managing a guy then named Humongous, who actually ended up being a big star—Sid Vicious. I decided that they can't fire me if I can tear the house down. I did everything I could to drive those people into a frenzy, and by the time we were done, the whole Mid-South Coliseum was chanting, 'Paul E. sucks! Paul E. sucks!' I had the place rocking.

"When I got in the back Austin Idol pulled me aside and said, 'Why are you managing somebody else, you should be managing me?' I said, 'I think I am being sent home tomorrow morning.' Austin Idol assured me, 'No, no, nothing of the sort.' He walked into Jerry Lawler's office and said, 'I want the New York kid to manage me. I want Paul E. Dangerously to manage me.' The next thing you know, I am the top manager in the territory, and we are shaving Jerry Lawler's head and we are front-page news."

So Heyman was rehired and managed the team of Austin Idol and Tommy Rich. He helped fuel a feud between Idol and Lawler with a match in which the loser got his head shaved. Lawler lost, so they go about shaving Lawler's head in a sold-out Mid-South Coliseum in Memphis. "The place is rioting," Heyman says. "It took place inside a cage, and Austin Idol is thinking, 'We are never going to get out of this cage.' The cops couldn't get us out. Fans were barracading the cage. Tommy Rich was drunk. He had just flown in from Japan, and he had helped Austin Idol beat Jerry Lawler. He was too smashed to realize how much danger he was in. I'm 21 years old, these people are trying to kill us, and I am thinking, 'This is great heat. I have made it.' I am too young and stupid to realize that these people are really trying to kill me. People wait a long time, a lifetime in this business, to hit a moment like that, and three months in, I am in the middle of it. It was the right place and the right time."

Wrestling is, by nature, a transient business, and often, to move up, you have to move around. Heyman moved on to work for one of the major wrestling organizations, the AWA, run by wrestling legend Verne Gagne out of Minneapolis. Heyman was sent to Las Vegas to help run the AWA television shows being produced there. And this put him in the middle of the politics of the wrestling industry, which rival or in many cases surpass those of any other business in America.

One of the most popular tag teams in the NWA was called the Midnight Express—Dennis Condrey & Bobby Eaton—and they were managed by Jim Cornette, the high-profile manager and promoter of Smoky Mountain Wrestling. But in 1987 Condrey disappeared and was replaced by Stan Lane. Condrey later resurfaced and contacted some friends in the AWA and said he wanted to team up with a former tag team partner, Randy Rose. The two had teamed up before Condrey hooked up with Eaton, so Condrey wanted to call them the Original Midnight Express. The AWA wanted Percy Pringle, who would go on to WWE fame as Paul Bearer, the manager of Undertaker, as the manager for the Original Midnight Express. But Tommy Rich, who had just joined the AWA, told Gagne that they should use Heyman for the Original Midnight Express promotion. So Heyman flew to Las Vegas, where they would tape four weeks of television shows at once at The Showboat hotel and casino. Heyman was managing the Original Midnight Express, but he was on a short leash. If they didn't like him, Pringle would manage the tag team.

"I had one chance to impress," Heyman said. "I went out there and did everything I possibly could to tear down the house and say as many controversial things as I possibly could. After the first hour, they said I was hired. They were on ESPN daily back then, different versions of the show all spliced up. So I had a platform where in a promotion filled with guys who had been seen for the past few years, I am the freshest face. The ESPN time slot is on every day around 4 P.M., and I am there doing the most insane interviews I could. The

Dennis Condrey, Paul, Doug Gilbert.

AWA was so old school in its mentality. A manager would walk on and say, 'I want to discuss armbars and toeholds and headlocks and dropkicks,' and I am out there saying, 'I am walking down the street in New York and hanging out with my friend Jon Bon Jovi, and Bon Jovi has a song out now, called "Living on a Prayer," and that is exactly what our opponents are, living on a prayer if they think they can beat my men.' I would tie topical references in with politics or a sensitive issue, and would use it to my advantage. Anything that was a hot button in society, I would talk about. This was not done back then, and it made me stand out and drew a lot of attention to me."

Staying on the move, six months later Heyman went to work for a small promotion starting up in Georgia called Southern Championship Wrestling. He also helped open a promotion out of Chicago at the same time called Windy City Wrestling. It was there, at the age of

22, that Heyman got a chance to start booking wrestling shows—determining who won, who lost, who was used, how they lost, what they said, basically scripting the entire show. Heyman loved it. "The creativity was great," he remembers. "I was responsible for not just one segment of the show, but every segment of the show. It was fantastic. Here I am at 22 years old, I am telling these veterans who wins and loses, and why. Windy City Wrestling catches on fire, and we are selling out shows all throughout the Chicago area."

He was still working with Southern Championship Wrestling as well, and while in Atlanta, Heyman ran into a familiar face, someone he remembered from his days as a kid photographer hustling his way into wrestling matches—a wrestler with a magnetic personality and a great feel for the business named Eddie Gilbert.

Gilbert, the son of Tennessee wrestler Tommy Gilbert, broke into wrestling in 1979 as Tommy Gilbert, Jr., in honor of his father. He later changed it to Eddie Gilbert and became a popular wrestler in the Mid-South Wrestling promotion. In 1986, Mid-South changed its name to the Universal Wrestling Federation, and Gilbert added the nickname "Hot Stuff." He started to play a role as manager as well, and managed wrestlers like Sting and Rick Steiner early in their careers, as part of a stable of wrestlers called "Hot Stuff, Inc." He also began his career as one of the best bookers in the business, getting the most out of unknown and unproven wrestlers. The UWF was later bought out by Jim Crockett Promotions and the NWA, where Gilbert went to work. But he chafed under the controls there, and wanted the independence to book shows. So he went back on the independent circuit, working for the United States Wrestling Association and then the Global Wrestling Federation. He moved on to the Contintental Wrestling Federation in 1989, where he hooked up with Heyman, whom Gilbert asked to help him with the booking in the CWF. Heyman moved to Montgomery, Alabama, where he worked as Gilbert's assistant booker and still made trips to Chicago to run two or three popular shows monthly for Windy City Wrestling.

They worked well together, and when Gilbert got an offer to join the old Jim Crockett Promotions—which was now about to become

Gilbert vs. Cactus Jack.

World Championship Wrestling, with Superstation television owner Ted Turner buying the operation. Gilbert told Dusty Rhodes, who was booking for the organization at the time, that they should consider bringing Heyman in the promotion. Heyman met with Rhodes.

"I was offered two different jobs—they wanted to groom me to be the color commentator, and they also wanted me to do something shocking, to shake things up there," Heyman said. "They were losing talent to Vince at the time, like Tully Blanchard. The deal was that I would bring in my Midnight Express team against Cornette's Midnight Express. They would be the babyfaces and I would be the strong heel. We negotiated the deal, and on November first, 1988, I went to Atlanta

and did this very different type of storyline on television. My team, the Original Midnight Express, jumped Jim Cornette's Midnight Express."

It was at WCW that Heyman, as Paul E. Dangerously, developed that manager character and his signature gimmick—a cell phone. "Back then cell phones were big and cumbersome, weighing about fifteen pounds. I always had a cell phone in my hand. 'Where's the phone, where's the phone?' I would say. I would crack people in the head with the phone. I would be talking to Wall Street investors on the phone." On the Saturday night WTBS show, Heyman, as Paul E. Dangerously, hit Cornette with the cell phone and he was gushing blood.

Rhodes was eventually moved out as a booker, and Crockett took over. He started a booking staff, which was essentially a writing staff, with a promoter named Jim Barnett, a wrestler named Kevin Sullivan, Gilbert, and Heyman. It was too many cooks for Heyman, who was gaining a reputation as one of the industry's up-and-coming creative bookers. The politics of booking by committee caused dissension—Ric Flair would take over booking after a power struggle—and stifled creativity, and Heyman, whose style rubbed some of the old-school members of the business the wrong way, was gone from WCW in 1993.

This would be a turning point for Heyman, and for the industry as well. He was 27 years old and had been in the business, in one form or another, for fourteen years now. "I was burned out on wrestling at the time," he said. "I was going to get involved in New York radio. I had some offers. One of the things I hated about wrestling was that the guys who had been in it for a long time would bitch and moan and say they could have done this better or that better, and why don't they do this or that, but they never did anything to change the industry."

Around that same time, the culture of America was changing. A rock 'n' roll president, Bill Clinton, took office. Eighty people died in Waco when government agents attacked David Koresh and the Branch Davidian compound. A car bomb exploded in the World Trade Center underground parking garage—all signs of a changing, tumultuous world. Culturally, the country was also going through changes. Johnny Carson had left the *Tonight Show*, replaced by Jay Leno. The music scene was being influenced by the Seattle grunge movement and groups like Pearl Jam and Nirvana. Hip-hop music had also come onto the scene and was starting to shape the entertainment industry. And the wrestling business, after the growth of *WrestleMania* in the eighties, was in a down spin, the product having grown stale.

While Heyman was considering his future, Jim Crockett was considering starting a third wrestling company to compete against Turner and McMahon, and do something different, which appealed to Heyman. And Eddie Gilbert called again and told Heyman he needed him to help with an independent Pennsylvania operation, and Heyman could pretty much do his thing there as well. So Heyman began working with both operations.

Eddie Gilbert had moved on to Philadelphia to work with a local wrestling operation there run by a jewelry store operator and wrestling fan named Tod Gordon. Gilbert had started running shows at a variety of locations—Philadelphia's Original Sports Bar, the Chestnut Cabaret, the Tabor Rams Youth Association, and Cabrini College in suburban Philadelphia, Gordon's promotion—created from what was left of the Tri-State Wrestling Alliance—managed to get some television time on SportsChannel in Philadelphia, starting in March 1993. Gordon used local independent wrestlers who were willing to work for $25 or $50 a show, and then highlight it with an older "name" wrestler, like Don Muraco or "Superfly" Jimmy Snuka—the typical formula that kept independent promoters in business. They called the promotion Eastern Championship Wrestling, and aligned themselves with the NWA coalition of small-town promoters that still existed, although the NWA was a shell of its former self. Snuka, who was once a headliner for Vince McMahon and was known for his high-flying style, was their first heavyweight champion, crowned on April 25, 1992. Two months later, the Super Destroyers were named the Eastern Championship Wrestling World Tag Team Champions, and three months later they created an Eastern Championship Wrestling World Television Champion, Johnny Hotbody.

In May 1993, the promotion moved to what would eventually become its permanent home, a warehouse-style structure in an industrial section of South Philadelphia, just off Interstate 95, at the intersection of Swanson and Ritner streets, called Viking Hall. It was owned by the South Philadelphia Viking Club, the neighborhood mummers group that marched in the Philadelphia New Year's Day parade known as the Mummers Day Parade. They stored their mummers floats in the building, as well as holding bingo events there. Viking Hall would soon become a wrestling version of the Boston Garden, or the San Francisco Cow Palace—an old, rundown, legendary location that held a special place in the hearts of fans.

Gilbert managed to attract a couple of veterans to Eastern Championship Wrestling—Shane Douglas, who was well-known on the independent circuit but had not been able to make it big in the majors, and Terry Funk, a member of one of wrestling's royal families and one of those "living legend" type of wrestlers that fans everywhere recognized. Gilbert and Funk helped kick off the new home of ECW

Gilbert vs. Funk.

by engaging in a Texas Chainsaw Massacre match. But Gilbert was dealing with personal problems (he would die two years later of a heart attack) and would have a falling out with Gordon in August 1993. When Gilbert left Eastern Championship Wrestling, the company was without a booker, so Gordon turned to Heyman for help. Heyman was already committed to the new promotion being started by Crockett, but he made a deal to work with both. Heyman booked shows for Eastern Championship Wrestling, with the idea of developing stars and then moving them up to Crockett's national promotion.

Heyman thought of the ECW job as a temporary arrangement. "I told Tod I was on borrowed time, and this was what I was going to do," Heyman said. "I am going to introduce all these wild new characters with all these local guys. I want you to know that I am going to piss off your veterans, because they are all going to lose to the young guys. I plan, within a month, to have one or two veterans left. One was Shane Douglas, who was a veteran, but was only 29 or 30 years old and had been in all the territories. He had pretty much burned his bridges wherever he went. He had just come out of WCW, and started there under Eddie. I give him the name 'The Franchise,' because in a promotion filled with neither good guys nor bad guys, he will be the one real heel. I will make people hate him. He will be our standard bearer. He will end up being our true heel champion that people will pay to see get beat."

The other anchor of the promotion was obvious—Funk. "Terry Funk understands this business," Heyman explains, "and, as an old-timer, Terry Funk will sit there and say, 'Let me make that kid. Let me build up a feud with this kid and then he will beat me. And then I will go and fight that kid, and I will smack him around, and he will beat me.' Terry Funk will go through that whole locker room and end up making everybody."

He would do just that, because, for one thing, Terry Funk was made for eternity in the wrestling business. He had nothing left to prove. And he would do that because he had a love for the business and wanted to see a new generation move the industry forward. It was more than a business for Funk. It was his family's legacy.

Dory Funk, Sr., was one of the all-time greats. His two sons, Dory Jr., and Terry, followed their father, who became a promoter in the Amarillo area, into wrestling after both of them played football at West Texas State. Terry Funk made his pro wrestling debut on December 9, 1965, against Sputnik Monroe in Amarillo. He would eventually become world champion by defeating Gene Kiniski. Terry and Dory, Jr., became star attractions not just throughout the South, but in Japan as well for a number of years in the early 1970s.

Terry Funk came back to the States and defeated Jack Brisco to win the National Wrestling Alliance World Heavyweight Championship in 1975 in Miami, but would continue to be a presence both in the South and in Japan. In 1983, Terry announced his retirement from wrestling and went on a tour of Japan. His last match was to have taken place in Tokyo, when he and his brother Dory were matched up against Stan Hansen and Terry Gordy. Terry Funk even went as far as giving an emotional farewell speech, but for him to leave wrestling was akin to stopping breathing. Terry Funk returned to wrestle for All Japan promotions in 1984, and also appeared in World Wrestling Federation matches in the mid-1980s. He also began working in movies and television shows, a favorite of Sylvester Stallone, who cast Terry Funk in his wrestling movie *Paradise Alley* and his film about arm wrestling, *Over the Top*.

He continued to wrestle, promote, act, and serve as a commentator throughout the business. He faced Ric Flair in 1989 for the NWA World Heavyweight Championship, kicking off a lengthy feud between the two legends. One year later, Terry Funk, wrestling in the United States Wrestling Association, beat Jerry Lawler to win their version of the heavyweight championship, twenty-five years after he broke into the business.

Though he was one of the legends of the business and an established star, Terry Funk continued to work with independent promotions and began making appearances in 1993 in Eastern Championship Wrestling. He would be the foundation that Paul Heyman would use to build a promotion—a legend from the past to create a vision for the future.

Tod Gordon with Shane Douglas.

chapter two

Laying the Foundation

Paul Heyman always had a lot of the mad scientist in him—the type that was willing to experiment with different ingredients in the hope of creating something new and exciting. He had ideas about how to do this, but never had the sort of laboratory that Tod Gordon was offering him in Philadelphia. There weren't a lot of options for Gordon after his fallout with Eddie Gilbert, a talented but troubled booker. So when he turned to Heyman to salvage this small wrestling promotion, he had to live with the idea that it was not going to be business as usual.

The formula Gordon had used to date in Eastern Championship Wrestling—nondescript local talent with a washed-up name veteran to lure people in—was history. Heyman had a plan for the promotion to create its own stars. And he started right off the bat with the first match of the first night he was in charge, creating a new tag team. It turned out he hit a home run with his first experiment—The Public Enemy, which would turn out to be one of the most popular tag teams the business has ever seen. And it started with two small-time independent wrestlers who had bounced around the business—the least likely candidates to be wrestling superstars.

Ted Petty was a 6-foot-2, 250-pound, 39-year-old veteran of the Northeast independent circuit who had flirted with the big time, with tryouts in WCW and a handful of matches for Vince McMahon. But Petty was never able to make the leap, so he wrestled for small promotions in small towns and supplemented his income by renting out a ring that he owned. Like most wrestlers, Petty—born in Woodbridge, New Jersey, and a graduate of Rutgers University—had been through a variety of personas and gimmicks over his fifteen-year career, at one time wearing a mask and calling himself The Leopard Mask and later The Cheetah Kid.

Petty, who died of a heart attack in 2002, often traveled with his own opponent: Mike Durham, a 6-foot-3, 260-pound kid out of Compton, California. He used the name Johnny Rotten, and while he was not a particularly good wrestler, he put on a good show as a punk rocker. Heyman had seen the two periodically on TV shows, and also once in a match in Singapore, and thought the two would make a perfect fit for an idea he had flying back from Singapore in the summer of 1993. He had been reading a *Newsweek* article about the cultural changes taking place in America, and about the problems for young men in places like South Central in Los Angeles and Washington Heights in New York. "I read a line in that story that said today we live in an environment that for the first time ever, there are teenagers who are more afraid of living than dying," Heyman recalls. "That line blew me away. I thought we should get these two white guys to do a hip-hop routine where they come out dressed as hoodies, with the baseball uniforms and the hot look in 1993. Their catch phase would be 'Can't scare us because we're the first generation of American children more afraid of living than dying.' Even though one guy was 39 years old, he didn't look it. I called them not Public Enemy, which was the name of the rap group, but 'The Public Enemy,' which was the name of the James Cagney movie where he shoves the grapefruit into Mae Clarke's face."

Heyman saw something in both of these unknowns beyond what they did in the ring, and what he did with Ted Petty and Mike Durham was the blueprint for what he would eventually do with ECW. He made them stars in interviews. "These were two of the funniest guys you would ever want to meet," Heyman said. "But Teddy never showed you that side because, number one, he was never on television enough, and number two, he wore a mask. So I took the mask off him and gave him the name Flyboy Rocco Rock, like Snoop Doggy Dog, and Durham, instead of Johnny Rotten, I called him Johnny Grunge. They became Flyboy Rocco Rock & Johnny Grunge, The Public Enemy. They would do interviews that were just over-the-top ridiculous. They were funny as hell, and then they would go out to the ring and brawl their asses off. They would go over the rails, which at the time was a huge taboo. They used weapons, they used frying pans, baseball bats. This was the act that caught everyone's attention because it was so over the top. In the ring, it was like a riot. And the reason we did it was, they really couldn't wrestle. Teddy could wrestle a little bit. He could put together a nice ten-minute simple match—armbar, headlock, takedown, whip into the ropes, and he could do some nice flying moves. But he wasn't going to put on a five-star match. It wasn't going to happen. Johnny couldn't wrestle. He could just fight." The Public Enemy was born, and their main gimmick was tables, using them to hit people with and throw people through.

"The theory was that you accentuate the positives and hide the negatives, and I said to Tod, 'We are going to open the show with The Public Enemy.'"

Heyman continued to go through his memory bank and Rolodex to build his new stable of stars. He remembered another independent wrestler who had impressed him when they had crossed paths; he was going by the name of Tazmaniac.

Peter Senerca, who would later be known as Tazz to ECW fans, was a Brooklyn-born tough guy, a compact powerhouse at 5-foot-9 and 250 pounds who had worked as a bouncer and security guard. He grew up playing football and competing in judo, reaching a second-degree black belt. He was going to C.W. Post College on Long Island when, anxious to make some money, he quit because he saw wrestling as an easy way to cash in on his physical skills. "I was going to college as a physical education major," Tazz explains. "My dream was to be a high school phys ed teacher and coach football. Then, as I was going to school, I realized gym teachers didn't make a lot of money and I started thinking I could do wrestling. One thing led to another, and I started doing it."

So in 1990, Tazz signed up for a wrestling school run by veteran wrestler Johnny Rodz, who would train many of the wrestlers who would become ECW stars. They started at an old boxing gym in Brooklyn, then moved over to Gleason's, the world famous boxing gym. The same day that Tazz started, he met another first-day student—a very big man, at 6-foot-3, 290 pounds, named Alex Rizzo. He was going by the name Alexander the Great. ECW fans would get to know him as Big Dick Dudley, one of the many members of the Dudley family. (Big Dick Dudley passed away in 2002 due to kidney failure.)

"I thought I was going to conquer the world of wrestling," Tazz said. "I was immature, and thought I could just walk into the business and kick the shit out of everyone and just make it. It didn't work out that way, it took a lot longer than I thought."

Tazz started wrestling in shows in Puerto Rico, where Rodz had some connections. And, like most wrestlers who are trying to break into the business, Tazz wrestled on the independent circuit in the northeastern United States. Life in the indies can be pretty chaotic, as Tazz learned in his experience with one of the legendary old-school wrestling families, the Savoldis.

"I was getting booked for this company called IWCCW in 1990," remembers Tazz, who was working on building up his character at the time, The Tazmaniac. "The owner was a guy named Mario Savoldi, and it was based in Parsipanny, New Jersey. They called me on the phone and asked me to go to Westchester, where they were doing TV tapings.

I didn't want to just go and get beat by some old guy and hurt my future in the business. I said, 'Yes, I will go there, no problem.' But they had a reputation for guys coming in there to do jobs [lose], so I said I would come in, but I would wear a mask, because I didn't want to just do a job. They said, 'No, you don't have to wear a mask. We don't want you to do a job. We want to promote and push you.'" (A push is when a booker helps a wrestler become more popular with fans, usually through winning matches.)

"I brought the mask with me anyway, so I could wrestle then under an anonymous name. I get up there, and there are a shitload of guys in the locker room. I look at the list, and they were doing three hours of TV, three weeks of shows, one hour, one hour, one hour. I was scheduled to wrestle against guys that I knew I was not supposed to win against.

"So Tazz confronted one of the Savoldis there, Tom, and said, 'What is the deal, you got me doing a job here? I got no problem, I will wear a mask, but I can't wrestle under the name Tazmaniac. That is not going to happen. I am trying to get this gimmick over.' They said, 'No, no, no, sorry, there was a miscommunication. You have to come do the job like that.' They were trying to fuck with me."

Tazz refused to go out there without the mask. "They got pissed off and started yelling, 'Who the hell do you think you are?' and all that stuff. At the time I was a real hothead. I had a chip on my shoulder, and I didn't give a shit about anybody. I said, 'Go fuck yourself.' All the Savoldis were there, and I am ready to throw hands. I said, 'Fine, I'm leaving.' They said, 'Go ahead and leave, you'll never work in the state of New York again. We're hooked up with the athletic commission and all that.' I told them I would do it under one condition, and they lied to me. So I leave."

A few months later, Tazz got a message that Paul Heyman wanted to talk to him. Tazz thought it was some of his friends playing a joke. But after several missed phone calls back and forth, sure enough, Tazz got Heyman on the phone, and Heyman said he had been looking to book Tazz for quite some time, and he wanted to get him in on a promotion he was booking for in New Jersey—for that same legendary wrestling family, the Savoldis. Tazz said it was very unlikely that the Savoldis would want him anywhere near their promotion, and he explained why. But Heyman told him it wouldn't be a problem.

Tazz remembers Heyman telling him, " 'I know what happened. I know they don't like you. I'm in with these people. Don't worry about it. You're taken care of. If you have to walk, I'm walking with you.' I am thinking, this guy doesn't even know me, what the hell is he talking about? He is going to walk if I walk? Whatever. I needed the money, $100 or $150. So I ask him, 'You're going to push me, right?' He said, 'I promise, I give you my word. If they try any bullshit, I am out of there.' "

The show Heyman wanted Tazz for was in Middletown, New York. He rode up to the show with two wrestlers, one of them Ted Petty. "I knew Teddy had known Paul for years, so I asked, 'What's the deal with this guy? Can I trust him?' Teddy said, 'You can trust him, but Paul is a character. He is off the wall. But if he says he will stand by you, he will stand by you.' "

They get to this old, upstate New York resort, where the match is scheduled to take place in a ballroom. Tazz walks into the building with his fellow wrestlers and is approaching the ballroom when he hears screaming back and forth: "Fuck you." "Yeah, well, fuck you."

Tazz walks into the ballroom, and he sees Heyman and Angelo Savoldi going nose-to-nose in a screaming match. Sure enough, Heyman stood by Tazz. "He kept his word," Tazz said. "They took care of me during the match. At the time, winning and losing was important, or so we all thought it was. So I won my match, they paid me the money, and I thought this guy Paul was a stand-up guy. He was done there, but we stayed in contact by phone."

Heyman asked Tazz to come to ECW, where he debuted on October 1, 1993, against another well-known independent wrestler, Sabu.

"I want you to come in and wrestle this guy named Sabu," Heyman told Tazz. "Have you ever heard of him?"

"Yeah, I met him a few months before at an independent show in Minneapolis."

"Do you think you can have a good match with him?" Heyman asked.

"Sure, it will be a great match," Tazz replied.

Tazz was just saying what Heyman wanted to hear. "I had no idea if it would be a good match," Tazz said. "I was just trying to get work."

Heyman told Tazz, who was doing his Tazmaniac gimmick, that he wanted to make Sabu and get him over with the ECW fans. He also told Tazz he had a lot of open dates ahead, and if this match went well, he could expect some more work.

This was how one of the legendary feuds in all of wrestling was born.

Sabu vs. Terry Funk.

Sabu, whose real name is Terry Brunk, was born December 12, 1964, in Detroit. He was born into wrestling royalty, the nephew of Ed Farhat, a wrestling legend known as The Sheik who became a star attraction in the Midwest, using the persona of a wild man from the Middle East who used foreign objects to cut up his opponents, objects that many times wound up being used on him, as witnessed by the scar tissue The Sheik had on his forehead. His biggest claim to fame was the fireball that he would throw in the faces of his opponents to blind them.

The Sheik had brutal matches with all of the historic names of his time in the ring—Freddie Blassie, Bobo Brazil, Bruno Sammartino, Jack Brisco, Dory Funk, Jr., and many others, in arenas like Madison Square Garden, the Maple Leaf Gardens in Toronto, and the Olympic Auditorium in Los Angeles. His home field, though, was Cobo Hall in Detroit, where he was also a promoter. The Sheik would also go to Japan to run a promotion there, and had some legendary matches against the Funks there as well. He even had a brief run in ECW before retiring at the age of 74 in 1998. He died in 2003.

The Sheik also trained a number of wrestlers, including Scott Steiner, Rob Van Dam, and his nephew, Sabu. As a wrestler, Sabu would carry with him the old-school mentality of his uncle and a style that would also incite and excite fans—without flames shooting out of his hand.

"I wanted Tazz to come in and wrestle with this guy I saw in Japan called Sabu," Heyman recalls. "He had a real hardcore cult following because he had scarred up his whole body by diving into barbed wire. I looked at Sabu and was mesmerized by him. He had a total disregard for his own being, and he looks like he will fight you to the death. To me, in developing the aura of ECW, Sabu was the main key to it all, because here was a guy that we could put up his picture on television, and people would say, 'That's different.' So I called Sabu and hired him, with the promise that when Jimmy Crockett and I started up and went national, he was coming with me. We would go together and make something happen. I wanted Tazz to come in and make Sabu look great."

They both wound up looking great. "We tore it up," Tazz says. "We did some wicked stuff. After that, I was booked for the next six and a half years. I ended up being in the right place at the right time, wrestling the right guy. Sabu was not selfish in that match. We went about twenty-minutes, and we went berserk. It was the beginning, for me and for Sabu."

Heyman also picked Tazz's brain for other prospective wrestlers on the independent circuit to build a new stable for Eastern Championship Wrestling, and Tazz told him about a good-looking kid from Yonkers named Tom Laughlin, later known to wrestling fans as Tommy Dreamer.

"I wrestle him at all the Northeast independent shows and we have a pretty good routine down," Tazz told Heyman. "I can suplex this kid on his head every night and never hurt him. The kid is tough as hell and takes a beating like no one I've ever seen. He is a pretty boy, so you will have to toughen him up, but he can take a beating."

Born February 14, 1971, Dreamer was 7 years old when his father, a hockey fan, sat down one night to watch the New York Rangers face the Montreal Canadiens. But the game had been snowed out, so instead they ran wrestling from Madison Square Garden, and after watching Bob Backlund wrestle Bulldog Brower, Dreamer was hooked. He wanted to be a professional wrestler.

A solidly built athlete at 6-foot-2 and 260 pounds, Dreamer played high school football and one year of football in college, but he never lost his desire to become a wrestler, and would sign up to train with Johnny Rodz, the same trainer who had taught Tazz and other future ECW wrestlers. "I got my brains beat in two days a week, Mondays and Tuesdays," Dreamer said. "Then I started working the indies, like everyone did. I got a few tryouts with the World Wrestling Federation at the time. I showed up one day in the ECW arena and was booked ever since."

Dreamer wrestled Tazz in his debut and lost, in a match every bit as good as Tazz had advertised it would be. After that match, Heyman called Dreamer a few days later and told him to come to the studio in Paoli, Pennsylvania, where they were editing the show for television. Heyman sat down with Dreamer in the studio and they watched his match together.

Heyman pointed to the screen, specifically to four people who gave Dreamer a standing ovation after the match.

"Did you see this?" Heyman asked Dreamer. "These people believe in you. This is Philadelphia. This is something. You have it."

Dreamer dismissed Heyman's little pep talk, but at the end of that TV show, Heyman had it close out with this line: "Wait a minute, wait a minute. These hardcore, bloodthirsty fans of Philadelphia are giving Tommy Dreamer a standing ovation. Maybe there is hope for ECW after all."

This would be a battle that Dreamer would fight throughout his early days of ECW—getting fans to accept him. Eventually, that would come on one memorable night.

"The fans respected my wrestling ability, but this was the 1990s, and they couldn't get over that I looked like a Buff Bagwell type, the prototypical babyface," Dreamer explains. "They couldn't get over my looks. No matter what, they would heckle me because of my looks. I wore suspenders. I had a shiny robe. They wanted to like me, but this was Philadelphia, where you had the Broad Street Bullies, and I guess they doubted my toughness."

Heyman didn't have much there when he took over booking Eastern Championship Wrestling. But he did have one guy whose toughness nobody doubted—a 6-foot-2, 250-pound bar owner named Jim Fullington, who would be known as the Sandman. He grew up in the Philadelphia suburb of Broomall playing football, basketball, and baseball and, like most kids, watching professional wrestling on television.

"I always wanted to be a wrestler since I was a kid," Sandman observes. "In 1989, there was this guy named Joel Goodhart who started this little company in Philly called Tri-State Wrestling Alliance, and I went to one of his shows. He was opening up a wrestling school, so on March 6, 1989, I started at this wrestling school, and by June 9, I had my first match."

Goodhart came up with the name Mr. Sandman for Fullington from a billboard off Interstate 95 near the arena for a bedding company called Mr. Sandman. He was pushed as a surfer, wearing green neon pants and carrying a surfboard in the ring. It was getting him work—he got some matches in Memphis under Jerry Lawler's promotion there—but it really didn't fit his personality.

"Jim Fullington was a big guy who hung out in neighborhood bars with his friends, drinking, and getting into fights with each other," Heyman says. "The loser would have to pay for drinks. He was a guy that enjoyed fighting, and didn't take it personally. He was a salty guy."

Fans could see through the surfer boy image, and Heyman could see that nobody was buying into it. "The Sandman came out to the ring with a surfboard, with Beach Boys music playing," Heyman recalls. "And the crowd would shit on him. This would be like Mel Torme opening up for Pearl Jam. It wasn't going to happen. It was horrible. And he was for shit as a wrestler. He wasn't very good in the ring.

"But the guy had a look, and he had charisma. He would sit around my locker room, smoking cigarettes and being very polite, thanking me for the opportunity to work here tonight, saying all the right political things. Then he would let loose something like, 'I just want to wrestle my match, get out of here and get drunk.'"

One day, Heyman and Gordon were talking about what to do with the Sandman, and the idea came up to show the fans that locker room attitude. "I say to Tod, 'I've got to let this guy go. He is dragging down the show.' And Tod says, 'But it is a shame that he can't get this personality over to the public.' He would be sitting there in the locker room in those body-building pants, sweatpants with printed designs, a ripped-up T-shirt, and smoking a cigarette."

What happened after that—who came up with what idea—is a matter of debate. Sandman remembers, "Tod Gordon convinced Paul to let me come out drinking a beer, and then smoking a cigarette."

Heyman says he told Gordon, "Why can't we present that to the public? Why can't he go out there and smoke a cigarette and drink a beer and be a bum? People like that. That is half of our audience. Let's present this guy as a guy who comes on and says, 'You know what I did yesterday? I smacked my wife in the mouth, and without her mouth, how am I going to make a living this week?' I said to Tod, 'He will be a cult hero. And you could make him a heel or a babyface any time you wanted.'"

So Heyman sat down with Sandman and said, "This Beach Boys thing ain't flying. I want to turn you into a new character. I want you to be you, just be an embellishment of yourself."

Sandman was willing to give it a shot, if it meant he would keep wrestling. After all, it wasn't much of a stretch. But he didn't think it would have the impact that it eventually did. "I didn't think it would be as big as it was," he admits. "It would be real easy for me to say now I thought it would be that successful, but really, I was just happy I was wrestling back then. I didn't have a clue. I was new to the business."

He listened to a few people who were not so new to the business—Mick Foley and Terry Funk—and began to have faith in the character and develop it, particularly his entrance, a legendary performance to the Metallica tune "Enter Sandman." "They were the ones that showed me how I identified with the fans," Sandman explains. "I was the guy at the end of the bar, drunk, who wants to play you in a game of pool, and then when you beat me, I want to beat you up. Everybody could identify with my character. It was hard to identify with some of these other guys. Everybody wants to be the tough guy at the end of the bar."

And so ECW found perhaps its standard-bearer for the future of the promotion. "As much as anyone else, Sandman was the embodiment of Extreme Championship Wrestling," Heyman recalls. "He was a huge part of our shows, the whole music entrance and smoking cigarettes and drinking beer and smashing the beer can until he bleeds from the head before he ever starts the match. His matches became secondary. Here was just a tough guy looking for a fight. People loved him."

There was another wrestler who had just arrived at Eastern Championship Wrestling whom Heyman would utilize and probably get more out of than any other promotion Troy Martin has ever worked with in his long wrestling career. After all, in ECW, Martin—known as Shane Douglas—was called "The Franchise."

Douglas, born November 21, 1964, in Pittsburgh, began training to be a professional wrestler under the legendary Dominic DeNucci. He began wrestling in 1982 and would gain some attention as one of the stars of the Universal Wrestling Federation. He went on to WCW, as part of a team with Johnny Ace called the Dynamic Dudes, but that fizzled, and Douglas—a talented wrestler with strong opinions and ideas about the business and his career—returned to the independent circuit. As has been the pattern of his career, Douglas bounced back and forth between the smaller and larger promotions. When he was briefly with WWE, Douglas won the TV title but struggled to be noticed. Going back to WCW in 1992, Shane won the tag team title with Ricky Steamboat. A year later, shortly after losing the belts to the Hollywood Blondes—Brian Pillman & Steve Austin—Douglas left WCW again and this time landed in Eastern Championship Wrestling, where he quickly became heavyweight champion in the summer of 1993. He would prove to be one of the building blocks of the new ECW.

Heyman was building up the faces of the promotion. But he needed a voice—an important part of any wrestling show. Ray Morgan was the legendary voice of the WWWF, and then the young Vince McMahon became part of the identity of the promotion as an announcer. Gordon Solie was one of the most popular figures in wrestling in much of the South from his work behind the microphone. A young kid growing up in, of all places, Stamford, Connecticut—the home of WWE headquarters—wanted to be the next Gordon Solie, the next big voice in professional wrestling.

Joe Bonsignore—who would be known to ECW fans as Joey Styles—was born in the Bronx, but his family moved to Connecticut when he was in middle school. Around that same time, Styles saw his first wrestling match on a 13-inch black-and-white television in his bedroom—the Wild Samoans against the Strongbow brothers for the tag team title. "I was hooked after that," Styles says. "My dream was to be a pro wrestling television announcer."

Styles picked Hofstra University to go to college for two reasons: it had a strong communications program with their own television studio, and it was close to the offices of the Pro Wrestling Illustrated family of magazines. He hoped to get an internship there to get his foot in the door of the business. While he was going to school, Styles wrote for the school newspaper, worked in the sports information department, and got his wrestling magazine internship—which got him backstage to a WCW show. It was there he met Paul Heyman.

"I worked for SportsChannel New York one summer, and I took a tape of my work there and showed it to Paul, and he liked it," Styles remembers. So, not long after Styles graduated from Hofstra in June 1993, Heyman began assembling the ECW talent, and made Styles his new announcer.

"He was trying to get work as a heel commentator, and nobody would return his calls," Heyman recalls. "I told him, 'Listen, heel commentator you are not. But a play-by-play announcer, which you could be very competent in, you could be. Instead of using one of the retread guys, I want to use you. You are someone no one has ever seen before. And I want to come in with a whole different way of doing things. When you see something exciting, I want you to scream, and when we shoot you we will tilt the camera MTV style, and zoom in on you.'

"'I don't want your commentary to be like all the other guys,'" Heyman recalls telling Styles. " 'I want you to speak to the audience and not just yell at the audience, and when the match gets exciting, scream your head off. I want you to wait for things to happen. I want you to look at what everyone else is doing, and I want you to be different. I want you to wear the nicest suits you can find, but don't be arrogant about it. We are going to give you a different image than anyone has ever seen in wrestling before. You are going to be Bob Costas. You will have Al Michaels's enthusiasm and Bob Costas's professionalism surrounded by all this insanity.' I never wanted him to be part of the hype or part of the show. I wanted him to be the Rock of Gilbraltar. In the middle of all this insanity is the voice of reason, Joey Styles. I brought him into this small editing studio in Paoli, Pennsylvania, and we started to craft our TV shows for SportsChannel Philadelphia."

Heyman needed someone to help him produce a new version of wrestling on TV, something befitting the new cultural era the country had embarked on. Later on that first year, he found someone in New York: a 29-year-old production whiz named Ron Buffone—who didn't know a lick about wrestling when he met Heyman.

"I grew up in the Bronx, and was not a wrestling fan," Buffone admits. "I hated it. I went to Iona College. I was majoring in computer information and sciences, and I hated it. I was in a band, and the band needed a music video. I took a couple of broadcasting courses, and did the music video for the band, and thought this was pretty cool. I could get into this. So I changed my major and graduated from Iona in broadcasting. From there I started my own company."

He would meet Heyman, who was looking for all new faces for ECW, both at the microphone in front of the camera and in the studios, and Buffone fit the bill—eager and looking to get in on the ground floor of something special. "When I met Paul, he was very personable," Buffone says. "He came with a couple of T-shirts and hats, and said, 'You guys hungry? Let's get some Chinese food.' So I liked him instantly. He gave me free shirts and hats and fed us. At the time, I didn't know who he was. I had never heard of him from WCW or anything. I learned all about what he had done afterwards. Paul has a million stories, and I would hear all these stories, and would be laughing behind his back sometimes after he left at some of his stories, like, yeah, right, because they were so hard to believe. Then I learned in the years I was in the business and started meeting the people he was talking about, I found that those stories were true."

Buffone had converted his old bedroom in his parents' home in Pelham Manor, New York, and eventually the ECW production work would move from the Paoli studio. They would hang an ECW banner on the wall of the Buffone basement family and run Styles through his voice-over work on the shows, and this small unit would start producing revolutionary work in the wrestling business.

"Productionwise, Ron Buffone is amazing," Heyman says. "He and I would fight from day one, and you would think we were going to get into a fistfight, nose to nose, but they were all productive because we loved each other so much. I would say something like, 'Let's build this music video and let's change the tempo of this to match that, and I need the whole screen to shake.' He would spend twelve hours, without me there, creating this effect where the whole screen would shake.

"I would say, 'Let's do that with The Public Enemy,' and he would say, 'No, they never shook things up, Shane Douglas shook things up, let the shake be on Shane.' I would say, 'Okay, I understand that, but this is why I want it with The Public Enemy,' and he would say something like,

'If it is going to be The Public Enemy, shouldn't it not only shake, but shouldn't the whole thing turn upside down?' Anything that I envisioned in video, with about $150,000 in equipment when these hip-hop artists were using multi-million-dollar studios, Ron Buffone could match anybody. He was a genius, and putting me and Ron in the same room to discuss producing a television show was dangerous. I was changing television as much as I was changing wrestling. We are doing more videos and effects and different graphic packages, and from the shitty little graphics package that Ron has, he is putting on graphics that match the NFL's graphics, with a $1,500 kit. The guy was amazing in terms of what he could pull off, productionwise."

Styles remembers with fondness the simplicity and uniqueness of their production work in the Buffone household: "You would do some work in the studio, then maybe walk over into the kitchen and read the paper. Ron's mother and father, who owned a restaurant for many years, would cook some of the greatest Italian food I ever had. Then we would go downstairs to the basement and do our on-camera work. There was a banner behind us, and I was looking at Paul Heyman sitting in a plastic lawn chair, with an ironing board as a table, with notes, telling me, 'Okay, I need a sixty-second on-camera saying this, or a thirty-second on-camera saying this,' and I would go ahead and would nail it. The show would be built through the night, or during the day while I was at work. I was going to either come in first thing in the morning, at five A.M., or be there seven at night after work, depending on when they got done. I would come in and do the voice-over first, and then with the holes left in the show, I would go downstairs and do my on-camera work and they would be inserted into the show as I would leave and sprint to catch the train to my regular job. A lot of times I would go in at about eight at night and work through the night, then wash my face and brush my teeth and go to my regular job with no sleep. That was the way it worked for years."

Heyman's first Eastern Championship Wrestling show was called *Ultraclash*, on September 18, 1993, at the ECW Arena in Philadelphia, before a crowd of more than a thousand fans who got a small taste of the future of wrestling.

In that show, Terry Funk and another wrestling legend, Stan Hansen, beat two other veterans, Kevin Sullivan & Abdullah the Butcher, by disqualification in a Bunkhouse match; Headhunters beat up Miguelito Perez & Crash the Terminator in a Baseball Bat match; The Public Enemy defeated Ian Rotten & Jason Knight; Tony Stetson retained the Pennsylvania Heavyweight Championship with a win over Tommy Cairo; Sal Bellomo beat Richard Michaels in a Strap battle; Super Destroyer #1 defeated Super Destroyer #2 in a Mask vs. Mask match; The Dark Patriot defeated JT Smith in a Scaffold match; Tigra won a Battle Royal; and Eastern Championship Wrestling Champion Shane Douglas beat Sandman to keep the title.

Heyman's influence on the show would be more apparent in the next promotion, a two-night event called NWA *Bloodfest, Parts 1 and 2*. There were not as many people in the crowd at the ECW Arena on October 1 and 2 for those shows, but they got a better look at Eastern Championship Wrestling, Paul Heyman–style.

About three hundred people saw Rockin' Rebel pin Richard Michaels; Malia Hosaka beat Molly McShane; Paul Diamond & Pat Tanaka, known as Bad Company, defeated Ian & Axl Rotten; Tony Stetson & Johnny Hotbody kept their Eastern Championship Wrestling Tag Team titles by beating Bad Company; The Public Enemy, Rocco Rock & Johnny Grunge, defeated Silver Jet and Gino Caruso; Sandman pinned Metal Maniac; Abdullah the Butcher, Terry Funk & JT Smith beat Don Muraco, Jimmy Snuka & Kevin Sullivan; then Sullivan and the Butcher fought to a double disqualification. Funk pinned Snuka in a Steel Cage match to win the Eastern Championship Wrestling TV title, and, in one of the most talked-about matches, Sabu pinned Tazz, still known as Tazmaniac.

One night later, back at the ECW Arena, Sullivan beat Abdullah in a Steel Cage match; The Public Enemy defeated Ian & Axl Rotten and Bad Company in a Triangle Steel Cage match; then Bad Company beat The Public Enemy in another tag team bout, and the Rottens defeated Don Allen & Chad Austin; Tony Stetson & Johnny Hotbody beat Sandman & JT Smith to retain the tag team titles; Sullivan pinned Caruso; Sir Richard Michaels beat Rockin' Rebel by disqualification; Snuka pinned Austin; Tazz pinned Tommy Dreamer; and in two ECW Heavyweight title bouts, Champion Shane Douglas defeated JT Smith by disqualification to retain the title, and Sabu pinned Douglas to win the title.

Though the crowds were not big, these shows were all about the TV product that Heyman was about to launch. "We just changed the way everything is done in Philadelphia," Heyman says. "We blast out Sabu. We blast out Tazmaniac. We do a match where Tommy Dreamer loses to Tazmaniac, but he took such a beating and kept kicking out, and taking a beating and kicking him out. It was an hour of television where every single segment, the bad guy won. We are heading toward our formula that there really are no bad guys or good guys, just guys that people will pay to see. But we had to do this slowly. So in every segment the guy that they didn't want to win won. In the final match Tazz wins, but it took such a beating to beat down Dreamer, that as we are going off the air and the music is winding down, the audience gives Dreamer a standing ovation.

"Joey Styles did all of his commentary in postproduction with my direction," Heyman recalls. "I knew the images we wanted to portray. It was all about getting over the letters ECW, you are watching ECW, this is ECW, and Joey has the line, 'On a night when nothing went right, on a night where so many heroes fell from grace, Tommy Dreamer, even in losing, has shown more dignity than anybody else here in this bingo hall tonight. Maybe there is hope after all.'

"For some reason, that resonated, and people just started calling the hot line and flooding us with requests," Heyman says. "People went nuts over this TV show, which was something they hadn't seen before in wrestling. We had no formula for TV. I wiped the slate clean on formula. I put on the best sixty minutes that I could produce every week, in whatever way we could, and because we were postproduced, that means that I could tape a match and never air the match. I could make it into a music video. I would splice together highlights of a match with a video, and air it, so you get to see the wrestlers in a different light.

"We did something different that is revolutionary to this day, and nobody understands how we did it, called the 'Pulp Fiction,' and the reason it was called that is because it always came back to that original premise," Heyman says. "We would shoot after the show, six hours worth of interviews, and I would chop them up. So you come into an interview segment, and we did our interviews different from what had been done before. I gave them thirty interviews, all jammed up, so it would be something like, 'Hi, I'm The Franchise, Shane Douglas, and don't forget, I'm coming down on November thirteenth, and my opponent, I'm going to kick his ass and you're going to like it,' and then boom, I would go to his opponent, in a totally different setting, and he would attack Shane Douglas . . . then I would go to The Public Enemy and they would say something like, 'Oh, Johnny, what are we going to do on November thirteenth? I don't know. Rocco, it is going to be a great fight,' and boom, you go to someone else, and they say something like, 'I don't like Philadelphia cheesesteaks,' and boom, you go back to Shane Douglas. You chop up these interviews and everybody is in different locations. These could go anywhere from six minutes to fifteen minutes on any particular subject, and everybody would have face time on television. Usually, it would only be the top stars who had face time on television. Well, then how do you get your young guys out there? So Tazz would talk and Dreamer would talk, and everyone would have air time."

One time, Heyman aired a thirty-minute sitdown interview, documentary style, with Shane Douglas about his career and ambitions—totally out of wrestling character. "I want to be known as 'The Franchise,' and I will have to prove myself," Douglas said. This show ran for thirty minutes in a sixty-minute show, without commercials.

"At the time, wrestling was trying to be such professional television that it was such a standard formula," Heyman says. "We kicked that out of the window. We come back from a break, and who knows what you were going to see? You might see an interview, a match, a music video, you never knew. We intentionally threw formula out the window and intentionally every week gave you a totally different type of show than what you saw the week before. The only thing that was consistent was that it was episodic—the storylines continued week to week. This guy is on a winning streak, this guy is on a losing streak. This guy is stalking this other guy's girlfriend, this guy's girlfriend is talking to this other guy. The storylines were consistent and long-term, but the formula for the show was Coke one week and Sprite the next."

Heyman held his first supershow—*November to Remember*—on November 13, 1993, at the arena, with a crowd on hand of about a thousand people. Sandman and Jim Neidhart fought to a double disqualification; Kevin Sullivan beat Tommy Cairo in a Shoot match; Johnny Hotbody & Tony Stetson defeated Ian & Axl Rotten to retain the tag team title, and then Johnny Gunn & Tommy Dreamer beat Stetson & Hotbody in a double pin to take the tag team title; in a singles match, Mr. Hughes pinned Johnny Gunn; Malia Hosaka beat Sherri Martel by disqualification; Salvatore Bellomo defeated Rockin' Rebel in a forfeited Chair match; The Public Enemy beat Bad Company in a South Philly Hood bout; Tazz pinned Tommy Dreamer; and in an Eastern Championship Wrestling Television title match, Sabu & Road Warrior Hawk defeated Terry Funk & King Kong Bundy, and when Sabu pinned Funk, because of stipulations made before the bout, Sabu won Funk's title.

"We did a thing where Sabu ended up beating Terry Funk for the heavyweight title," Heyman recalls. "I went to Funk and and asked him, 'Who do you want to make?' And he said, 'I want to make Sabu.' And he says, 'I want to make Shane Douglas, too.' I didn't take it that we would make one guy first and the other. I figured Terry was so great, we could make them both.

"There would not have been an ECW without Terry Funk," Heyman states. "He was the only veteran from that era who had the reputation of being legitimately tough, but also had the business sense that, 'I've got to get the next generation ready for there to be a business, for there to be an industry for me to leave something behind to.' Terry had that mindset. A lot of the veterans back then were unwilling to get the young guys ready, a lot of the veterans were still clinging and clutching to their spots . . . I want to be 'the' tough guy, I want to be 'the' champion, 'the' top guy. Terry Funk said, 'I can make him, I can make him, too . . . Let me make him, I'll do something special with him,' and he did, with everybody he worked with."

Once Sabu beat Funk for the title, Shane Douglas went on the Eastern Championship Wrestling show and called Funk out.

"Let's get one thing straight," Douglas said before the camera. "I am the number one contender. I'm young. I'm good-looking. I'm The

Franchise. I'm not some old guy like Terry Funk, hanging on. I'm not some guy clinging to the last vestige of my career."

Funk walked on and said, "Don't ever disrespect me again. You may think I'm like all these other old guys, but I will smack you in the mouth." Funk then proceeded to slap Douglas around on the show, which set the stage for Eastern Championship Wrestling's next event, *Holiday Hell*, on December 26, 1993. With about a thousand people at the arena, Mr. Hughes beat Sandman; Rockin' Rebel defeated Don E. Allen; Kevin Sullivan & Tazz beat JT Smith & Tommy Cairo to retain the tag team titles;

Sabu taking it to Funk once again.

Chad Austin pinned Pitbull #1; Pat Tanaka pinned Rocco Rock in a Body Count match; Shane Douglas pinned Tommy Dreamer, who then later won a Lights Out Battle Royal; and Sabu beat Funk—with a little help—in a no-disqualification bout to win the ECW heavyweight crown.

"It's Sabu vs. Funk again for the title," Heyman recalls. "This time, just as Terry Funk is about to win the championship, Shane Douglas comes out and knocks him out. Shane Douglas knocks out Terry Funk, and Sabu wins the match. Now we go on TV and find out that this enraged Sabu, because Sabu's uncle was the Original Sheik, who trained both Sabu and Rob Van Dam. Joey Styles told the story. Sabu is furious because the one man that the original Sheik could never beat was Terry Funk. And here was Sabu, going to beat Terry Funk all on his own, and Shane Douglas is going to take credit for it. So Sabu is looking for Shane Douglas. And Terry Funk has been deprived of his title, so he is looking for his title. And Shane Douglas is pissed at Terry Funk because Terry Funk embarrassed him, and he is also gunning for Sabu because Shane Douglas wants the title."

The tension is building between Sabu and Douglas. "We do a TV taping the first week of January," Heyman says. "There was this huge blizzard, and we had to offer free beer and hot dogs just to get a hundred and fifty people into the building. It was a free taping, free beer and free hot dogs on a Sunday afternoon, with nine inches of snow out there, and we only got a hundred and fifty people. But we gave them a forty-five-minute match between Shane and Funk in which both guys were just covered with blood, and nobody wins—which we never did, because from the moment I took over, there was a winner and a loser in every match. We didn't do disqualifications, we didn't do countouts, because I hated that, and if we did, it meant something. Here we were, four months in, and we did our first nonfinish. When the match was over, we had Sabu attack them both."

That December *Holiday Hell* match was noteworthy for one other reason—it marked the major show debut of a 6-foot-6, 270-pound wrestler from Tampa with a Hulk Hogan connection named Mike Alfonso who would come back years later and become ECW Champion Mike Awesome, who pinned Randy Starr.

Paul with Mike Awesome.

"I watched professional wrestling as a teenager," Awesome said. "I was always interested in it. My Dad's sister married Hulk Hogan's brother, and they produced a son who was about a year younger than me, my cousin, Horace Hogan, who also wrestled and whose real name is Michael Bollea. He and I grew up together. Because his uncle, Hulk Hogan, became a popular wrestler while we were in high school, my cousin got interested in it. We talked about it, and it got me interested in it."

So Awesome began training with Steve Keirn in Tampa, and made his debut on February 26, 1989, at the Eddie Graham Sports Complex in Orlando. He would eventually wind up in Japan, which is where he found his ECW connection. "I was working in Japan, and so was Sabu," Awesome recalls. "We became friends, and he started working with ECW. He came back to Japan and told me, 'Mike, there is this company, it is really cool, and you have to work there.' I was pretty busy in Japan and not really that interested in it. But he finally talked me into it. I used my own frequent-flier miles to go to Philadelphia and wrestle an ECW match. After that, Paul agreed to use me." Awesome would leave ECW and then come back, as did many wrestlers over the years.

The seeds were being planted for change in 1993. They began to take root the next year.

chapter three

Going Extreme

There was a momentum building now in Eastern Championship Wrestling for something special to happen, centering on the heavyweight championship and the three stars involved in the developing storyline. Terry Funk is looking for Shane Douglas. Funk is looking for Sabu. Sabu is looking for Douglas, because Douglas stole the title, and Shane is looking for both. So for the February 5, 1994, show at the ECW Arena in Philadelphia, Heyman came up with the notion of doing a three-way match, or what they called a three-way dance—three wrestlers battling each other in the ring. Typically, in such a match, the first wrestler to score a pin on somebody wins. Heyman came up with something different, and it would forever be known as *The Night the Line Was Crossed*.

"Three guys start, somebody gets eliminated, and then the two survivors fight it out until there is only one winner, so you are guaranteed two losers and one winner in one match," Heyman explains. "Usually these matches were done in Mexico. It was more of a Mexican specialty. Sometimes they were very exciting, and usually they were a real clusterfuck. But now, my concept was, with these three guys, let's make this different than any other three-way match that anyone has ever seen. Besides the fact that we are going to have two losers and one winner, what else can we do?

"The theory was that when the match was over, Sabu would be a cult hero, Funk would continue to be the legendary hardcore hero, and Shane Douglas would emerge as the one hated guy in ECW, and since he was our champion, that was the way I wanted it. The only way to do it that I could think of and the only way to shock people and the only way to create a worldwide buzz and get press in Japan and all over the Internet and let everyone see that it took a lot of balls to do—I took three heels, turned two of them in one match babyfaced, made one guy the heel of the promotion, and put the title on him. My figuring was to have no falls in the match. Go the complete hour and do a draw. It could be a great match, you could have that whole place going crazy at the end." (A match with a time limit that plays to a draw is called a Broadway.)

The match turned out to be more than Heyman and Tod Gordon and everyone in Eastern Championship Wrestling could hope for—a pivotal first step for the new era of wrestling.

"The whole night was amazing," Heyman says. "Everything clicked. It was one of those shows where everyone was on their game, and the audience was going nuts and loving every moment of it. Then we had that match. They wrestled a brilliant match, and we layered the match so at the end you would be cheering for the two guys and dying for someone to beat Shane. The last 30 seconds the people were on their feet going crazy, and when the bell rang and people had just realized they saw a sixty-minute match, the whole building just stood up, and instead of chanting, 'Sabu! Sabu!' or 'Terry! Terry!' everyone chanted, 'ECW! ECW!' It was one of those moments in life where everyone understood something special happened. After all this hard work, we were an overnight sensation. As the audience chanted louder and louder, 'ECW! ECW!' we all realized we had just hit it."

The promotion quickly capitalized on the event. The TV show featured all the chanting and celebration after the match, with Styles offering the perspective on the night: "For those of you who were not at the ECW Arena this past Saturday night, you may have missed what many are now calling the greatest wrestling match to take place in this country in quite some time. Forget the stupid gimmicks. Forget the showboating for the camera. Wrestling has returned to the United States of America."

A press conference was held after the show, with twelve Japanese photographers on hand, and flashbulbs going off. Funk appeared before the cameras, his face covered with blood.

"I love this more than I can tell you," Funk said, breaking down and crying. "My father died in the ring. My family has owned the Amarillo, Texas, territory for years, and I have always wrestled to earn a living, but no promotion has ever captured my heart like this one. I love ECW with all my heart. I love the ECW fans. I love the ECW promotion, and I love all the young guys in the back who have fire in their eyes that is unmatched."

A few minutes later, Shane Douglas came into the press conference. Appearing before the camera with Styles and Gordon, Douglas, wearing a Pittsburgh Steelers hat, standing there with Sensational Sherri Martel, let his feelings be known, blasting with both barrels: "I've got a couple of words for you. Tonight I took the so-called self-proclaimed Terry Funk, and I beat his ass right in the center of the ring. I took Sabu, the crazy man of wrestling, and I beat his ass in the center of the ring. I sent them both back to the dressing room, Mr. Gordon. As a result of that, I want you to declare me right now in front of this TV camera, in front of the entire world, as the ECW Heavyweight Champion—to prove I am The Franchise. Sherri, you saw it, the whole world saw it. Philadelphia, you witnessed it live. Professional wrestling as it was meant to be—ass-kicking, take no names, beat the hell out of whoever is in front of you. Terry Funk, I smashed your knee to oblivion. When I took you with that chair outside of the ring, even the crazy man Sabu and his people looked at me and said, 'Oh my God, it's the end of an era, finally put to rest the Funk family.'"

Tod Gordon tried to interrupt Douglas, but he pressed on: "You keep your mouth shut. You can fire me if you want to, you can take me out of this territory if you want to. But you can't stop The Franchise. Someplace, sometime, I will be heavyweight champion."

Funk walked in and said, "I don't understand what you are doing. We all walked into this match with a reason for the audience to hate us. And when the match was over, everyone chanted, 'ECW!' Didn't you feel that magic? Aren't you proud of yourself tonight? Why are you being such a jackass?"

Douglas looked at Funk and said, "You know, you're right. I feel terrible about myself. And as a matter of fact, my conduct is not befitting a champion. And Terry, I want to hand you this title belt."

Douglas handed Funk the title belt, and Funk acted like he didn't know what to do with it. He said, "Why are you doing this?"

"I'm only handing you the title, you old piece of crap, because I know how much pleasure I will get taking it back from you," Douglas replied.

Funk took the title belt and threw it in Douglas's face, and Douglas smacked Funk. They got into a big fight, and everyone went crazy.

"It was such a realistic-looking press conference, and everybody bought into it," Heyman recalls. "Now, that is where 'The Line Was Crossed.'"

It was vintage Shane Douglas—angry at the powers that be and the slights he felt he had been dealt during his career.

"Shane Douglas was pissed off at WCW and Ric Flair and would say anything on the mike and vent his frustration with the industry," Dreamer explains.

He wasn't the only one who was frustrated over the business. "If you watch early ECW, Paul Heyman was pissed off and hell bent to take down WCW," Dreamer states. "I believe when Paul left WCW, he was actually supposed to come and do the whole Paul E. Dangerously for Vince, but he was just waiting, and then he started with the whole ECW thing. Paul had painted Eric Bischoff and WCW as the most vile people and organization that you could ever work for. You were joining the Taliban if you joined WCW and Eric Bischoff. Eric Bischoff was Satan."

Heyman doesn't dispute that view of WCW: "I didn't like them and they didn't like me. I didn't like the way I was treated. They didn't like the way I treated them back. I pretty much told them to go fuck themselves when they were treating people like shit. And I don't think they enjoyed that. This was during the Bill Watts administration, and Bill wasn't really a people person."

After *The Night the Line Was Crossed*, there was more reason to look toward the future than to live in the past. Dreamer says you could tell that it was a turning point for the promotion: "At the end of the match, all the fans were standing on their feet and applauding all the wrestlers' hard work. It was, like, go time for this company. You knew something special was here, and we started running more and more towns after that."

And things were moving quickly. "We took off like a rocket from there," Heyman says.

The word was spreading, via the limited Internet available in the early stages of that mode of communication. Eastern Championship Wrestling was starting to get requests for tapes not just from the entire United States, but also from Japan and Australia. Fans there had heard about the shows in which wrestlers were put through tables and ladders were used as weapons, and all sorts of extreme performances, and they wanted more.

Heyman ran into resistance when he went to do a show in New York with Jim Crockett, with whom Heyman was supposed to eventually work on a new national promotion to compete with World Championship Wrestling and World Wrestling Federation when Heyman was done with this "temporary" Eastern Championship Wrestling job. "Jim Crockett didn't understand it as much and started to second-guess everything," Heyman states. " 'Why would this guy bring a table into the ring, and why wouldn't this be a disqualification?' Well, it

Terry & Dory Funk vs. The Public Enemy.

would be a disqualification, except people hate disqualifications, and I'm not going to have the referee call for a disqualification. I'm simply going to have them fight it out. This is a pseudo-scripted version of Ultimate Fighting, but it is in a wrestling ring. It is not real, but we are not going to do disqualifications and stuff. We are going to give them a winner and a loser, because that is what people wanted to see.

"One of the main things I tried to preach was that it is not just important what we had to do," Heyman continues. "It was equally as important what not to do, and we really had to learn from the mistakes that were killing the wrestling industry in the United States. One of those things was the nonfinish, the disqualifications and the countouts. We were going to avoid that at all costs.

"All of a sudden, Jim Crockett, who was one of the biggest proponents of my 'Let's change the business' mentality, started to get very conservative once he saw the product, despite the fact that people were going crazy for it. Jim said, 'We have to slow this down.' He was in shock. He wanted to go back to 1986, but you had to be progressive, not retro. Other people were doing retro and were dying. We were doing progressive and people were going crazy for the product."

So Heyman abandoned his plans to join Crockett on a new national venture, and with Gordon, plans to take Eastern Championship Wrestling national. He met a media consultant named Steve Karel, who handled the production on the Jim Crockett project and had worked in ABC advertising sales. He also had a show that was on a lot of sports channels called *Muscle Sports, USA,* and was in the bodybuilding business with the National Physique Committee. Heyman brought Karel into ECW. "He was a hard-nosed businessman and very tough in negotiations and knew how to use lawyers," Heyman says. "Steve had his show on MSG and Sunshine Network and he had his show on Prime Sports Midwest. In the expansion of ECW, he was a necessary component to start getting this TV show on in other areas besides Philadelphia. Immediately we got on the Sunshine Network in Florida, our first expansion."

That cost money. The Philadelphia show was free, but Eastern Championship Wrestling had to pay to get on other networks—an expensive but necessary component for expansion in 1994 and for building up the new stars they were hoping to get over. They had to expand—to show these up-and-coming wrestlers that there was a future with ECW—or else risk having them move on to the other companies. This was something that ECW would constantly battle against throughout its existence. They had to show they were growing, and that every market was a new market for them to conquer. These wrestlers were putting their bodies on the line, crashing through tables and putting on shows the likes of which fans had never seen before. To do that, they needed to believe in the promotion, and the chance for their careers to grow with it. So expansion was vital to ECW's survival.

Besides being on television in Florida, Eastern Championship Wrestling made plans to put on shows there and start running smaller shows in Delaware and New Jersey. The Public Enemy were becoming stars and engaged in a feud with the Funk brothers. Shane Douglas and Sabu were also growing in popularity.

ECW followed *The Night the Line Was Crossed* with their next big show, *Ultimate Jeopardy,* on March 26, 1994, in Valley Forge, where Crash the Terminator defeated Pitbull #1; Jimmy Snuka beat Tommy Dreamer in a Steel Cage match; Tommy Cairo defeated Sandman; The Bruise Brothers beat Paul Diamond & Pat Tanaka; and, in a War Games match, Shane Douglas, Mr. Hughes & The Public Enemy beat Tazz, Terry Funk, Road Warrior Hawk & Kevin Sullivan.

The show *When Worlds Collide* took place on May 14, 1995, at the ECW Arena, where Tommy Dreamer beat Rockin' Rebel; Jimmy Snuka defeated Kevin Sullivan; in a handicap elimination bout, JT Smith & The Bruise Brothers beat Shane Douglas, Mr. Hughes & The Public Enemy; Sabu & Bobby Eaten beat Terry Funk & Arn Anderson; and the person who might have been voted least likely to be a professional wrestler beat 911—Heyman's former giant bodyguard—for the TV

911 towers over Sabu and Paul.

title in a disqualification. His name was James Watson, but he went by the name Mikey Whipwreck in the ring, and he would become an ECW legend.

Born in Buffalo, New York, on June 4, 1972, Whipwreck was trained by Sonny Blaze, who, as the story goes, didn't even charge him for the training because he doubted this 5-foot-7, 180-pound kid with more guts than talent would ever be a professional wrestler. He desperately wanted to be in the business, though, and wound up in Philadelphia working as part of the ring crew at the ECW Arena. One day, Heyman saw Whipwreck practicing some moves on his own in the ring. He had been begging Heyman for a shot, and he finally got one. "Mikey Whipwreck was the lovable loser," Heyman explains. "He never had an offensive maneuver. People started to get behind him because he took such great beatings."

Joey Styles, commenting during a Whipwreck match, summed up the Mikey Whipwreck appeal: "Mikey Whipwreck is taking the beating of his life. I've never seen this kid land a punch, a shot, a kick, anything on anybody ever."

It was during *When Worlds Collide* that a weapon was introduced that would play an influential role in the development of the promotion—the Singapore cane.

In March 1994, America was transfixed by a case in Singapore involving an 18-year-old United States citizen named Michael Peter Fay. He had been convicted on vandalism charges, and part of his sentence was to be struck with a cane six times. The case dominated the headlines here and created a wave of outrage over the punishment. President Bill Clinton asked the Singapore government to waive the caning, which he called "excessive." But they refused, and went ahead with the caning of Michael Fay.

"In wrestling there was this weapon used called kendo stick, a martial arts weapon, bamboo sticks all tied together," Heyman recalls. "Nobody ever used it as a prop all the time. I said, 'Let's do a Singapore Caning match. The Sandman will use the kendo stick, but we are not going to call it a kendo stick. We'll call it a Singapore cane.' Who knows the difference? People don't know what they cane you with over in

Singapore, so people called it the Singapore cane. Now, nobody refers to a kendo stick as a kendo stick anymore. It is always a Singapore cane. There was a martial arts show that was on ESPN not long ago, and they never referred to a kendo stick as a kendo stick. They called it a Singapore cane. It became part of the pop lexicon."

They were looking for a feud partner for Sandman, so they planned something with his former best friend, Tommy Cairo. They used Nancy Sullivan, Kevin Sullivan's wife who had served as his valet in wrestling, as a character called Woman, and hooked her up with Sandman. "Nancy was very popular with the crowd, despite the fact she managed Kevin Sullivan, who was a heel. We did a thing where the Sandman started to be managed by Nancy, and all she would do is light a cigarette. He would take out a cigarette, she would light it for him. She would always have one line on television, something like, 'You know, I don't know about you, but lighting my man's fire puts me in the mood for violence.' Sandman would look over and say something like, 'What Woman wants, Woman gets, and if she wants violence, she is with the right guy.' People were eating this up."

So they had Tommy Cairo come on television and take Sandman to task for his relationship with Woman.

"You know, my former best friend, the Sandman, has become a real jackass," Cairo said. "He smacked his wife. Then he is always at the bar ignoring his kid when his kid needs help with homework. Now he is running around with Woman, and totally ignoring his wife. Okay, two can play that game."

In the meantime, Sandman's wife, Lori Fullington, had appeared with him on television and was called Peaches when he still had the surfboard. Cairo went on TV to do an interview with Joey Styles and said, "Sandman, pay attention to this . . . I have been training and I have been hanging out in my backyard, eating peaches."

Everybody got the reference.

Cairo and Sandman were scheduled to have a Singapore Cane match at the May 14 show. Sandman went on TV, with Woman, for an interview. Sandman's beeper went off during the interview.

"You've got another phone call," Woman said.

"My beeper hasn't stopped beeping all day," Sandman said. "Tommy Cairo, let me lay this out for you. You're banging my wife? I'll tell you the same thing I tell everyone else. You owe me money. I figure my wife is good for three romps in the hay a day. I'll charge you $25 a romp. That means you owe me $75 a day. You have probably been with her for ten days, that means you owe me $750, Tommy Cairo, and I'm collecting this Saturday. Pay your bills, Tommy Cairo. You can drink my beer, watch my TV, you can raise my kids, but damn it, if you bang my wife, you're paying your bills."

When they met in the ring, as Cairo came out, everyone in the arena started chanting, "Pay your bills! Pay your bills!" And Sandman gave Cairo a Singapore Cane beating.

Next came the *Hostile City Showdown* on June 24, 1994, at the Philadelphia arena. Tazz defeated Pitbull #1 in a Dog Collar match; Chad Austin & Don E. Allen fought to a no contest; Tommy Dreamer beat Hack Myers; The Bruise Brothers defeated Shane Douglas & Mr. Hughes; Tommy Cairo beat the Sandman; The Public Enemy went to a no contest with Terry & Dory Funk, Jr.; and, in a match that would help set the stage for another leap forward for ECW, Sabu beat one of the most colorful characters to ever walk into a ring—Cactus Jack, known in real life as Mick Foley.

Foley had several personas while bouncing around the independent circuit. He made a name for himself in WCW wrestling as Cactus Jack with his hardcore style of wrestling and his willingness to take unheard-of punishment and sacrifice his body. According to Foley, in an arrangement with Kevin Sullivan and WCW, a so-called talent exchange was supposed to take place between ECW and WCW that would benefit both companies. As it turned out, it would not work out that way for ECW, just one of the many bitter disputes between the two companies. But for now, the relationship was cautiously civil, though Heyman wasn't thrilled with it. This was an arrangement worked out between Sullivan and Tod Gordon, who worked out a deal for Foley, as Cactus Jack, to come wrestle in ECW against Sabu in *Hostile City 1994*.

"Kevin Sullivan, when he came back to WCW in the spring of

1994, he had just come from ECW, and he loved it," Foley remembers. "He loved the character development and the crowd, and I believe he was the one who wanted to establish the relationship. I went over as a favor, because a lot of real hardcore fans saw the matchup of me as Cactus Jack and Sabu as a hardcore dream match.

"I had seen Sabu on tape many times," Foley continues. "I saw he was taking the hardcore style and innovating it with some athletic moves. He was taking what I had done, and adding a touch of athleticism to it, and in so doing he kind of ushered in the ECW era. I think without Sabu you wouldn't have seen the popularity of hardcore. He kind of set the bar that other ECW wrestlers tried to live up to, and that carried over into all of the other organizations and aspiring independent wrestlers. You could argue if his style changed wrestling for better or worse, the same way you could argue whether or not my style did. But I don't think there is any arguing that without him, it would be a different game today."

It turned out to be a rough night for Foley. "The arena was hot, with no showers. After the match I ended up herniating a couple of discs, and I wound up being taken to the hospital at about 4 A.M., in incredible pain. I also broke out into hives over about 50 percent of my body, which I guess was caused by waiting around for hours to do postmatch interviews, rather than taking a shower. But taking a shower was not an option in that building. I have no idea what move caused the herniated discs. It could have been just the straw that broke the camel's back. I had a lot of wear and tear on my body by 1994."

Before he left the arena, though, he did an interview that ended with him showing his disdain for WCW by spitting on his WCW Tag Team title belt: "It's your friend, Cactus Jack, bringing you tidings from WCW. What this belt here says is that Cactus Jack is one half of one of the best tag teams in the world. It means a lot to me. These people say it is the first belt that Cactus Jack has had in a long time, and indeed it is very dear to me." Then he spit on the belt and threw it down. "Not anymore. Not anymore. You might think it is nice for Cactus Jack to come in and give one of the performances of his life, lose, and walk away saying I still got a title. But it is not true. Bang bang. Because tonight, I lost the three titles I held for the last five years—most suicidal wrestler, ugliest wrestler, and Jack Kevorkian's favorite wrestler."

Foley said spitting on the WCW title created some hard feelings at the rival promotion. "That show caused a lot of friction between me and WCW, because they thought I was faking the back injury, which was not something I had ever done, and I also ended up spitting on the WCW Tag Team title. They didn't seem to care for my rationale that I was trying to show that despite the fact that I had left ECW with my championship title, I had also felt like I left it without my pride and dignity, because Sabu had proved to be the more extreme of the two of us. Over at WCW, they weren't into philosophical discussions when it came to saliva on their beloved belts. I still maintain that the people in charge would not have been so upset, Ric Flair in particular, if they had actually seen the interview instead of just hearing about it. What I was doing, I was saying that the tag team belt was important to me, but not as important as my pride, which I felt like I had lost that night in the ECW arena. I was told, 'Hey, help these guys out.' And I wanted to help them out not only with what I could do in the ring, but with what I could do with the mike. I thought Sabu deserved to be established as the top guy, and I thought I would do what I could to make that happen."

Heyman says that Foley's coming over to ECW was not because of any talent exchange, but because of legal actions taken against WCW over copyright infringement. "We ended up many different times nailing WCW on a lot of different things," Heyman says. "WCW violated our copyrights by putting on shows; for example, they had a show, *When Worlds Collide*, which was also the title of a show we had done earlier. We sued them, but we sued successfully so many different times. It was almost always settled out of court, but they kept on coming after us in different ways and stepping on their own johnson. One thing that happened was that we were given access to Mick Foley. He came in as Cactus Jack and came on our television show. He worked a match with Sabu, and Sabu beat him. This was a dream match, because Cactus Jack was the god of the hardcores. He was known the world over as the best hardcore wrestler, and now Sabu beats him."

Cactus Jack heads over the rail into Terry Funk and the crowd.

The next month—*Heat Wave 1994* on July 16 at the arena—Sabu & Tazz defeated The Pitbulls; Tommy Dreamer beat Stevie Richards, then lost to Mr. Hughes; Sandman beat Tommy Cairo; Ian & Axl Rotten defeated Rockin' Rebel & Hack Meyers; Mikey Whipwreck defeated Chad Austin; Shane Douglas beat Sabu; and in a Barbed-Wire match, The Public Enemy defeated Terry & Dory Funk, Jr. They followed that up with *Hardcore Heaven 1994* on August 13. Chad Austin beat Tommy Cairo; Hack Meyer defeated Rockin' Rebel; Tazz and Jimmy Snuka beat The Pitbulls; 911 defeated Mr. Hughes; Sabu defeated Too Cold Scorpio (the series of matches between the two over the years would be one of the highlights of ECW); Cactus Jack and Terry Funk wrestled to a no contest; and there would be one more match—one more moment in what was becoming many big moments in a promotion that was the talk of wrestling fans. This was the night when the Sandman defeated Tommy Dreamer in a legendary Singapore caning that helped put Dreamer over with the fans.

Dreamer lost to Sandman, and the loser had to be caned. Sandman delivered one blow after another, yet Dreamer, bloodied, kept getting up. At one point, he walked over and grabbed the microphone from Woman and said, "Thank you, sir, may I have another?" He walked over to the rope to be caned again. As it went on, the fans chanted, "Tommy! Tommy!"

"It hurt, taking that beating with the cane," Dreamer recalls. "What they do now, those canes have little ties around them, and when you have the ties, if they are pulled tight, it has the impact of a bat, and if they are pulled all the way up, it still hurts, but it is less of a blow. Sandman and I, being retarded, we just kept them tight the whole time. We didn't know if you moved it up, you could lessen the blow. It hurt, but I knew what I had to do. When adrenaline took over, and I saw the fans . . . the first couple of canes, they were cheering, but then as it went on, even my worst critics were yelling, 'Tommy, stay down!' They could see my blood, my back opening up, and my lips quivering, because I was in pain. They were yelling, 'Stay down!' They couldn't believe I was getting up. It was kind of like a real-life Rocky situation, where they wanted Rocky to stay down, but he kept getting up and kept on fighting. I know that was Paul's initial reaction, because I was Italian. 'This kid is tough, and this is Philadelphia and all that.'

"That was a turning point in my career, but it was also a turning point in ECW," Dreamer says. "It was a form of redemption through violence for me and for the fans. It is the best drug in the world, that rush from the fans. It is amazing. That is what always kept me going, pretty much—the fans."

Ron Buffone said you could see the transformation among the fans after that caning. "Once Tommy took that horrendous caning from the Sandman, when he said, 'Thank you, sir, may I have another?' the fans decided he wasn't just a pretty boy," Buffone recalls. "The fans respected that you were willing to put your body on the line. And ultimately, the fans make the wrestlers. If you are not getting the response you want from fans, then you are not doing your job, and Tommy certainly did his."

Sandman also remembers it as a turning point, for the both of them: "Tommy Dreamer and I made each other."

But ECW would be known for taking a storyline and playing it to a level never seen before in wrestling—which is what they did with Sandman and Tommy Dreamer.

At an October show at the ECW arena two months later, the feud was supposed to come to a climax with an I Quit match. Fans were stunned when during the match, as Sandman lit up one of his customary cigarettes, Dreamer shoved it in his eye and used Sandman's Singapore cane to cane him across the face. As the story went, Sandman was blinded by the cigarette and the caning, which led Dreamer to stop attacking him and start yelling to Woman, "I didn't mean it! I didn't mean it!" Sandman was writhing on the floor, a towel covering his face. Other wrestlers, both babyfaces and heels, were hovering over him, showing their concern. Sandman was wheeled out of the arena on a gurney by Heyman and paramedics. Even a savvy crowd like that at the ECW Arena couldn't quite make out if what was going on was real or not. And what happened after that only made the whole thing seem more real. Woman screamed at Dreamer, "You bastard! You son of a bitch!"

Remarkably, Sandman carried the story to the extreme, staying home for a month, and nobody saw him around town. "He never left his house," Heyman says. "He never answered his door. His wife answered the door. It was unheard-of back then for somebody to stick to the storyline to this degree."

On the next show, Woman declared she would no longer manage the "useless" Sandman, and Dreamer wrestled without any spirit or enthusiasm, showing that the blinding had caused him great pain. A month later, Sandman came to the arena, with his eyes bandaged, for what was supposed to be a final interview. Now blinded, he was going to retire from wrestling. While Joey Styles was doing the interview, Sandman's wife, Peaches, came to the ring and made up with her husband. Woman, armed with a Singapore cane, ran up and started beating Peaches and then threatened to do the same thing to the blinded Sandman. Dreamer ran to the ring to stop it and save Sandman, but while his back was turned, Sandman took the bandages off, grabbed the cane, and slammed it over Dreamer's head, with blood pouring down the fallen wrestler's face.

"It was one of the most shocking moments in early ECW and one of the loudest, because, boy, did that hook the audience," Heyman says.

"When ECW was first starting, there were a lot more gimmicks in professional wrestling," Dreamer recalls. "It was more geared toward children. ECW was mainly that 18-to-24 male demographic of testosterone-filled, ass-kicking wrestling with hot women. There was also a lot of blood, which was a no-no in WCW and WWE. And also there were a lot of women getting their butt kicked by men. Some wrestling fans on the Internet were offended, and some people weren't, but there were a lot of people talking."

The feuds, the hardcore battles with tables, ladders, and chairs, the barbed wire, the storylines—all contributed to the talk that this promotion was something wrestling fans had to see.

While Heyman had abandoned his plans to work with Jim Crockett on a new, national promotion, he had not forgotten about it. He still had visions of making such a move, and now saw Eastern Championship Wrestling as a vehicle to do that. And he felt the summer of 1994 was the right time to make that move.

"My goal was to create a new generation of a wrestling promotion, what I saw as the evolution of the industry," Heyman explains. "My theory was—and I had not clued anyone, including Tod, in on this—was that the business was at a turning point. We are the buzz of the business. Vince is in the middle of his federal steroid trial on Long Island. WCW is now being run by Eric Bischoff, who is just raiding Vince's talent, but doesn't know what to do with them. And the business has not yet caught on to what it needs to do. So we are the hip, alternate wrestling promotion.

"People are flying into our shows from all over the country and from Japan. They do a whole tour from Japan, with fifty people coming over for our show. It is exploding. We moved into Florida—and we are paying for that time—and now we are up on the satellite. We are looking for other markets to go into. We get cable television throughout New Jersey. It is time to make another move."

Heyman saw two ways to raise the level of the promotion: to change its name from its regional identity, and to break away from the old-school National Wrestling Alliance, which Eastern Championship Wrestling was still connected to. Various independent promoters were part of the NWA, which—ever since WCW broke away and went out on its own—was no longer a powerful national force in wrestling. "It didn't have any real political clout," Heyman says. "They hired an attorney in Charlotte who drew up the bylaws stating what you had to do to be a member in good standing in the NWA, which of course means nothing. Just because you put NWA on your poster or TV ad doesn't mean you are going to get two hundred extra people, so it is really a waste of time. Their big claim is NWA goes back to the days of Harley Race and Ric Flair, which is true, but this isn't really the NWA of old. This is a bunch of nobodies strung together."

Wrestling has its share of backstabbing and double-dealing outside the ring among promoters. Heyman had some problems with a local promoter from southern New Jersey named Dennis Coraluzzo, who had been doing business with Tod Gordon. Heyman said that Coraluzzo was sabotaging Eastern Championship Wrestling shows. "Dennis was jealous of Tod's success and tried to run shows five minutes away from the ECW Arena, right across the bridge in Cherry Hill, New Jersey. Maybe he'd draw fifty people while we are selling out the arena in 1994," Heyman says. "Dennis would call the fire department in Philly as a local citizen, claiming that the ECW Arena was overcrowded and dangerous and in violation of fire codes. So every month I am getting head counts done by the fire department at all my shows, and the fire marshal is checking the sprinkler system an hour before an event begins, and it is a real pain in the ass—cheap, dirty promoter tactics that have been around since the carnival days."

While Heyman was contemplating a way to make a statement about establishing his new promotion nationally, Coraluzzo had petitioned the NWA board that he wanted to hold a tournament for the NWA title. He claimed they needed to crown a new NWA champion. Heyman saw this as a way to make his statement.

Heyman went to Gordon with a plan to break away on their own, and to use the NWA title tournament to do it. They sent a letter to all the members of the NWA, suggesting that Eastern Championship

Wrestling host the NWA title tournament, since they had the most television exposure, in Pennsylvania, Florida, and New Jersey and on satellite TV as well. But they included in the proposal an offer to have Coraluzzo be part of the event, a black-tie affair, with Coraluzzo and Gordon sitting together and then making the championship presentation together in the ring. It was a great opportunity for a small-time promoter like Coraluzzo to get some exposure. So he agreed, and the tournament was set up for the August 27, 1994, show at the ECW Arena.

The title tournament was announced at the Philadelphia arena on August 13, 1994, during *Hardcore Heaven*. In that show, Tazz & Superfly Snuka beat The Pitbulls; Jason Knight defeated Mikey Whipwreck for the ECW TV championship; Hack Meyers beat Rockin' Rebel; Chad Austin beat Tommy Cairo; Sandman won over Tommy Dreamer in a disqualification; Sabu defeated Too Cold Scorpio; and Terry Funk and Cactus Jack battled to a no contest, but gave the promotion a scene that would live forever in ECW lore.

At the end of their match, after Funk and Foley had beaten each other up, The Public Enemy ran into the ring and beat up both Funk and Foley. The crowd didn't appear to know how to react—they couldn't decide if they liked it or didn't like it.

What was supposed to happen was that Funk and Cactus Jack (Mick Foley) were going to reverse the attack on The Public Enemy and leave them in the middle of the ring unconscious, and then challenge them at the big show for the titles. But Funk improvised. He dove out of the ring and got a chair, threw it into the ring, and nailed Johnny Grunge in the back of the head. Then he waved for the audience to throw in their chairs. The audience threw their chairs into the ring, and The Public Enemy was buried underneath the chairs. The arena erupted with chants of "ECW! ECW!"

"Terry and I started to fight them off together," Foley recalls. "And Terry asked a fan for a chair. Before we knew it, one chair was followed by another, and another, and another until it was literally raining chairs in the ECW arena. Terry bailed out after about a hundred chairs, and I stood there. Looking back, it should have crossed my mind how potentially dangerous the situation was. Once I got clipped

Chris Benoit taking ECW wrestling to another level.

in the head, I left the ring. Meanwhile, The Public Enemy was buried beneath the chairs. They were down there for a good five minutes. That's something that can never be repeated, it was so spontaneous."

It was repeated, though, over and over again, as part of the taped introduction for ECW throughout its existence. So now, in addition to the NWA Heavyweight title tournament, a grudge match between Terry Funk & Cactus Jack and The Public Enemy was set up for the August 27 show.

If that wasn't enough, the August 27 show would feature the ECW debut of two of a group of wrestlers that created a whole new segment in the promotion—no barbed wire, tables, ladders, or chairs, but remarkable technical wrestling skills that would appeal to the fan base. Dean Malenko and Chris Benoit would make their first ECW appearance, part of a group that would also include Eddie Guerrero.

"Chris Benoit, Eddie Guerrero, Dean Malenko all came in, and you

The Rise & Fall of ECW

have some great wrestlers there," Tommy Dreamer recalls. "It was just the place to watch good wrestling."

Chris Benoit was part of that stable of wrestlers. He was born in Montreal on May 21, 1967, raised in Edmonton, and trained by the legendary Stu Hart, along with Bret and Owen Hart and future ECW wrestlers Lance Storm and Chris Jericho. He began wrestling in 1986 with Hart's promotion, Stampede Wrestling, and then went to Japan to wrestle with New Japan Pro Wrestling, going under the name of Wild Pegasus. He would be known in ECW as The Crippler.

Dean Malenko descended from wrestling royalty. He was born on August 4, 1960, in Tampa, Florida, the son of a rough-and-tumble wrestler named Boris Malenko. His early career consisted of wrestling in independent promotions and in Mexico and Japan before coming to ECW.

Eddie Guerrero also came from a wrestling background. He was born October 9, 1967, to one of the greatest wrestling families in Mexico. Eddie's father, "Gory" Guerrero, was heralded as one of the greatest wrestlers in Mexican history. His older brother, Chavo, was a great wrestler, and Chavo's son and Eddie's nephew, Chavo, Jr., is carrying on the wrestling tradition. Eddie Guerrero's brother Hector was also in the business.

Eddie Guerrero was raised in El Paso, Texas, and went to college at the University of New Mexico on a wrestling scholarship. He would get into professional wrestling in Mexico in 1987. He went to Japan to wrestle with New Japan Pro Wrestling and then returned to Mexico to tag team with Art Barr, becoming a huge star in Mexico. The style of wrestling popular in Mexico is *lucha libre,* featuring spectacular, high-flying moves. Guerrero was supposed to come to ECW with his partner, but Barr died unexpectedly.

Benoit recognized they were offering something different for ECW fans. "The guys there were slamming people through tables and hitting them with chairs and kendo sticks, and I was going out there and just wrestling," he said. "You had me and Dean at the time and Eddie, and we were like straight wrestlers. We were very different, and that was appealing to the fans."

Guerrero welcomed the chance to show his skills to an appreciative, passionate audience. "The fans loved it," he says. "It was great because there were hardcore fans who wanted to see blood and guts and pans, but Paul gave us the time to go out there and wrestle. Paul Heyman gave me the opportunity."

Heyman saw it as another part of the ECW foundation. "They brought a style that was different then, from the taped fists and barbed wire and baseball bats and brawls all over the arena," he explains. "They brought a pure wrestling ethic to ECW, that again helped us expand our audience, because we didn't just have the violence and the tables and the chaos. We also had the best wrestling that you couldn't find anywhere else. And that was a necessary component in building the ECW audience."

Wrestling is an unpredictable, volatile business. Something usually goes wrong, as it did the day before the August event. Funk decided the day before the show that he wouldn't show up, which left the ECW brain trust in a difficult position, with the show less than twenty-four hours away.

"The next day, Tommy Dreamer and I leave for Philadelphia," Heyman recalls. "We leave early and get into town. I get Tod Gordon and Shane Douglas, Mick Foley, and The Public Enemy all in a hotel room, and I tell them what happened and asked, 'Who do we call?' But we are thinking the wrong way. We are thinking of a big name we could call. What do we tell the audience? It's noon now, and Foley says, 'I don't know who we are going to get.' It's eight hours before the show. We've got to get a guy on a plane, negotiate a price . . . we need somebody from within. And then there was one of those moments where everyone was on the same page at the same time. It was almost a scene out of a movie, and we all looked at each other and said, 'Mikey Whipwreck. The Lovable Loser. Holy shit!' We can do this with Mikey, if Mick Foley—Cactus Jack—teams with Mikey. We will have Cactus come out to the ring and say, 'There is only one man who I would face The Public Enemy with, and he is the toughest man alive. That is Mikey Whipwreck.' The place will go crazy."

In a packed ECW arena, with about a hundred Japanese fans who flew in for the show, Benoit lost to Too Cold Scorpio; 911 beat Matt Borne; Dean Malenko defeated Osamu Nishimura; Shane Douglas beat Tazz; Too Cold Scorpio defeated 911 in a disqualification; and Shane Douglas defeated Malenko, setting up the final match of the tournament for the title—Douglas vs. Too Cold Scorpio.

What happened next, when Douglas was awarded the NWA belt, only Heyman, Gordon, and Douglas knew about. With the belt draped over his shoulder, Shane took the microphone and addressed the fans: "To the Harley Races. To the Barry Windhams. The Ric Flairs. I accept this heavyweight title. Wait a second. Wait a second . . . to the fat man himself, Dusty Rhodes. This is it tonight, Dad . . ." He took the belt in his hand. "God, that's beautiful . . . and Rick Steamboat . . . and they can all kiss my ass." And he threw the belt on the mat.

"What in the hell is he doing?" a bewildered Styles asked the TV crowd.

Douglas continued, "Because I am not the man who accepts the torch to be handed down to me from an organization that died, RIP, seven years ago. The Franchise, Shane Douglas, is the man who ignites the new flame of the sport of professional wrestling."

Douglas walked over, picked up the ECW belt, and said, "Tonight, before God and my father [his father had died the year before] as witness, I declare myself, The Franchise, as the new Extreme Championship Wrestling Heavyweight Champion of the world. We have set out to change the face of professional wrestling. So tonight, let the new era begin—the era of the sport of professional wrestling, the era of The Franchise, the era of the ECW."

As Douglas dropped the microphone and stood in the ring, fans began chanting, "ECW! ECW!" at a near deafening roar.

"When Shane Douglas took the NWA World Heavyweight Championship, with its lineage dating back to 1905 with George Hackenschmidt and Jim Londos and threw it down, and proclaimed the Eastern Championship Wrestling title as the Extreme Championship Wrestling World Heavyweight Championship, it ushered in the era that we were looking to create," Heyman says.

It caught everyone by surprise—fans and other wrestlers alike.

The Franchise with *the* title.

"When Shane grabbed that belt and threw it down, it was crazy. I couldn't believe what was going on," Dreamer recalls. "Nobody knew what was going on. Paul and Shane were the only people that knew."

Stevie Richards remembers it as a defining moment for ECW: "That is probably one of the most historic moments I have ever witnessed in my career. It was unbelievable to see that happen and to see the fallout between Dennis Coraluzzo and the NWA board and Paul Heyman and the ECW, which basically made the ECW even stronger afterwards."

In an interview that night, Coraluzzo showed he had clearly been caught off guard by the move. "What happened tonight was a disgrace," he said. "I'm disappointed at it. Shane Douglas is the NWA Champion. He threw the belt down. He had no right to do that."

Even that interview was a setup of Coraluzzo, according to Heyman. "Now here comes Coraluzzo to the back, and I'm not done with him yet. I'm going to show him how to play people. I walk up to him and say, 'Now, wasn't that great? Think how great you are going to draw at your show.' He says, 'What do you mean?' I said, 'Don't you see, you are the NWA representative. I want you on my TV show right now. We're going to do a press conference, and you are going to say what Shane Douglas did is a disgrace. It is typical of the ECW to condone this type of action. I've never liked those people to begin with. And furthermore, Shane Douglas, whether he throws down the title or not, is the NWA Champion, the World Heavyweight Champion in our eyes, and there is no getting around that, and he will defend the title whether he likes it or not.'

"I had him do the promo three times. I said, 'That was good, Dennis, let's do another one.' When he was done, I said, 'With the great angle we have, I want you to call me Tuesday night after the TV show and we will arrange dates for Shane Douglas to come and defend the title. You know what? It would be great if he drops it to one of your guys, and you bring that guy here to the arena and defend the title here against another one of my guys.' He said, 'Oh that would be great.' But by the time he had gotten home, someone had smartened him up that he had just gotten double-crossed in a big-time way. And we did. We sent a message about fighting back and playing dirty with us. It was one of the most famous double crosses in wrestling in the 1990s."

Not everyone thinks it was handled the right way. "To this day, I don't like it," Styles says. "I didn't think it was right. The NWA was not in on it. They did not know they were being taken advantage of. But once WCW broke away, there really was no NWA to speak of. It didn't mean that much. But I didn't like the idea of lying to Dennis Coraluzzo. I thought it was in poor taste. I was not a fan of the way it happened."

Soon after, in another interview, Tod Gordon made the historic announcement that officially gave birth to Extreme Championship Wrestling. "As of noon today, I have folded NWA Eastern Championship Wrestling," Gordon said. "In its place will be ECW—Extreme Championship Wrestling. And we recognize The Franchise, Shane Douglas, as our World Heavyweight Champion."

Heyman said the word *extreme* seemed a perfect fit. "A word that was being used more and coming into popularity back in 1994 was the word *extreme*. It hasn't reached the point that it would eventually. In 1995, the word exploded, but as soon as I heard the beginnings of it, I knew, this was something to tap into." Douglas would, on and off, hold the title four different times over his ECW tenure and probably be the most identified with the heavyweight championship. But it would never be enough for him, as Douglas maintained throughout his career that he never got the recognition that he deserved.

"Shane Douglas was very serious, and sometimes I think he took himself too seriously," Al Snow maintains. "He was a terrific guy and a great worker, but very frustrated and very bitter about the business. I remember when he first broke in as Terry Orndorff, and he had all this potential and promise, and so many people touting him as the next big thing. It was within his grasp, but he just kept missing the brass ring, and I think that drove him even more in ECW, to prove, as he called himself, The Franchise. He was very intelligent."

His drive often made him misunderstood, Tazz claims: "Shane Douglas has been misunderstood by a lot of people. The character, The Franchise, I was a fan of. He was this cocky, brash attitude, smart, and a cool character with a lot of layers there. I thought Shane Douglas made The Franchise that way, with Paul Heyman giving him the platform. But I think he is misunderstood behind the scenes at times, because he is an outspoken guy, a passionate man. He is a very blunt guy, and doesn't sugarcoat things. I respect him a lot. I wrestled him a lot and learned from him and liked being in the ring with him."

Dreamer says Douglas was well suited for the role of being the guy who turned away from the past and looked to the future of professional wrestling. "He was an amazing talker," Dreamer admits. "I had a lot of great matches with The Franchise, Shane Douglas. We went to a 58-minute draw in 117-degree heat. We did it in the summer in the arena with no air conditioning, and a big thermometer in the building said it was 117 degrees."

The August 13, 1994, show was not over yet, though. There was still one more match for the ECW Tag Team title—Cactus Jack & Mikey Whipwreck against The Public Enemy. The crowd was thinking that it would still be Cactus Jack & Terry Funk against The Public Enemy, but Cactus Jack came in the ring and introduced Mikey Whipwreck, which sent the crowd, already at a fever pitch, ratcheted up even more.

In Mike Foley's book, *Have a Nice Day*, Foley recalls the pairing with Whipwreck: "Without Funk, we knew we needed a gimmick, and I felt like Mikey was it. I went into the ring alone to the sounds of Steppenwolf's 'Born to Be Wild.' The fans were aware that Funk was not in attendance, but no substitute had been named. When Public Enemy hit the ring, I grabbed the house mike and said I would be returning shortly with my partner. Joey Styles called the action as I disappeared behind the curtain. 'Who is Cactus Jack going to find? What tough guy, what tremendous athlete, what former world champion will he return with . . . it's Mikey! Oh, my God, it's Mikey!' I came through the curtain dragging Mikey by the arm, as he tried desperately to get away.

"I started in with The Public Enemy, and Mikey promptly ran away to the back, leaving poor Cactus Jack defenseless against the ECW Tag Team Champions. After a few minutes of this beating, when all looked lost, Mikey reemerged—and in true ECW fashion, he had a foreign object. But it wasn't a chair or any other normal instrument of destruction, because that wouldn't be Mikey-like. Instead, he held a flimsy piece of paneling that looked as threatening as a gaggle of baby geese. Flimsy or not, the paneling made a hell of a noise upon impact, and he took turns bringing it down on the heads of The Public Enemy. When the paneling broke, Mikey Whipwreck—the man of no offense—began throwing lefts and rights to the jaws of both men. The roar of the crowd rose with each blow, until he was laid out with a vicious double-team move. As he lay unmoving, Grunge and Flyboy Rocco Rock began the attack on me.

"As we went over the railing, I noticed Mikey still lying there, motionless. Now we were in the crowd, and still no Mikey. For five minutes I took abuse while Mikey lay motionless inside the ring. Finally we returned, and Rocco went to the top rope for what would surely be the coup de grace. As the Flyboy stood perched atop the ropes, I got up and stumbled, falling into the ropes, sending the Flyboy testicles-first into the turnbuckle below. He screamed on impact, fell into the ring, and tripped over Mikey, who still hadn't budged. With Rocco prone, and holding his testes for comfort, Mikey found the strength to drape an arm over him. I stopped Grunge from interfering, and the referee made the historic count. One, two, three, and ECW had new tag team champions. There was a whole tour of Japanese fans sitting ringside at the show, and when I saw them, I hopped over the rail and celebrated, as the Japanese media flashed away."

For Mikey Whipwreck, the lovable loser, to beat The Public Enemy was inconceivable. Taking a page from the 1980 Winter Olympics American hockey team, Joey Styles declared, "Do you believe in miracles? Mikey Whipwreck has won the tag team title."

In a hilarious interview after the match, Cactus Jack said, "Mikey, The Public Enemy is mad. You know what that means?"

To which Mikey Whipwreck answered in a quivering voice, "It means I'm gonna die."

Cactus Jack grabbed Mikey Whipwreck around the neck and hugged him and said, "Mikey likes it. He really, really likes it."

It seemed like everyone liked what ECW was doing, but not everyone was getting a chance to see it, given its limited TV distribution. Like an evangelist, Heyman had to find a way to spread the message, and TV was the answer.

Mikey Whipwreck proving his mettle to The Public Enemy.

chapter four

The Fire Spreads

Extreme Championship Wrestling was now a promotion that was garnering tremendous word-of-mouth among wrestling fans. They closed out the 1994 year with two more strong shows—*November to Remember* and *Holiday Hell.*

In *November to Remember,* Tommy Dreamer defeated Tommy Cairo; Too Cold Scorpio beat Mr. Hughes; JT Smith defeated Hack Meyers; The Pitbulls beat Axl & Ian Rotten; Chris Benoit went to a no contest with Sabu in a bout that would be remembered because it was reported that Sabu broke his neck because of an errant move by Benoit, who then wound up getting counted out, along with Too Cold Scorpio, in their bout; Dean Malenko beat Tazz; Shane Douglas successfully defended his ECW Heavyweight title; and in a rematch, Cactus Jack & Mikey Whipwreck lost the ECW Tag Team belts to The Public Enemy.

They followed that up with the *Holiday Hell* show, on December 17 at the ECW Arena, with Mikey Whipwreck beating Don E. Allen; Tommy Dreamer & Cactus Jack defeating the Sandman & Tommy Cairo; Dean

Malenko beat Ray Odyssey; Stevie Richards defeated JT Smith; Chris Benoit beat Hack Meyers; 911 defeated The Pitbulls in a Handicap match; The Public Enemy beat Sabu & Tazz for the ECW Tag Team title; and Shane Douglas remained champion with a win over Ron Simmons.

"Sabu, with a broken verterbra, had come back with a collar two weeks after he was hurt and wrestled," Heyman remembers. "When it comes to work ethic, Sabu was the most passionate performer you would ever see, because nothing could keep him out of the ring, not even a broken neck."

Heyman began building up Sabu and Tazz as tag team partners. "Starting at the December show, I had The Public Enemy put Sabu through tables," he says. "Sabu had been putting people through tables, and now he was being put through tables. It would build up to Tazz becoming Sabu's partner. They do a Double Tables match. You can't imagine again, inconceivable that The Public Enemy would lose this type of match, a Tables match, to Sabu, even though it is Sabu's gimmick to put people through tables. We do a match and put the titles on Sabu and Tazz. In runs Chris Benoit, who throws one member of The Public Enemy, Rocco Rock, on a table and then hits Sabu. Malenko puts a table on the top rope. Benoit climbs up on the rope, brings Sabu with him, and hits a power bomb off the table on the top rope and throws Sabu through Rocco Rock, who is on a table in the ring. Now Benoit is a monster because he broke Sabu's neck before. Fans believed there was this huge grudge with Sabu and Benoit. Now we are creating this scenario where Benoit and Sabu still have this issue going, and now Tazz is involved, and we now have Benoit doing something to The Public Enemy. Now The Public Enemy come out on TV, and say, 'Oh, we're going to get our hands on Chris Benoit and Dean Malenko.' But first Benoit and Malenko are going to go after the titles of Sabu and Tazz, because this is Sabu's chance at revenge."

ECW kicked off 1995 with a *Double Tables* show at the arena on February 4, which featured Tommy Dreamer beating Stevie Richards; Mikey Whipwreck beating Paul Lauria; Ian Rotten defeated Axl Rotten; The Pitbulls & Jason the Terrible beating The Young Dragons & Hack Meyers; Shane Douglas defended his ECW Heavyweight Championship successfully against Tully Blanchard; Cactus Jack beat Sandman; and, in a Double Tables match, Sabu & Tazz defeated The Public Enemy.

There was one other match that night that was noteworthy, because it marked the debut of one of the most popular and colorful wrestlers in the business, one who had toiled for years in the independent circuits and had gained a reputation among his cohorts as a wrestler's wrestler—Al Snow, who lost to Chris Benoit.

Allen R. Sarven—Al Snow—was born on July 18, 1963, in Lima, Ohio. As a young man he was determined to become a pro wrestler, but he had a tough time getting started. "I broke in at a time when the business was still closed and very protective," Snow says. "At that time, before there was the proliferation of schools, you had to basically find someone to train you and take responsibility for you, which was pretty hard to do. If you were shit, that reflected on the guy who recommended you and trained you, and then he would not get work, because if he put you over as being so great, and you weren't, then he must not be very good himself.

"I spent two years making calls and trying to get in," Snow remembers. "I went to Arn Anderson's tryout camp and basically got tortured and beat up, my nose broken. I encountered Jim Lancaster at the camp and convinced him to train me. I had my first match May 22, 1982." Thirteen years later, he made his first appearance in ECW.

"I had the nickname 'The Best Kept Secret in the Wrestling Business,' which was a great compliment for the first two or three years, but then it gets kind of old," Snow says. "I kept fairly busy and worked on a regular basis, but three or four years after I started, the independent territories started dying off, and it was hard to get work. I had worked anywhere and everywhere. I worked in Minnesota, Kansas, Michigan, all over.

"I went to Japan, and when I came back, there was a show in Michigan, and everyone was booked on the card. Sabu was on the card, and we had known each other. He was in ECW at the time. Sabu's opponent didn't show up, so I worked with him, and we had a great match. It was like everyone's eyes had opened up and started looking at me different. Sabu suggested that I come to ECW, and I did."

Soon after, though, Snow also got the attention of Jim Cornette, who offered him a spot in Smoky Mountain Wrestling. At the time this was an area where wrestlers moved up to World Wrestling Federation. Snow says, "I was already working for Paul E., but he had no problem with me working for both companies. Paul E. said great, and then he quit using me. I worked for Smoky Mountain that year, and the week of my birthday, I went down to WCW for a tryout, and up to Stanford for an interview, all in the same week. I chose to go with Vince. That was the first time I was with ECW."

It would be during his second stint in ECW that Al Snow would have his career-defining moment.

At that February 25 show, at the ECW Arena, which featured the return of Terry Funk to ECW, Chris Benoit & Dean Malenko defeated Sabu & Tazz for the ECW Tag Team titles; Too Cold Scorpio beat Hector Guerrero; Jason Knight & Paul Lauria defeated Hack Meyers & Mikey Whipwreck; Cactus Jack topped D.C. Drake; and The Pitbulls beat Joel Hartgood & Chad Austin.

Meanwhile, to move beyond a small, unique promotion into a force to compete with the big boys, ECW had to spread the word. Everyone knew the way to do that was through television, so ECW moved their production to a studio in Paoli, outside of Philadelphia, and from Ron Buffone's home in Pelham Manor. Steve Karel began working to pick up new markets. The biggest market was New York, and that is where the biggest battle took place.

"Madison Square Garden Network did not want us on the air," Heyman recalls. "We were having the toughest time getting them to take our show. I made the statement, 'Put me on Sunday nights at 1 A.M., I don't give a shit.' They said no. I did an interview on the Internet and somebody asked me, 'Are you going to move into New York?' I said, 'I am trying to get in on Sunday nights at 1 A.M.' Once our fans heard this, they went crazy. They started bombarding MSG with letters and phone calls, tying up the MSG switchboard, asking when ECW was starting.

"They complained to the Dolans, who owned Cablevision and MSG. And Jim Dolan called me and asked, 'Who are you and why is your audience bombarding my office?' I said, 'I'm Paul Heyman, and you guys won't put me on the air. I'm trying to buy a time slot Sunday nights at 1 A.M. for $5,000 a week and you won't sell it to me.' He said, 'You'll give me $5,000 a week for Sunday nights at 1 A.M? I said, 'Yes, I will.' He said, 'Sold.' Steve negotiated the rest of the deal, and we got on the air in New York in early 1995."

This was another turning point for ECW, but it was just the start of the ongoing battles that ECW would have throughout its tenure. At one point during their early days on MSG, programming officials went ballistic and pulled the show after seeing a bloody match in which Sabu went through a table. They agreed to put it back on, but one hour later, at 2 A.M. on Friday-night. "The only problem was the HUT levels are much higher at that time—houses using televisions," Heyman says. "Also on Friday nights, MSG is played in all the bars in New York, all the strip clubs. Sunday nights, nobody is out. Friday nights, everybody is out. All of a sudden, people are in bars asking, 'What the fuck is this stuff?' I'm putting out videos and insane clips, and people are saying, 'What is this stuff? I've got to get some of it. This is great!'"

Heyman kept the momentum going by introducing new faces and storylines to ECW and building one character after another. The new, raw promotion is showcased in the *Three Way Dance* on April 8.

Mikey Whipwreck won by disqualification over Ron Simmons; Axl Rotten beat Ian Rotten in a Hair vs. Hair bout; The Pitbulls beat Tony Stetson and Johnny Hotbody; Hack Meyers defeated Dino Sendoff; and in the three-way dance for the ECW Tag Team Championship, The Public Enemy won over Dean Malenko & Chris Benoit and Tazz & Rick Steiner. The two new faces were Eddie Guerrero, who finally arrived and won the ECW TV title by beating Too Cold Scorpio, and a dark character that had once wrestled as Scotty the Body, but was now known as Raven.

Scott Levy—Raven—was born on September 8, 1962. He was trained by Larry Sharpe and Jake "The Snake" Roberts, and made his debut in February 1988, as Scotty the Body, in the northwestern United States. He moved on to several other promotions, among them Mid-

Raven and Tommy Dreamer.

Southern Wrestling and the Global Wrestling Federation, before making his debut in WCW in 1991 as Scotty Flamingo. Two years later he
joined World Wrestling Federation as a manager named Johnny Polo,
and did some announcing and other work for the promotion before
leaving in 1994. ECW offered him a chance. "They started to move him,
because he had a bright mind, into office clerical work," Heyman explains. "He would be the guy who would call you up and say, 'Hey, I'm
just letting you know they need you to make this show because this
guy is hurt, and you can also pick up a booking in the Chicago show as
well.' And Scott was miserable. He wanted to be a wrestler. He grew his
hair long, and looked like real disenfranchised. And I was looking for a
poet of the macabre. Much like The Public Enemy was cutting edge in
1993 and 1994, now everyone was trying to copy their act. I needed
another rebel. I knew I needed somebody who could sit there and
honestly discuss how he understands why Kurt Cobain couldn't handle the pressures of success. Somebody who could honestly discuss
the angst of today's kids. Again, somebody like The Public Enemy,

who could discuss being the first generation of American kids more afraid of living than dying. We needed someone new to tap into that audience. Even with Kurt Cobain having killed himself in the summer of 1994, the anti-establishment—not grunge music, because that died with Cobain—Green Day was taking off, Phish was taking off. It was like revenge of the mud people. The next generation of grunge happened right after Cobain died. They were disillusioned and disenfranchised, and I needed someone to tap into that, but in a very strange way. I knew I wasn't going to get those kids to come to wrestling. I knew it was not their thing. But because it was so topical, and everyone is so threatened by them and disgusted by these kids, if I could have a guy who could legitimately discuss these issues—you would want to see him get his ass kicked.

"I see Scott Levy again, with his hair long and a leather jacket on. I ask him, 'What do you want to call yourself?' He said, 'Raven.' I said, 'Okay, is this like the Crow?' He had kind of a babyfaced character in mind, kind of like the movie. I said to him, 'Would you be willing to walk a line with me on this one? Would you be a poet of the macabre?' He needed an editor, and needed someone to give him a concept. I would have him go on TV at first and quote Voltaire. I'd have him quote Jim Morrison. He would say these things, and I said your catch phase would be, 'Quote the Raven nevermore.' I said, 'And you are going to be a heel.' He said, 'Okay, so why would people hate me?' I said, 'Okay, let's figure this out.'"

They did this by creating a storyline with Tommy Dreamer. Even though Dreamer had gone a long way to winning over fans with the Sandman feud, where he was caned, Dreamer was still not where ECW wanted him to be.

"Tommy Dreamer was a homegrown babyface, and we just couldn't get the hardcore fans to accept him," Heyman states. "We had just gotten through the blinding thing—the *November to Remember 1994*—where Sandman came back and peeled off the bandage. The audience, no matter what we did, still wasn't accepting Dreamer. Even though he had this amazing feud with the Sandman, it became all about the Sandman and not about Dreamer."

Raven went on TV and said things like, "My mission is not complete. I am here for a purpose, and my purpose is my pain, because I feel your pain, and you know who you are. Quote the Raven nevermore." And he would strike this crucifix-like pose that became a signature gimmick for Raven. Fans weren't quite sure what to make of it, but they were captivated by it.

In March, before the April show, Raven went on TV and declared his intention to come to ECW. "My purpose is simple," he said. "I'm going to get Tommy Dreamer. Tommy Dreamer and I went to camp together. Dreamer was always popular, and I was never popular. That is what happens when you are an only child, with an abusive drunk father who beats on you. No one wants to hang out with you. 'Hey, let's go to Raven's house. No, no his father might beat me up, too.' When I was in camp I had a girl. She was the fat girl at camp. Tommy Dreamer and I fought over this girl. And you know what, Tommy Dreamer? I never forgave you for stealing her, and I promise you, you will feel my pain."

The "fat" girl turned out to be a beautiful woman named Trisa Hayes, who was born March 14, 1969, in Kalamazoo, Michigan. She got into wrestling briefly in 1988 in Stampede Wrestling in Calgary, as Brian Pillman's sister. She was dating Pillman at the time. In 1995, while attending a Super Bowl party in Miami with baseball player Ron Gant, Hayes, who had appeared in *Penthouse* and other magazines, met Raven and told him she wanted to get back into wrestling. Paul saw the magazine layouts, and, on Raven's recommendation, invited her to ECW to be a character called Beulah McGillicutty.

"She was so ridiculously hot and had this innocent, sweet face, and I knew this was the perfect way for Raven to become the all-around heel," Heyman says. "We would have him be abusive toward her, and everyone will want to see Raven get his ass kicked."

Raven also added another part to his act, a lackey named Michael Manna, born on October 9, 1971, in Philadelphia, Pennsylvania, and trained by Mike Sharpe. He went by the name Stevie Richards and had been languishing for three years as a preliminary wrestler in the promotion but seemed to be a perfect fit for Raven's sycophant, another victim of Raven's abuse to fire up the fans.

Dreamer was scheduled to face Raven for the first time at the April 8 show. Beulah McGillicutty made her debut as well. She took a can of hair spray and sprayed it in Dreamer's face, and Raven hit Dreamer with the DDT and won the match. They matched up a week later at the arena, and it was a raucous bout, even by ECW standards. A bloody Dreamer laid Raven out on the canvas with a chair and the referee, and was about to give Raven the DDT when Beulah, wearing a schoolgirl outfit, came in and started pounding Dreamer on the back. Dreamer

turned around and grabbed Beulah by the ears, picked her up to put her in a piledriver, and of course the schoolgirl skirt was down and showed her pink panties. He turned her to all four sides of the arena, and the fans went crazy. Dreamer piledrived Beulah in the middle of the ring, and stood over both Beulah and Raven. Dreamer extended his arms in a Raven pose. The whole audience started chanting, "He's hardcore! He's hardcore!" and then "Dreamer! Dreamer!" and then "ECW! ECW!" From that moment, Tommy Dreamer was a made man.

"The fans really truly accepted me then," Dreamer recalls. "I started wrestling with a T-shirt instead of the suspenders. My goal was to make those people like me, and there were a lot of little things I did that Paul [Heyman] helped me out with. He used to manage Arn Anderson, and I remember when I would go to the ring, people would go to high-five me, and as I would go to hit their hands, they would pull them back, and Paul said, 'Don't do it. Don't ever do it again.' I was like, 'Why?' He said, 'When Arn Anderson comes out, the fans respect him. Make these people want to touch you, as opposed to you wanting to touch them.' Also, if you looked at what Hulk Hogan would do, he would always look up to the rafters and point to the people. I got that from Paul helping me. It worked, and Paul pointed out that a great babyface, the men respect him and the women want to fuck him. That is kind of what I was."

This would be the start of a feud that would be the backbone of ECW. "The feud between me and Raven was probably one of the best feuds in ECW for the simple fact that I never beat him," Dreamer explains. "For three years, I never beat him. Every time I would come close, I would somehow not pull it off.

"Paul had allowed myself and Raven a lot of creative freedom, which was a blessing. A lot of times in this business, you are told, 'This is what you have to do,' instead of someone telling you, 'What do you want to do?' What? It was Raven and Dreamer, but then we started incorporating other people. So many things shot off that and so many people's lives were affected by it."

In the strange world of wrestling, strange things happen. Seven years later, Beulah—Trisa Hayes—married Tommy Dreamer. "We were just friends when I first met her," Dreamer says. "I really didn't like her. Most of the greatest stuff in wrestling is stolen. I remember Jerry Lawler piledriving Rick Rude's valet. That is what I wanted to do. That was why we did it. She got over as well on her own. She was trying to be a heel, but she was a hot girl, and this was Philadelphia, and they just accepted her as a babyface."

Women—beautiful women—were a big part of ECW, and there were a number of them who became stars in the promotion besides Beulah. There was Woman, Elektra, Dawn Marie, Kimona Wannalaya, and a former Catholic school cheerleader from Philadelphia named Francine Fournier, who was known in ECW as "Francine, Queen of Extreme."

Francine, born February 19, 1972, in Philadelphia, was working behind a desk for a life insurance company when she came to a life decision—she wanted something with more excitement than life insurance. "One night I was flipping through the channels when I found Eastern Championship Wrestling," Francine remembers. "There was a commercial on TV, saying if you wanted to be a wrestler or a manager, call this number. I watched it for about a month, then I decided to give them a call. I didn't know anything about wrestling or the business. I called and went down to meet Tod Gordon, and started going to wrestling school.

"I was the only girl. It was four guys and myself, and J.T. Smith was my trainer. I trained with the men to wrestle. I did everything they did. Every week I said to myself I was going to quit. I was 21 years old and weighed 110 pounds. One of the first things they make you do is run the ropes, and when I would get done running the ropes, my whole right side would have deep purple bruises. There were times when I couldn't move my neck, and I would be black and blue all over. I would say I'm not going back next week. But then I would feel better, and keep going. There wasn't a week that went by where I didn't go to training. I just stuck it out, and I'm glad I did.

"I went to wrestling school for seven months. I did a couple of independent shows while I was going to school. Then I met Paul and started doing ECW house shows, and then they put me on television."

Francine got her start working as a "devoted fan" of Stevie Richards, and gained the respect of the wrestlers quickly. "Once the other wrestlers saw my work ethic and all the bumps I would take, they considered me one of the boys," she says. "I tried just as hard as everybody else, and never said no. Whatever they wanted me to do, I did. I gave them respect, and they gave me respect right back. I tried to prove myself as much as possible and did whatever they wanted me to do, no matter how crazy it was. I would say, 'Okay, that's great,' and I would just do it with a smile on my face, and I think that won them over."

The Queen of Extreme, Francine Fournier.

The April 8 show was also supposed to feature the culmination of a tag team feud among Benoit & Malenko, Sabu & Tazz, and The Public Enemy. "Benoit and Malenko beat Sabu and Tazz for the titles. Now we have tag team champions that The Public Enemy want to face and Sabu and Tazz want to face. At the same time, Sabu and Tazz and The Public Enemy want to face each other," Heyman recalls. "We have the classic makings for a three-way dance. We spend the whole month of March building this up, at every show. Anytime The Public Enemy is in the ring, or Sabu and Tazz, or Benoit and Malenko, we are building this up. Everybody is chasing everybody, and everybody has a reason to chase the other guy. This was intricately booked dating back to the night that Benoit hurt Sabu, which was an accident that we capitalized on. From that moment forward, we were building up to the three-way dance."

But in a volatile, emotional business like wrestling, plans can fall apart in one night, as they did on this night. Sabu had gotten a lucrative offer to wrestle in Japan, on the same date as the April ECW show. Sabu was not particularly thrilled about being teamed with Tazz. They legitimately hated each other. "He did not like teaming with Tazz," Heyman says. "He hated it. They didn't get along.

"Sabu wanted me to pull him out of the tag team, and I said as soon as the three-way dance is over, I'll do it, but I can't pull you out now," Heyman reports. "There is no way. This three-way dance is going to be the hottest tape we ever had. He said, 'Let's shoot an injury angle.' I said, 'No, I don't want to shoot an injury angle. I am the one that is giving you a full-time living, and we're building something together here. We are about to explode with the biggest tape selling we ever had.' Sabu had a choice to make. He chose to go to Japan. He called me from Japan on Friday and said, 'Look, I just want to let you know I am here. You run four- or five-hour shows. Just hold that show for me.' He was talking about making a flight right after his match and coming home. He said, 'I get in at 11 P.M., and once I clear customs, I'll be at the arena by midnight. You can do a four-hour show. Just buy me some time, and I'll do it.' I said, 'I can't take that risk. What if you take two hours to clear customs? And who says you are going to make that flight? I can't risk it.' I said that he had to get back on the plane now. He said, 'I can't do that.' Nobody knew what I was going to do.

"I called my old friend Rick Steiner. I said, 'I need you for one shot. We are going to do a three-way, and I am teaming you with Tazz.' He said, 'I will be there, no problem.' I knew in my heart what I had to do. About five minutes before the show began, I went to Tod Gordon and said, 'I'm going to fire Sabu.' He said, 'Oh, yes, you have to.' I said, 'No, I am going to fire him in the middle of the ring. I'm going to let the audience fire him.'"

Heyman grabbed Tazz and 911 and told them they would be walking out to the ring out of character, to tell the audience what was going on. Heyman got into the ring, took the microphone, and addressed the crowd: "Sabu gave us a committment and decided that because he was offered more money someplace else that he would not give you what you paid to see and he would not give me the courtesy of a phone call when he swore to God on Sunday night before we all went into production that he would do that when I said, 'If

you are not going to be in the arena, if you are going to fuck the audience that made you a star in this country, let me know and I will handle the interview.' He said, 'I swear to God I will be there.'

"Everyone back there busts their ass for you, and everybody back there has been building this thing together since September 1993, and everybody has made sacrifices. If you want him back, I will bring him back and all will be forgiven, and if you don't want him back . . . time will heal all wounds, and if you want him back sometime, just let me know."

Heyman says he didn't know how the audience would respond. "The audience just gasped, because he was the hottest guy we had. I look over at Tazz, and he gives me this look like, 'Holy fuck, man. This is where it ends. We blew it. We did something that the audience is going to hate the promotion for: fired their hero.' But one person in the audience screams out, 'Fuck him.' I look over because I don't know if the guy is pointing at me and talking about me. I don't know who he is saying fuck to yet. Someone else yells, 'Yeah, yeah, yeah,' and in a few seconds, the whole building in unison is chanting, 'Fuck Sabu! Fuck Sabu!' and it got louder and louder. I put down the microphone and looked at the audience as if, 'Okay, you made your decision.' And we all left the ring and went on with the show. No one asked for a refund, and he wasn't back until November 1995."

Tazz was angry—angrier than normal—at Sabu for bailing on him. "Sabu and I did not get along," he says. "I couldn't stand him and he couldn't stand me. I was really angry with Sabu when he left. Paul Heyman had me walk to the ring with him and 911, and Paul went into the ring and publicly fired Sabu. It was the real deal."

Tazz and Sabu had a unique relationship. In many ways, they made each other, but they hated each other as well. "Sabu was the best," Tazz says. "I don't know how to explain him. There were times when we hated each other's guts. We were tag team champions at one point, and we hated each other. We were at the Marriott in Philadelphia, at the airport, and Paul Heyman was in the room with us, and we were going to throw each other through the window. Paul had to calm us down. We just didn't get along. We were both supercompetitive with each other. But, God, without Sabu, I don't think I would be where I am today. He made me. The reason why I got into ECW was to wrestle Sabu in 1993. I was there to make him, and in the end, I think we made each other. He was ahead of his time, the whole table-breaking thing was him, in Japan, with FMW, and then The Public Enemy and the Dudley Boyz did it after that. Sabu was a crazy bastard with a good heart. He has a tough texture on the outside, but inside he was good people, a good human being. We used to get under each other's skin a lot, but I miss being around him. I think he was great. His style was spectacular. He was so smart and knew how to make his moves mean something. He was a master at his craft."

When Heyman fired Sabu, it was another revolutionary moment in wrestling, where the fans were brought behind the scenes and shown the real dealings of the business. "Paul never lied to the fans," Dreamer claims. "Anything that got out to the Internet or to a magazine, Paul, a lot of times, would address it by going into the ring and talking to the fans. He lied to the wrestlers, but he never lied to the fans."

Chris Jericho remembers how Heyman would lie to the boys. "It was my job to get the crazy plane tickets and plane fares that Paul E. would arrange for me, often calling me about a half hour before I had to leave my house for the flight," Jericho says. "I remember one time I got home at eleven at night and was supposed to leave the next morning. There are very few flights from Calgary that will get into Philly in time. I called him every hour and no answer, 11:30, 12:30, left messages, and finally at 5:30 in the morning I left a message telling him he could '. . . take your TV title and stick it up your ass. I don't care what you do, I'm not coming in. Forget your stupid promotion. See you later, buddy. Forget it. I am not coming, no matter what.'

"A minute later he called me back and said, 'Hey, what's going on? I tried to call you and your phone wasn't working, and I just couldn't get you, and here is your flight information. What's going on, buddy,' and blah, blah, blah. By the time I finished talking with him, it was impossible not to like this guy. I had called him and told him I was never going to work for him again, and ten minutes later I was packing my bags with minutes to spare to make it to the airport."

Heyman had been the driving force behind the ECW expansion, and now he would become the owner as well. Tod Gordon was having financial problems and other issues, and in the first week of May 1995, Heyman took over total control and responsibility. "That responsibility, including a couple of hundred grand in debts that had been run up, including about $25,000 in TV station fees, and $35,000 in production fees, and plane tickets, and other expenses," Heyman explains. "Tod remained on and helped out when he could, in some business things or securing an arena, and remained the on-air commissioner, for rulings and such."

The organization moved the merchandising operation to New York—that stepped up sales—while the ticket operation was run out of Philadelphia, with the ECW Arena as the anchor. Much of that action had consisted of violent slugfests, with tables, chairs, ladders, canes, and whatever weapons could be used to fuel these brutal battles. But Heyman had also been cultivating another part of the promotion, using Chris Benoit, Dean Malenko, and Eddie Guerrero to present the fans with pure wrestling—moves and holds and fast-paced action. He would now place an emphasis on that part of the promotion, opening up another area to grow and bring in more fans.

"ECW was known as the blood-and-guts company in the early days," Dreamer recalls. "Then everyone started doing crazier stuff, like breaking tables. Then we brought in all these new wrestlers like Chris Benoit and Dean Malenko, and turned it around to a wrestling company."

Heyman said he wanted to use the ECW TV Championship to create this different personality with the promotion. "With Dean Malenko and Eddie Guerrero, I wanted to make the TV Championship different than the heavyweight championship," he said. "I wanted to give it its own personality. At first, in 1994, it was the title that Mikey Whipwreck had won. He won it by accident, he took beatings and survived, he was the miracle kid. Then we took the TV title off him and put the tag team title on him with Mick Foley. But as we got into 1995, I wanted to make the TV title more of the pure wrestling championship. I gave the title to Too Cold Scorpio, and started having him doing really nice wrestling matches with people, usually the third or fourth match of the night, so no one would complain about it being boring or yell, 'We want blood, we want blood.' This would be the fifteen minutes a night of chain wrestling, is what they call it—whip into the ropes, duck under, drop-kick, grab a headlock, flip the guy over, and you both arch up to your feet. Wrestling, grappling."

Heyman told Eddie Guerrero, "I want you to come in and beat Too Cold Scorpio for the TV title, and dedicate your victory to Art Barr [Guerrero's former tag team partner who had passed away]. I know that will mean something to you. And I want to get you in a feud with Dean Malenko. I want Malenko to be the heel. I want to make this a wrestling feud."

Heyman planned on switching the title back and forth between Malenko, Guerrero, and Benoit, which was unusual for ECW, which did not often use their titles for such gimmicks—flip-flopping champions quickly and doing all sorts of outcomes with the championship among the three wrestlers. Guerrero beat Too Cold Scorpio at the April 8 show to win the TV belt, then wrestled Malenko to a draw at the April 15, 1995, *Hostile City Showdown,* which also featured Raven winning over Tommy Dreamer in a disqualification; Axl Rotten beating Ian Rotten; Tsubo Genjin defeating Tony Sexton; Sandman taking the ECW Championship from Shane Douglas; The Public Enemy beating The Pitbulls for the ECW tag team title; 911 beating Ron Simmons; and Cactus Jack defeating Terry Funk for the ECW Heavyweight Championship.

The May 13, 1995, ECW Arena show was known as *Enter the Sandman.* Guerrero and Malenko wrestled to another draw, and then Guerrero beat Marty Jannetty; the feud between Axl and Ian Rotten continued, with Axl winning a "barbed wire baseball bat barbed wire chair match"; Tazz & 911 defeated Tsubo Genjin & Hiroyoshi Iekuda; Hack Meyers beat Tony Stetson. Sandman beat Cactus Jack and then Shane Douglas for the ECW Heavyweight belt; and in a Double Dog Collar match, The Public Enemy beat The Pitbulls again to successfully defend their ECW Tag Team Championship.

It continued to be a hot summer at the box office and on TV for ECW, with one big show after another raising the profile and spreading the reputation of the promotion. One of the featured promos that summer was a referee named Bill Alfonso, known as Fonzie. He was supposedly appointed by the Pennsylvania State Athletic Commission, and created a lot of heat. "We had him do everything, every bullshit wrestling decision known to man," Heyman notes. "We did every ripoff finish, because we had never done it before, and we put all the heat on Fonzie. We did things like reverse a decision, which we never would do. We had him call for a disqualification because someone threw a punch. We had him stop a match because someone would have a little cut over their eye. It was some of the most insane heat you had ever seen."

Cactus Jack vs. Sandman.

The Dreamer-Raven feud was going strong, as was Sandman and Mick Foley's. A tag team war was raging between The Public Enemy and a team that had arrived on the scene from Smoky Mountain Wrestling in Tennessee called The Gangstas. Jamal Mustafa, known as Mustafa Saed, and Jerome Young, a former bounty hunter known as New Jack, were The Gangstas, and they were one of the most violent teams in ECW, using anything you could think of for weapons, from crutches to staple guns.

ECW also introduced a gimmick that would spawn perhaps the most successful act in ECW history, though the Dudleyz would take some time to find their proper place in the business. At the July 1, 1995, *Hardcore Heaven*, Dino Sendoff & Don E. Allen wrestled to a no contest with Chad Austin & The Broad Street Bully; Hack Meyers defeated Big Malley; Too Cold Scorpio beat Tazz; Stevie Richards & Raven beat Tommy Dreamer & Luna Vachon for the ECW Tag Team Championship; Axl Rotten beat Ian Rotten; The Public Enemy defeated The Gangstas; in an ECW World Heavyweight Championship bout, Sandman beat Cactus Jack, and the Dudley Boyz defeated The Pitbulls.

The Dudleyz were a stable of wrestlers supposedly related to one another, and initially were part of Raven's Nest, one of many characters who would connect as Raven followers. The story went that the Dudleyz were all half brothers, and in their debut, there were three— Dudley Dudley, the only pure Dudley because both of his parents were named Dudley; Big Dick Dudley (Alex Rizzo, 6-foot-3, 285 pounds, and trained along with Tazz by Johnny Rodz), the big enforcer of the group; and Lil' Snot Dudley (Anthony Michaels), the underdog, who was injured in a boating accident after *Hardcore Heaven* and was replaced by Dances with Dudley (Adolfo Bermudez), so named because he was the result of their father's visit to an Indian reservation. There would be many more Dudleyz over the years, but the two that would break away and carve out a huge niche of their own were Bubba Ray Dudley and D-Von Dudley, who would emerge on the scene a year later.

The roll that ECW was on took a turn in the opposite direction in the summer of 1995. During a show in Fort Lauderdale, Tazz broke his

Dudley Dudley, Big Dick Dudley, and Snot Dudley.

neck in a tag team match with Eddie Guerrero against Dean Malenko & Too Cold Scorpio. "Scorpio and Malenko were taking it to me pretty good," Tazz notes. "I was trying to tag Eddie, and I couldn't get to him. The next thing you know they gave me a spike piledriver. Malenko came off the second rope, grabbed my boots, drove my boots down while Scorpio had me up for the piledriver, and boom. I didn't get a chance to protect myself. I landed on my forehead and jacked my whole neck back, and that was it. It was just a nasty move where I thought it was going to be one move, and it ended up being a different move, and when your timing is off in this business, it is catastrophic. I was scared. I didn't have any feeling in my body for a few seconds, although it felt much longer than that."

But Tazz still managed to finish his match, and after the show, with the help of Tommy Dreamer, went to a nearby hospital. "When Tazz broke his neck in Florida, he finished his match and kept saying, 'Damn, my neck is hurting,'" Dreamer recalls. "I walked him into the hospital. We would always travel together. They asked him, 'How did you get in here?' He said, 'I walked.' They said, 'There is no way you walked in here.' He said, 'Yeah, I did, I walked in here.' They said, 'Well, sir, you have a broken neck.'"

It was frightening on several levels for Tazz, who, with his wife, had just bought a house and had no signed contract with ECW. "The company was just starting to make a little money," Tazz remembers. "I had just gotten back from my honeymoon, maybe a week after my honeymoon. Paul stood by me, paid me for every week, even though I was out for about nine months. We were just barely getting by as a company, and he couldn't afford that. We had a deal with a handshake, not a written contract. I never signed a paper contract with Paul Heyman, always a handshake, even when I was ECW Champion, and it was big. We always had that trust. I didn't have insurance. I was young. Paul said he would stand by me, and he did. I will never, ever forget it. Paul was loyal to the crew and the crew was loyal to Paul."

The other setback came in the Guerrero-Benoit-Malenko storyline. Heyman planned on having Guerrero and Benoit meet for the ECW Heavyweight Championship, with Benoit winning and being a long-term title holder. But at the end of the summer, all three left ECW for WCW, which sent a shock wave through ECW and created controversy that exists today over how it happened.

Heyman accused WCW boss Eric Bischoff of raiding ECW. "ECW was the first victim of the Monday night war [between WCW and WWE]," he states. "In August 1995, WCW stole Chris Benoit and Eddie Guerrero and Dean Malenko, all in one swoop."

Dreamer says that ECW had become too popular to ignore by the two larger promotions: "I think ECW started getting noticed, and the other companies needed more talent."

Bischoff dismisses the notion that he "raided" ECW talent. "I need to point out that one man's raid is another company's acquisition," he asserts. "We never raided anybody. We never raided the WWE, despite everybody's opinion to the contrary. We never raided ECW. We never raided anybody. Think about it, did Vince McMahon raid all the local territories when he accumulated talent? They made a decision that they would rather work for Vince McMahon as he was expanding his national territory, as opposed to working for local promoters. Was that a raid? Certainly not in Vince McMahon's mind and certainly not in the minds of the people who work for WWE currently, or in the fans' minds, or mine. Did some talent leave ECW and come to WCW? Of course they did, because: A, they probably weren't getting paid, and they had to in order to pay their bills and feed their families, and B, they recognized that WCW was a much stronger, much more secure, a much larger international platform for them to ply their trade. Did they make that choice to come to WCW? Of course they did. Did some of them make the choice to go to Vince? Of course they did. But that is not a raid, despite what Paul Heyman and others would have you think."

It certainly created some bitter feelings between WCW and ECW, beyond perhaps the normal competitive tension. "Eric Bischoff is full of shit, and much like a lot of other people, never gave ECW the credit that it deserved," Heyman claims. "Eric Bischoff stole Chris Benoit, Eddie Guerrero, and Dean Malenko, same way he signed Chris Jericho from ECW, same way he stole the cruiserweights from ECW. It was a smart move by Eric Bischoff to do it, because he was in competition with Vince, and he had to have the talent, and he found them in ECW before anyone else had a chance to sign them. It was smart by Bischoff to do it. I just don't like the fact that he never said, 'Yeah, I stole that from ECW.' Because he did. It was blatant. We sued him over it a bunch of times."

That sort of tension didn't exist between ECW and World Wrestling Federation, as witnessed by the later cooperative efforts between the two promotions. "I didn't think it was the right thing to do that we would just raid his talent roster and give nothing back," McMahon says. "We put Paul on the payroll to compensate him in some way for taking a lot of the talent that he had. Contrary to that, of course, was Eric Bischoff, who would take his talent as well and not give him anything. Gleefully, not give him anything."

But even in the departure of three of its biggest stars, ECW showed it was a different promotion. It was the last night in ECW for Guerrero and Malenko, and the fans were told so when the two met in a Two Out of Three Falls match. The two wrestlers didn't relish facing what they expected to be a hostile crowd, and perhaps there was no more hostile crowd on the face of the earth than an angry ECW crowd. But it was also a crowd that appreciated what wrestlers did in ECW, putting their bodies on the line to produce great shows. That was the emotion that took over the audience for Malenko and Guerrero's last night in ECW. "Others who had left had heard chants like, 'You sold out,' 'Fuck you,' 'We hope you die,' and all kinds of different chants," Heyman explains. "But these guys got showered with respect. The audience was chanting, 'Please don't go.' Both Guerrero and Malenko were moved to tears during the match. It was a moving night. They wrestled to a draw, very rare in ECW. It was a regular card at the ECW Arena that we showed the highlights on television. Again, doing what no one else had done, we taped the match and we aired it throughout the course of an hour as one episode of television, a very famous episode of ECW TV.

"In the past, no one would ever say a wrestler was leaving one organization for another," Heyman continues. "You just beat a guy on his way out. If we followed the golden rule of wrestling, we would have had Eddie Guerrero get up in the ring and have Sabu put him through a table, and it would be the end of Eddie Guerrero. Then we would have Dean Malenko come out and have someone beat the fuck out of him and run him out. We went the opposite way. We showered them with respect, and when their match was over, unbeknownst to them, we all were coming out to the ring, the whole locker room. We put them up on our shoulders and shook their hands. We wanted to show everyone we were the fans' promotion. We appreciated everything they did for ECW. It was so cool. It was such an emotional moment. And everyone thought I was nuts. All my confidants thought I was crazy. They said, 'You have to beat them out the door.' I had a lot of resistance to what I wanted to do, but we were going to do this my way."

This is the way Joey Styles called it on the video: "If you are not here tonight to see this live, I don't know that the camera, or anything else, can convey and capture the feeling in this arena tonight, the overwhelming emotion that is overtaking everyone in this building."

Still, despite all the warm feelings, there was a lot of fear about what would happen next in the promotion after losing three major attractions. Ron Buffone turned to Heyman in the studio while putting together the TV show and said, "I now know it is over. There is no way we can recover from this. We have been so publicly punked out. I am scared this is the end."

Heyman, though, had options, and tapped one that had captured his attention in Mexico—a group of wrestlers who were making a name for themselves in *lucha libre* wrestling, in particular, Rey Mysterio, Jr., and Psicosis.

Rey Mysterio, Jr., was born in San Diego, California, on December 11, 1974. He was trained by his uncle, another great *lucha libre* wrestler, Rey Mysterio, Sr. The young Rey was so good and talented that, at the age of 15, he made his professional debut, which had to take place in Tijuana, since he was too young to be licensed in the United States as a professional wrestler. Despite his small size—5-foot-3 and 140 pounds—he developed a crowd-pleasing acrobatic style and found someone who could compliment him in battles in a rival who went by the name of Psicosis. Heyman had seen some tapes of the two and was very impressed. "It was the hottest thing I had ever seen, and it wasn't even the main event," Heyman recalls. "It was in the middle of the card—two young kids, stealing the show every night. I knew this could replace Benoit, Malenko, and Guerrero. It was a whole different style, *lucha libre*. Nobody had seen it in this country. WCW had it in its lap, because they co-promoted one *lucha* show in Los Angeles, put it on Pay-Per-View, and fucked it up, didn't follow up on it. It was just another example of WCW not understanding where wrestling was heading."

Heyman called a booker and wrestler in Mexico he knew named Konnan.

"They took Benoit, Malenko, and Guerrero," Heyman said to Konnan. "If you were me, and you had the golden pass to take anyone from Mexico, and use them when it is convenient and doesn't interfere with your business, who would you pick? It can't be you. You can't come in person. You can't lead the way." (Konnan would, however, soon join ECW.)

Konnan told Heyman, "Mysterio and Psicosis."

"Is it okay with you?" Heyman asked.

"Paul E., they are going to blow away everything you have on your show," Konnan said. "Nobody can follow them. I am learning it now. Nobody can follow them. It is the hottest thing you have ever seen."

They would make their debut at *Gangstas Paradise*, a September show that would come at a time when it appeared ECW might be on the ropes after the loss of Benoit, Guerrero, and Malenko. It turned out to be one of the bigger nights the promotion had seen yet.

The Pitbulls beat Raven & Stevie Richards for the ECW Tag Team title in a Two Out of Three Falls–Double Dog Collar bout; Tommy Dreamer pinned Raven, but Fonzie came out and reversed the victory as the state athletic commission representative; 911 finally got his hands on Fonzie, whom he had been chasing all summer, and choke-

Lucha libre finds a home at ECW: Mysterio vs. Psicosis.

slammed him; Mikey Whipwreck & The Public Enemy defeated Too Cold Scorpio, New Jack & Sandman in a Steel Cage match; and a new tag team named The Eliminators came to ECW and joined Jason in defeating Tazz & Rick & Scott Steiner.

The Eliminators consisted of two very talented athletes—Perry Saturn and John Kronus. Saturn—born Perry Satullo on October 25, 1966, in Cleveland—came out of the army, where the story goes that he was an airborne ranger. He used his physical prowess when he came out of the service to become a wrestler, and began training with the legendary Killer Kowalski in Malden, Massachusetts, in 1988. Two years later, as Saturn, he made his debut in the United States Wrestling Association. He also wrestled under the name The Iron Horseman as a cowboy in Kowalski's promotion, the International Wrestling Federation. Like many other wrestlers, he also wrestled in Japan with New Japan Pro Wrestling in 1993.

Saturn also worked as a manager of a bar in Boston, and it was there he met a bouncer named George Caiazo, who was interested in becoming a wrestler. Saturn sent him to Kowalski for training and then formed a tag team with him, giving Caiazo the ring name John Kronus. Kronus was a unique 6-foot-3, 280-pound force of nature in the ring, and along with the unpredictable Saturn, would form a devastating tag team.

"Perry Saturn would scare me to death," says Mike Nova, who would also join ECW in 1995. "Him and John, Perry would have to treat him like a kid. Kronus was the best natural athlete I ever saw in the ring. He was 6-foot-2, nearly 300 pounds. I remember all of us in the ring one day fucking around with a crash pad. We were trying to do the Shooting Star Press, the Billy Kidman move, and none of us really had the balls to do it. He went up to the ring and did it, not only effortlessly, but he did it three-quarters of the way across the ring. He and Too Cold Scorpio were two of the greatest flyers I had ever seen."

Saturn and Kronus broke in as a team with the United States Wrestling Association in 1993 and won the tag team titles there in 1994. Heyman brought them into ECW, where they were managed by

Jason and won the tag team belts three times in the promotion and created some of the action-packed, brutally fought feuds in the ring with The Gangstas and The Pitbulls. Saturn also worked as a trainer for ECW's wrestling school, House of Hardcore. The team would break up after Saturn tore knee ligaments in 1997. When he returned, he decided he didn't want to team with Kronus any longer.

In the middle of all the chokeslams, the tag team battles, and the wild scene taking place that September night at the ECW Arena, Heyman introduced Rey Mysterio and Psicosis to ECW fans.

When Mysterio and Psicosis got to the arena, Heyman met with them.

"Hi, how are you guys doing?" he asked. "Thank you so much for coming. Konnan tells me all about you. Put your match together and I will get back to you later."

Heyman left them alone for about twenty minutes and then returned and said, "Do you guys know what you want to do yet?"

Mysterio asked, "What are our parameters?"

Heyman replied, "You have none. If you both went to heaven, and God said, 'Put on the most entertaining match to simply blow me away, and I'm giving you one chance to do it, or you both go to hell, but if you do it, you and your families will be up here in heaven with me,' what match would that be?"

He walked away again, leaving the two wrestlers stunned. If this was WCW or WWE, they would be going through a carefully planned and choreographed match.

Before the show started, Mysterio came up to Heyman and said, "Please, you've got to tell me what you want."

Heyman said, "Okay, here it is. Steal the show. I am giving you the platform. You can go into the rails, you can use tables and chairs. Be smart, though. Just because you can do it doesn't mean you should, and just because you should do it doesn't mean you have to, and just because you have to do it doesn't mean you're going to. Steal the fucking show. Do it any way you have to—wrestle, brawl, bleed, fly, anything you want. Show these people you are the best in the world. Rey, do you believe you are the best in the world?"

Mysterio answered, "I believe I'm one of them."

Heyman turned to Psicosis and asked, "Do you think there is any better heel than you?"

Psicosis answered, "No, I think I am the best in the world."

Heyman kept trying to ease their fears. "Okay, so twenty chair shots ain't your style, right?"

Psicosis said, "No."

Heyman went on. "Ten tables ain't your style, right?"

Psicosis said no again, and Heyman replied, "But maybe one table, one chair, maybe one kick to the balls. Be smart. How much time would you like? Is thirty minutes too long?"

Psicosis answered, "Yeah, thirty minutes is too long."

So Heyman asked, "Is twelve too short?" to which Psicosis replied yes, and they agreed on twenty minutes.

Heyman looked at them and said, "Okay, go home when it is right. You want to make me look good, right? Here's what I want. I want Rey to win. I want Rey to win with a finish that nobody has seen here before."

Mysterio told Heyman, "I do this thing, man. I stand up on the top rope, the guy runs at me, I flip over his shoulders, I come up with a sunset flip, we both flip twice, and I end up hooking his legs. I did it once and people loved it."

Heyman said, "Okay, that's your finish. Now that we know it, I don't want to tell you anything else. My ring is your canvas. Paint me a Picasso. If you are over, then you are invited back for all my shows. If you're not, then you tried. This is me giving you a chance to have the most famous match of your lives. Go for it."

Heyman said he had nothing to lose by leaving them on their own to make the match. "I knew if they gave me a classic, people would think I was a genius. If they bombed, then people can say I tried. If I am wrong, then I am wrong, but at least I took the risk, and if I am right, I am the guy who gave them the chance. They will make me look good."

Mysterio and Psicosis went on to steal the show with their high-flying, fast-paced *lucha libre* match. "It was fabulous, and it saved me, because now people knew if they wanted to watch extreme *lucha libre*, they had to watch my show," Heyman declares. "Now I have all the Hispanics in New York watching me, too. All of a sudden we are getting all these orders for tapes from Texas and California because they want to see these guys. And it also sent a message—anyone can leave ECW. We will replace everybody. Earlier in the year, we replaced Sabu and didn't miss a beat. Now we lose three of the greatest wrestlers in the world—Benoit, Malenko, and Guerrero—and on the very next show, we replaced them with two Mexican wrestlers that Vince and Bischoff thought could never get over. They were seen as midgets. Someone said to me, 'You've got midgets on your show. Jumping beans, jumping beans.' But people were blown away."

Mysterio recalls his introduction to ECW: "Konnan spoke very highly of me and Paul Heyman brought me in. I owe Konnan so much and he is still a very close friend and neighbor of mine. He has a brilliant mind for the wrestling business.

"I remember walking in that first day and asking Paul, 'What can we do? Can we use tables or chairs?'" Mysterio says. "Paul answered, 'Do whatever you guys want. Just go out there and have a good time.'"

One month later, Mysterio and Psicosis would meet in a much-celebrated Two Out of Three Falls match that would overshadow all their others, in particular because Psicosis would be the winner. "That Two Out of Three was perceived as the last match, even though it wasn't," Heyman explains. "It was perceived as the blow-off, you put the heel up clean, no cheating, just let him win. That was so risky because people were, 'Oh my God, it will kill Rey.' But it wouldn't kill Rey. It would help make him, because it would show people you never know who will win between these two. You have to give credibility to Psicosis because he is so good."

A description of how each fall was won shows the acrobatic *lucha libre* style that captured the attention of fans: The first fall is Mysterio's. He nails it by taking off and goes flying out of the ring, over the top rope and into Psicosis, who is out of the ring, knocking him back over the guardrail and into the seats. The crowd is going wild, chanting, "ECW! ECW!" Mysterio gets up and climbs into the ring slowly, looking as if he is hurting. Psicosis is even slower getting up, but both wrestlers eventually get back into the ring. They start hurtling back and forth against the ropes, then Mysterio dives into the air, grabs Psicosis with a flying leg scissors, and flips him over, then gets the quick pin.

The second fall goes to Psicosis when Mysterio does a cartwheel and wraps his legs around Psicosis's head. He throws Psicosis to the mat. Psicosis gets up and Mysterio comes flying backward off the ropes for another leglock around Psicosis's head in a springboard moonsault from the second rope, but this time Psicosis drives Mysterio into the mat with a Tombstone Piledriver, which nearly puts Mysterio out. Psicosis holds Mysterio down for the count. Psicosis wins the second fall, as Mysterio lies nearly motionless on the mat.

In the third and final fall, Psicosis whips Mysterio into the steel rails. Psicosis picks Mysterio up and slams him into another rail. Psicosis sets up a table, lays Mysterio out on it, gets a chair from a fan in the crowd, and slams the chair into Mysterio's stomach. Psicosis then gets back in the ring and climbs to the top rope, jumps, and lands on top of Mysterio with a leg drop, breaking the table. Psicosis picks Mysterio up and tosses him back into the ring. He takes Mysterio's head, puts it between his legs, and delivers a powerbomb. As Mysterio lies on the canvas, Psicosis brings a chair into the ring and smashes it over Mysterio's chest and face. Psicosis lays the chair on top of Mysterio, climbs to the top rope, dives off, and backflips onto Mysterio and the folded chair lying on top of him. Psicosis gets the cover and the victory over Mysterio.

This kind of action existed in an atmosphere in which Heyman let the wrestlers—the artists—paint their own picture. "It was one of the only companies that really had no restrictions on time limits or moves," Mysterio recalls. "It was just go out there and do what you do best, which was wrestle."

But that was just one part of ECW—the wrestling. The talking was a big part of the success of the promotion, and Heyman was about to welcome someone who would talk his way into ECW history and launch his own remarkable career in the process.

chapter five

Ruth and Gehrig

Steven Williams—born December 18, 1964, in Victoria, Texas—was a typical tough guy from the Lone Star State. The 6-foot-2, 250-pounder played football at North Texas State University and then went to work at various odd jobs. Eventually, wrestling seemed like a good fit for him, and after being trained by Chris Adams, he made his debut in 1989—not as Steve Williams, because there was another wrestler with that name, but instead taking the name Steve Austin, after the nearby town.

"Stunning" Steve Austin wrestled in Texas with the United States Wrestling Association for two years and in 1991 joined WCW, where he began to make a name for himself, winning the TV title and hooking up with a faction in the promotion called The Dangerous Alliance. That group, which featured Rick Rude, Larry Zbyszko, Bobby Eaton, and Arn Anderson, was led by a colorful, outspoken manager named Paul E. Dangerously. Paul E.—Paul Heyman—would leave WCW, but Austin stayed and continued to move up in the promotion, holding the WCW Tag Team title with Brian Pillman on a team known as the Hollywood Blondes. That was the first incarnation of Steve Austin—a tough but pretty-boy blond. It was not the persona that would make him one of the biggest stars in the history of the business.

Austin went on a tour of Japan in 1995, where he suffered a severe injury—a torn tricep. Soon after, he suffered another injury—this one much more personal. His boss at WCW, Eric Bischoff, fired him over the phone, a move that angered Austin.

The word spread to Heyman that Austin had been fired. "The fact that he had been injured and Bischoff fired him, that was a real shitty move," Heyman states. "I figured Vince would give him a job. I managed Steve in WCW—not his legitimate manager, but his wrestling manager—and I thought, given the right platform, Steve would be a huge star. I had a great relationship with Steve. There was a WCW magazine back in the fall of 1992, and I used to write a column called 'The Danger Zone,' because I was Paul E. Dangerously. I wrote an entire column that Steve Austin, by the year 2000, would become the biggest single star in the business. I knew it."

Heyman called Austin when he heard the news. "Hey, how are you doing?"

"Hi, kid, what is going on?" Austin said, in that gruff, readily identifiable voice of his.

"I heard you got fired."

"Yeah, the motherfucker, he fired me on my answering machine."

"What?"

"His secretary called me and fired me on my answering machine."

"Come on," Heyman said.

"Paul, I was sitting here at home drinking a beer," Austin said. "I didn't hear the phone ring. There was a beep from the machine and I heard, 'Steve, this is Jeanie Engle calling for Eric Bischoff. Please call

Eric Bischoff.' There was another message, 'Steve, this is Jeanie Engle calling. Eric Bischoff needs to talk to you.' And then another one that said, 'Hi, Steve, Jeanie Engle calling. Eric said don't bother calling him back, just wanted to let you know we are going to send your release papers. Thank you for your contribution to World Championship Wrestling. We wish you all the best luck in future endeavors. Bye.' End of message."

"You mean they fired you on your answering machine?" Heyman said in disbelief.

"Damn right, motherfuckers."

"So when do you start for Vince?" Heyman asked, anticipating that Austin would be recruited by McMahon.

"Two problems," Austin said. "My arm is still all fucked up and I'm still rehabbing, and I got a couple of months left to go."

"What is the second problem?"

"Nobody's called me."

Heyman was stunned. "Wow."

"You called me," Austin said.

"Do you want to work for me?"

"Fuck, yeah, I want to work for you. I love your show."

"Really?"

"Fuck, yeah."

"Steve, I want you to show people what you got."

"I'm sitting here with a beer in my hand and my feet up on the sofa. What do you need from me?"

"Just come in here and tell your story."

"Okay, who do you want me to tell it to?" Austin asked.

"Everybody. Come up here and rip those motherfuckers to shreds."

"You've got to be kidding me."

"No, you've got to air that."

"Fucking A, I'm going to air that," Austin said, excited about the prospects.

"Anything you want to do, just let your personality show," Heyman offered.

"I'll do it under two conditions. Number one, I want to have my first match back for you, and I want to wrestle Mikey Whipwreck, and I want him to beat me in the middle of the ring."

Heyman laughed. "Okay, why would you want that?"

"Because that's business," Austin said. "I love that kid and the way he works, and it would be a pleasure to work with him."

Heyman wanted to take the heavyweight championship out of Sandman's hands, and they figured, why not put it around Mikey Whipwreck's waist? "I needed Sandman back to being a babyface, and the way to do it was to take the title off him and have him just beating the fuck out of people, because when he loses everything is when people love him. So when he lost that title and started caning the fuck out of people, they loved him again."

Austin appeared on the scene doing some of the greatest promos ECW had seen, as this former WCW star went on TV and ridiculed and ripped his former bosses. He wore a black wig and imitated Bischoff, saying things like, "Welcome to *Monday Night Nyquil*." He would work to hone his promo style in ECW, where he would also find the inspiration that would lead to the character that would later make him a star—Stone Cold Steve Austin.

Another future wrestling superstar would tape a set of promos that summer that would make wrestling history—Cactus Jack. They began at *Wrestlepalooza 1995*, on August 5. Raven, Stevie Richards, Snot Dudley, and Big Dick Dudley were scheduled to face Tommy Dreamer, Luna Vachon, and The Pitbulls in an eight-man tag team bout. When Cactus Jack arrived at the ECW Arena that night for his match, he got a surprise from Paul Heyman.

Heyman wanted Cactus Jack—Mick Foley—to turn heel. "I was planning on talking to Mick at that show about turning heel at one of the upcoming shows," Heyman says. "But we had an eight-man tag team match booked, and Luna Vachon missed her flight in Florida, and we fired her. She was one of Dreamer's partners. Mick was scheduled to do a run-in in another match. When he got to the building, he had been stuck in some heavy-duty traffic and got there right before the show."

Heyman pulled Cactus Jack aside and said, "I am sorry this is not a long-term conversation. I wanted to sit down with you after the show tonight. But I want to turn you heel. I want to turn Cactus Jack heel."

Foley didn't give it much thought. "That was almost unthinkable because I was such an established figure in the hardcore world, and would presumably be a difficult guy for the fans to boo," Foley declares. "But I just looked at him and said, 'Okay, let's do it.'"

Tommy Dreamer, with the ring emptied out at this point in the match, finally got his nemesis, Raven, and delivered a DDT. As he went for the pin, Cactus Jack—supposedly Dreamer's tag team partner—came into the ring and kicked Dreamer in the head. Then he lifted Dreamer off the floor and did a double DDT on a chair. Cactus Jack grabbed Raven and pulled him on top of Dreamer for the pin. The crowd was stunned.

If ECW fans were shocked, they were blown away, as were even the other wrestlers, by two promos Cactus Jack would shoot later that month and in September: the anti-hardcore promos.

Here is the one Cactus Jack shot in August:

"I'm going to take you back to a deciding point in my life—a time when I believed in something. A time when I thought that was my face and my name made a difference. Do you remember the night, Tommy Dreamer? Because it's embedded in my skull, it's embedded in my heart, and it's embedded in every nightmare that I will ever have. As Terry Funk took a broken bottle and began slicing and dicing Cactus Jack, the pain was so much that—I'll be honest with you, Tommy—the pain was so much that I wanted to say, 'I quit, Terry Funk, I give, I wave the flag, and I'm a coward—just please don't hurt me anymore.' Then I saw my saving grace. You see, Tommy, I looked out in that audience, my adoring crowd, and I saw two simple words that changed my life: 'Cane Dewey.' Somebody had taken the time and the effort and the thought to make a sign that said, 'Cane Dewey.' And I saw other people around, as every moment in my life stopped and focused in on that sign and the pain that shot through my body became a distant memory, replaced by a thought which will be embedded in my skull until my dying day! Cane Dewey. Cane Dewey. Dewey Foley is a three-year-old little boy, you sick sons of bitches. You ripped out my heart,

you ripped out my soul, you took everything I believed in, and you flushed it down the damn toilet. You flushed my heart, you flushed my soul, and now it sickens me to see other people making the same mistake. You see, Tommy Dreamer, I have to listen to my little boy say every day, 'Daddy, I miss Georgia,' and I say, 'That's too bad, son, because your dad traded in the Victorian house for a sweatbox on Long Island. Your dad traded in a hundred-thousand-dollar contract, guaranteed money, insurance, respect, and the name on the dotted line of the greatest man in the world, to work for a scumbag who operates out of a little pissant pawnshop in Philadelphia.' You don't expect me to be bitter?

"Tommy, when you open up your heart, when you open up your soul, and it gets shit on, it tends to make Jack a very mean boy. And so, I say to you—before I take these transgressions out on you—to look at your future and realize that the hardcore life is a lie, that these letters behind me are a blatant lie, that those fans who sit there and say, 'He's hardcore, he's hardcore, he's hardcore,' wouldn't piss on you if you were on fire, you selfish son of a bitch! But I want you to understand, Tommy, though he's hurt you time and time again, Raven wants you to understand that the hatred I have in here is not for you. No, no—far from it. You see, Tommy, I'm not doing this because I hate you—I love you, man! I only want the best for you—but when I hear that WCW called up your number and you said, 'No, thank you'—well, it makes my blood run cold. As cold as that night in the ECW Arena. And so I got a moral obligation. You see, Tommy, I'm on a path of righteousness, and righteous men wield a lot of power. So if I've got to drag you by your face to that telephone and dial collect and say, 'Hello, Eric, it's me, Cactus, and though I know I've burned my bridge, and I'll never be taken back with open arms, I've got a wrestler who would gladly trade in his ECW shirt for a pair of green suspenders. And Tommy, just think of that sound in your ear when Uncle Eric says, 'Welcome home, Tommy Dreamer, welcome home.'"

He followed that with another memorable promo in September 1995:

"You know I'd like to apologize for my behavior. I'm embarrassed, certainly, I feel a little stupid about the way I acted on this show a few weeks ago. It's just that I get a little emotional when I talk about wrestling, because wrestling's been my livelihood for the past ten years. It's enabled me to live out my childhood dream. So for me to come out on a show such as the ECW television program and badmouth the wrestlers there—well, I'm sorry. But I think in order to understand what's going around my head, you have to understand where I come from and what my goals were when I got into wrestling.

"See, back in 1985, there was a program called 20/20 that challenged the wrestling industry, which kind of portrayed it in a negative light. Tommy, if you're listening, try to understand that I was about the biggest wrestling fan in the world. And for me to stand in front of that television set and see people running down a business that I loved and held dear—even though I knew very little about it—to see my friends laughing at me saying, 'That's what you want to get involved in?' That night I went to bed not with visions of sugarplums dancing through my head, but of broken bones, of battered bodies and bloody corpses, saying to myself, 'If it's the last thing I do, if I have to hold myself up for a human sacrifice, the world will respect professional wrestling.' Oh, and that dream came true—yes, I've sacrificed myself for the past ten years, leaving the better parts of my past lying on concrete floors from Africa to Asia to South America to right in the middle of the ECW Arena. And what's it really done? Where have we really come to?

"Lying in a hospital bed in Munich, Germany, seeing my ear being thrown into a garbage can, not being able to take it on the trip back because I didn't know the German word for 'formaldehyde.' And having a nurse walk into my room, looking at that piece of my body that's lying at the bottom of the garbage, and saying, 'Es ist alles Schauspiel!' which means, 'It's all a big joke!' Excuse me! I didn't know you opened up the diseased lung of a smoker and said, 'Oh, my golly, I thought smoking was supposed to be good for you!' Do you open up Terry Funk's nonfunctioning liver and say, 'Hey, I didn't know that four decades of heavy drinking took this kind of toll!'? So, if they show that much respect for other patients, what made me any different? Because I was a wrestler. And professional wrestling will never be respected, no matter how many teeth I lose, no matter how many ears I lose, no matter how many brain cells have to die. And so it comes down to the point where it's just not worth it, and, Tommy Dreamer, you've got to start looking at this realistically.

"Wrestling is a way to make a living—nothing more and nothing less—and as long as it's strictly business, well, you may as well be cuddled in the welcoming arms of World Championship Wrestling. Because ECW fans will be the death of you. You see, they realized, and they were smarter than any of us, that they rule ECW wrestling—not us. What happened, Tommy? You came back from All Japan wrestling with your trunks and your boots and said, 'By golly, I'm really going to wrestle.' Did Giant Baba hand you a dozen eggs and say, 'Here, crack these on Jumbo Tsuruta's head'? You're a disgrace to the profession, Tommy, you're becoming a damn fool. And I can't sit back and take it, because I've got a moral obligation. Tommy, try to understand—I am but a fouled experiment in human sociology, and I can accept that. But never in my sickest dreams did I imagine that there would be other wrestlers taking dives onto concrete floors, committing human suicide on my behalf—like I'm the patron saint of all the sick sons of bitches. Is that all I stand for, Tommy? Is that all I stand for, to stand in an arena where J.T. Smith lands headfirst on the concrete and hears the fans yell, 'You fucked up, you fucked up?' Well, fuck you. Who the hell do you think you are?

"We're not a wrestling organization anymore—we're the world's damn biggest puppet show. I'll be damned if I'm going to walk into an arena and let any of you call my match. One, two, three—jump. One, two, three—jump. Well, not me, because I'm nobody's stooge, and Tommy Dreamer, if you had a little bit of pride, or a little bit of common sense, you'd understand that those people don't love you— they laugh at you! You took some of the worst beatings the sport's ever seen, and they still laughed in your face. And to think that I stood there with my arm around you and endorsed you, saying, 'He's hardcore, he's hardcore, he's hardcore.' And for that I deserve to die a terrible, painful death, Tommy, because I feel responsible. And I got to go to bed at night, and I'm not sure where I'm going to spend eternity. And you, Tommy, are my salvation. Because, by delivering you to a better organization, where you can be appreciated, loved, and held with just the littlest amount of respect in the Turner family, then maybe there's a chance for me, too. Please, Tommy, for my sake, think it over, because a yes to Cactus Jack would mean a great deal to me— and a no—well, I'd have to take that as you putting a big A-OK stamp of approval on my eternal damnation. I'm counting on you, you selfish prick. Don't make me hurt you, because I can. Don't make me do it, because if I do, with God as my witness, it won't be in front of those little scumbags at the ECW Arena—it'll be just me and you,

Tommy, and you won't know when it's coming, and you won't know where. So unless you want to damn me to the depths of hell, answer my call and say, 'Okay, Cactus, you win. I'll put on the suspenders, I'll groom that mustache, and I'll call Uncle Eric and say, Count me in.' Because not only would you be doing yourself a big favor—not only would you be helping your life, you'd be saving mine. You'd be saving . . . mine."

Foley describes his process for getting in the right frame of mind for those promos as pretty much like method acting: finding a motivation for the character. "I was told once that a heel—a bad guy—has to believe he is right. No matter how flawed his logic, in his mind, his actions have to be justified. I simply thought back to a fan that was holding up a sign that said, 'Cane Dewey.' I kind of laughed it off when I saw the sign, but when I mentioned it to my wife, she almost got physically sick. I thought about the fan who had gone home and actually took the time to write a sign and encourage me to beat a 3-year-old kid. I made it very real in my mind. So the approach I was taking was that the fans wanted too much out of us, and that I was apparently the only one who caught on to it, and it angered me that Tommy Dreamer wouldn't accept WCW's invitation to join their crew. It was almost like I was the Jacob Marley of the ECW, and was the only one who realized the bad road these wrestlers were on. And there was some legitimacy to that.

"I was offering myself up as an example of someone who had messed up in his wrestling life, who had burned his bridge in WCW, and I have to say that WCW worked much better in an anti-hardcore program than WWE would. While our fans may not have liked Vince McMahon, at least they respected him. But they had a hatred and lack of respect for Eric Bischoff, who was the head of WCW. I was looking at the idea of trying to redeem myself by helping others, and I, like a lot of people, was always a little scared of religious zealots, so I became one, and worked a little religious zealotry into the mixture. I basically got angry because of Tommy Dreamer turning down my offer of help. He was dooming me to eternal damnation. I was trying to redeem myself, and couldn't do it without his cooperation."

Foley declares that it was the atmosphere in ECW that helped him create such promos. "What was nice about it was that you could really experiment with it and come up with some far-out ideas, and fans listened. They really listened. There were actually two sets of these anti-hardcore promos. There were the hardcore anti-hardcore promos, like the ones I was telling you about, where I had seen the light, claimed I was hardcore, and did it in a fashion that was very much not to the fans' liking. I was trying to figure out how to get the fans to really hate me, and I just systematically took away everything they liked about me. If they liked the beard, I shaved that. If they liked the hair, I wore it neat and in a ponytail. If they liked the hardcore image, I would take that away and do nothing in a match."

And Foley credits Heyman for creating that atmosphere. "It was awesome to work with Paul Heyman. He gave me all the room I needed, almost complete creative autonomy. He would be in the room when I would do the interviews. It was not as if he was not aware of what was going on his show. He loved it and encouraged me. I don't know if he ever took issue with what I said, and there were times when I was doing the anti-hardcore hardcores, as opposed to doing the hardcore anti-hardcores, that we had to stop the cameras several times because I was laughing so hard. For example, I would say, 'What is the wimpiest possible food someone could eat?' and Paul would say, 'A watercress sandwich,' and I would do my interview and say something like, 'Wait a minute, I believe I have a piece of watercress stuck in my teeth,' and I would attempt to floss using the microphone cable, because I was missing a couple of teeth, and I would say something like, 'See, I'm missing teeth because I'm hardcore,' that type of thing. I had my daughter's birthday party, and I was grossing kids out because I was missing an ear. They were polar opposites, there was really intense stuff and really hokey stuff. ECW fans accepted both of them."

The promos didn't just blow away the fans. The ECW wrestlers were amazed as well by the creativity. "When Mick Foley became a heel, that was a huge moment in the business," Tommy Dreamer says. "He had been this hardcore icon, and I brought him in as my partner, and he pretty much did a whole thing where he said hardcore wrestling gets you nowhere, and he was beating me up not for hate, but for love. I had offers to go to WWE and WCW, and he was trying to tell me, 'Take the money, because the fans don't care about it.' He was pretty much saying how much his body hurt, and that he lost his ear for what? What are you going to do when you retire and all this. He cut his greatest promos against me, and his favorite promos as well, which was all anti-hardcore stuff, which, coming from Mick Foley, was something amazing."

Sandman, who was not easily impressed, was in awe of Foley's ability to create heat. "Cactus Jack was one of the smartest guys I met in the business and did some of the best promos in the business," he states.

Ron Buffone was there to shoot those promos and knew they would have an impact. "You know when you are holding that camera and you are shooting a promo, you know when you have something special," he explains. "You know when you feel it, that this is great, and sometimes you are looking through the viewfinder thinking, 'Wow.' I always got that feeling with Steve. I got that feeling with Cactus. The stuff that he would do was brilliant. The stuff he came out with, 'Where did that come from? Wow!'"

So, at the same time, ECW had Steve Austin and Mick Foley—two of the future legends of the business—doing some of the best interviews ever seen in wrestling, for this blazing-hot Philadelphia-based wrestling promotion that had started out of a sports bar but was now making the big boys sweat.

"I had Babe Ruth and Lou Gehrig," Heyman recalls. "I had the greatest home run hitter and the greatest RBI guy. They were the best. It was phenomenal. The beauty of it all was that it allowed me to air them in their entirety or break them up amongst the pulp fiction montages we were doing. So I could air a nine-minute Mick Foley interview, or I could air a minute at a time, and intersplice other people around him, because you were always waiting for the next shoe to drop on the interviews. It was tremendous television."

One of those greats, Austin, made his presence felt during the October 28, 1995, ECW heavyweight title bout—a Ladder match—between

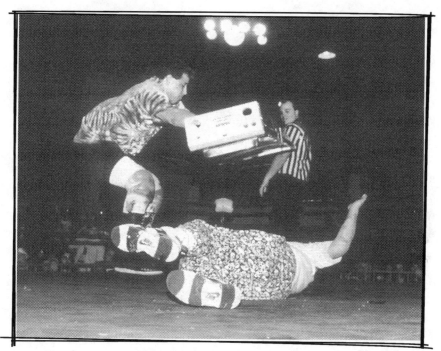

Mikey Whipwreck cuts Sandman down to size.

Sandman and Mikey Whipwreck. As usual, Sandman's intro took about twenty minutes, but it was a sight to see, set to the Metallica song "Enter Sandman." He strutted around the arena with Woman in tow, smoking a cigarette and drinking beer—a version of Austin before he became Stone Cold.

Mikey Whipwreck climbed into the ring, and Sandman, who had climbed to the top of the ladder in the ring to be used as a weapon in the match, comes down and towers over Mikey Whipwreck. As the ring introductions were made, a long-haired blond Steve Austin, dressed in garb that both reflected the Sandman and Mikey Whipwreck image, came out of the locker room and walked up to the ring, pointing his finger.

Austin got in the ring, took the microphone, and said, "A couple of people got smart with me on the way to the building today and said I was a Hulk Hogan wannabe. One of them said I look like Hulk Hogan. I've been crapped on for four years. I believe I deserve a break."

He climbed up the ladder and said, "I didn't get to climb the ladder to the top of WCW like this. I'm up here all the way at the top, and I look down and I see two jabronees and"—pointing to Woman—"from the places I've been, about a five-dollar piece of ass." As the crowd roared, Austin continued, "Whipwreck, you amaze me, son, because you're a go-getter. You ain't got no quit in you. You don't know what the word quit means. I respect you for that, but you are still just a loser in my book, son. This is Steve Austin talking to you, and if I am calling you a loser, you can damn well bet it is the truth."

Then he turned to Sandman and said, "Keep drinking a few more beers, smoke a few more cigarettes. You are sure really, really cool. Brother, I am going to get your ass in the ring and run circles around you, and when your tongue is hanging out down by your feet and I am walking off with the damn belt in my hands, you're going to wonder what the hell was I thinking, that's Steve Austin."

Austin turned his attention to Mikey Whipwreck again and said, "Mikey Whipwreck, this is not one of the misfits back there in that godforsaken dressing room, man. This is Steve Austin."

Then he pointed to Woman and said, "Don't get me wrong, hey, I can rustle up five dollars, and if I had a clothespin to put on my nose, I'd give you a try. Don't be looking at me pissed off, honey, because it is you that married a midget, not me. I wish both of your guys best wishes. I hope one of you kills the other because whoever comes out on top, you are looking at the next champ right here."

As soon as Austin left the ring, Sandman ran over and attacked Whipwreck on the ropes, hitting him with his can of beer, kicking him and putting him down on one knee. But at the end, a bloodied Sandman was laid out on the canvas, with the ladder on top of him, as Mikey Whipwreck dived from the top turnbuckle and hit a splash on top of the Sandman, getting the pin, and the crowd roared its approval for this bizarre twist—Mikey Whipwreck, the lovable loser, was the ECW Heavyweight Champion.

Fans at the October 28 show also got more than they bargained for when a match between Dreamer and Cactus Jack was scheduled, with Terry Funk in Dreamer's corner for support and Raven in Cactus

Jack's corner. After Cactus Jack turned heel, he proceeded to perform terribly in the ring for several weeks after that, further angering the fans and getting over as the heel. Heyman, as part of the storyline, accused Cactus Jack of stealing money, while Cactus Jack kept building up WCW and tearing down ECW. So Dreamer was there not only to meet Cactus Jack for revenge, but also to carry the banner of ECW and give the fans their money's worth, since they felt so cheated recently by Cactus Jack. They would get their money's worth and then some. At one point in the match, Cactus Jack stood on the ring apron and attempted to lead cheers for WCW, forming the letters with his arms, à la "YMCA." Dreamer beat up on Cactus Jack, who fought back hard until he screamed at one point after hitting Dreamer, "Oww! I think I broke my hand!" He grabbed the ring microphone and addressed the frenzied crowd at the arena.

"Ladies and gentlemen, as you can see, I suffered tremendous damage to my hand, and as a result, I just can't go on," Cactus Jack said. "The pain is too great. I am truly sorry, but I'm afraid that this match is over. The bout will be ruled a no contest."

To which referee Jim Molineux replied, "Cactus Jack, this is ECW—there's no such thing as no contest."

"Then do your job and count me out," Cactus Jack said.

"Cactus, why are you being such a pussy?" Molineux shot back.

Cactus Jack walked back to the dressing room. Bill Alfonso—"Fronzie"—came out and said that Cactus Jack, according to the Pennsylvania State Athletic Commission rules, had every right to be counted out. Alfonso began counting Cactus out, and Terry Funk decked Alfonso, took the microphone, and tried to lure Cactus back to the ring. "Cactus Jack, you're a goddamn coward, you son of a bitch," Funk said. "Your wife is a whore. Your mother is a whore. Your children are both whores. . . . Bischoff is a homo."

Cactus ran out to the ring, where he was pummeled by Funk and Dreamer. Suddenly, Raven appeared and hit Dreamer and Funk in the back with a chair. Raven pulled out a ten-pound weight and a roll of athletic tape and taped the weight to the top of the boot of Cactus Jack, who used it to kick Funk in the testicles. Funk went to the back of the arena, and Raven and Cactus double-teamed Dreamer. Funk returned, but Raven and Cactus Jack beat up Funk and Dreamer until Alfonso came back out with a chair that was to be set on fire, using a kerosene-soaked towel. Cactus Jack hit Dreamer and Funk with the unlit chair and the kerosene-soaked towel, knocking them down. The chair was lit, and Cactus Jack raised it up to hit Funk, but Dreamer dove in to protect Funk, who told Cactus Jack to use the chair again. He did, but this time the towel came off the chair and looked as if it had set Funk on fire. Cactus Jack tried to catch Funk, who was running around seemingly on fire. What happened was that the towel hit Funk and then rolled off him, but it still burnt him on the arm and at least one fan in the audience. It set off panic in the arena, as workers started spraying fire extinguishers, and chaos—more than the typical chaos—was everywhere. When Funk got back to the dressing room, he was screaming and throwing furniture around.

"Funk and Cactus come up with a stunt that they had done several times in Japan, where they are going to set a chair on fire," Heyman explains. "The way that you do this is you wrap a towel around a chair and douse it with lighter fluid, and set it on fire. This is not like a flaming table, where you just use the Ronsonal—barbecue lighter fluid—and it just dissipates. This is a cloth, so it doesn't dissipate. That towel is going to burn. What they suggested was that at the finish of the match, Dreamer has Mick Foley beat, Raven gets involved, Funk comes in, the fight between Funk and Cactus gets out of control, they get Funk and Dreamer down, they light the chair on fire, Funk gets the chair and nails Cactus. Dreamer goes for the DDT on Raven. Balls shot to Dreamer, and DDT to Dreamer on the flaming chair. Cactus gets Dreamer as Raven and Funk fight off.

"Well, when Funk swung the chair, the towel broke loose, and the fire was bigger than they thought. It burned the rope that tied the towel to the chair. The towel came off the chair and flew onto Funk's back. Funk rolled out of the ring. His shirt was on fire. A fan reached over and tried to put him out. Funk burned his arm pretty good, but the fan really burned his fingers. To make matters worse, the crew at the ECW arena, seeing there was an incident involving the fire, went crazy and started spraying fire extinguishers all over the place. Then the lights went out. It was a convergence of bad luck—one, two, three. Funk is on fire, the fan reaches over to put it out and burns his hand and starts screaming, 'Help me, help me.' The lights blow as the arena people caused this panic, spraying fire extinguisher every-where. We are about to have a stampede.

"We had this spotlight that I had set up, not connected to the power supply," Heyman continues. "We hooked it up to an alternative power supply, because we knew this spotlight was so bright it could blow the fuses in the building. The sound guy brought it, and brought the extra generator for it. That was the spotlight for Raven and Dreamer. So I am looking over in the dark while this mass panic is going on, and I see that Raven has Dreamer chained up. So I said, 'Hit the spotlight.' We hit the spotlight on Raven and Dreamer, and got everyone's attention, and it made for great footage, too."

This set up *November to Remember*—November 18, 1995—with so many twists and turns and any number of features that alone would have made any single show. Put together, the promotion was boiling over with heat.

Where to begin? How about bringing back Sabu?

Heyman had fired Sabu in April for taking a match in Japan and vi-olating his commitment to an ECW show. But he saw Sabu about seven months later in Chicago, where Heyman says they made peace. "At the time, Sabu was miserable on the independents. We did a show right after the fire, where we put on some ECW *lucha libre* matches, with Konnan and Rey Mysterio and others, at The Amphitheatre in Chicago. It was a Spanish show, and we put on some ECW matches. It was the first time Sabu and I had seen each other—he was on the show, too—since the week before I fired him. We were very cold to each other, but when we were in the same room with each other for a minute, you could tell one was waiting for the other guy to say, 'I really miss you.' I missed him and he missed me. One was just waiting for the other to make the first move, and we ended up on the phone the next week. I said, 'I had this fire thing happen, and I really want to give the fans something big when they come back. I think you are the answer.'"

So at the start of *November to Remember* at the ECW Arena, Heyman walked out to the ring and took the microphone. "Last time here we had a very bad incident with fire," he announced. "It was bad. You have to look no further than me, because the buck stops with me. If there is anyone responsible or to be yelled at, I am the guy. We always make things up to the audience, and we're going to make this up to you. We want to thank you for coming here tonight. We want to thank you for your support. We want you to know that it is not about personal agendas here. It is about giving the audience what you want. The only thing I will tell you is that if I could turn back the clock, I would. But you can't. So why don't we say that we at least tried. So if you don't mind, and there is no fire or fire extinguishers, let's dim the lights and turn back the clock."

They dimmed the lights, and when they came back on, Heyman was standing in the ring with Sabu, which sent a roar through the building and pumping the crowd up before the first match even took place.

If they were going to bring back Sabu, then why not Tazz, who was nearly recovered from his broken neck? He came back for this show as a special referee for a feature match between ECW Commissioner Tod Gordon and the heel referee, Bill Alfonso.

It would be a new Tazz, an angry, badass character that would skyrocket as one of the anchors of the ECW promotion. "We were bringing Tazz back, and this was under a new gimmick," Heyman recalls. "He was going to be our ultimate fighter–style wrestler. We were going to market him as the toughest guy on the planet. He was going to be a lot of what Austin's character became. A lot of what Austin was, the beer drinking came from the Sandman, but the attitude came from Tazz. Tazz gave the middle finger, the whole thing.

"We were going to bring back Tazz, and I knew he could be a big monster babyface, but you needed to give him a year and a half as a heel. And again, wanting to break all conventions and the way things were done in the past, I knew that the biggest feud in ECW, and the match we would end up going on Pay-Per-View with, was Tazz against Sabu. And much like I was going to make people wait forever to see Dreamer defeat Raven, I wanted to make people wait forever to see Tazz wrestle Sabu."

Tazz welcomed the change, and like Cactus Jack, called on real emotions to create his persona and deliver compelling promos. "I was bitter, and for real, because no one sent cards or letters or any-thing, nothing from the fans," Tazz explains. "I was talking on the phone to Paul one day and saying, 'This is bullshit. These people don't care about me.' I went off, and Paul said, 'You need to do that in the ring.' I said, 'Paul, you know I am no good on the microphone, I can't do it.' He said, 'You can, and you need to let that out.' He kept trying to get me to talk on the microphone. The Tazmaniac character had died—we killed it—a couple of months before I broke my neck, and we were still trying to find this new character.

"All we knew about this new character was that he was going to be from Brooklyn, like I was, and I was going to wear orange and black, and going to have an attitude," Tazz remembers. "That is a little vague, but that is what the character was at that point. We would let it evolve into whatever it was going to evolve into. And then, boom, I break my neck. Paul had this genius idea that if you are so bitter, tell them on the microphone. Tell them how you feel about that. He had me do this thing as a special ref to help Tod Gordon and not help this evil referee who was going to become a character wrestler—Bill Al-fonso—and I would help the heel, Fonzie, and punch the shit out of Tod Gordon. I would cut the thing on the microphone: 'No one cared about me. Not one card, not one letter. No one gives two shits about Tazz. The only one who cared about me was Bill Alfonso. He helped pay my bills.' It was all a heel promo, and very heated at the time in late 1995. It was strong. It was a breakout promo for me, and it was all because of Paul. No writers, none of that bullshit, just Paul gave you some input and you just found a flavor for yourself."

Early in the evening, during a match between Konnan and Jason, Tazz came out to the ring in a referee's shirt to work the bout, and took the microphone.

"I want to let everyone know that my neck is not healing right, and this is what I have to do to pay my bills and feed my family," Tazz said. "I have to be a referee. So if anybody has a comment about it, we can go outside after the show and have a conversation in the parking lot, because my hands still work fine. I just can't get medical clearance to wrestle. And everyone in this building knows that if I really want to wrestle, nobody can stop me. So Konnan, are you ready for this match?"

Konnan answered, "Yeah."

"Jason, are you ready for this match?" Tazz asked.

Jason started to answer. "Tazz, I would like to tell you something—"

But Tazz shut him up and said, "Jason, I don't think you heard me. I'm a referee. I don't need this shit. So shut your fucking mouth. Now, are you ready to wrestle?"

Jason replied, "Well . . ."

Tazz said, "Sounds like a yes to me. Ding."

Konnan nailed Jason and beat him with an inverted power bomb in three seconds.

Later, Tod Gordon and Bill Alfonso had their match, and it was a bloody affair. Five minutes into it, they were hitting each other with cookie sheets, and they bumped the referee. When they bumped the referee, Tod Gordon knocked out Bill Alfonso with a cookie sheet. He covered Alfonso, and Tazz ran down in his referee's shirt and counted, "One, two," and then stood up without continuing the count.

Tod Gordon stood up and demanded, "What are you doing?"

Tazz nailed Gordon and decked him. He threw Bill Alfonso on top of Gordon and counted, "One, two, three."

Bill Alfonso, the most hated man in the ECW, pinned the commissioner, Tod Gordon. It was, for ECW fans, an unbelievable scene.

Then Tazz got on the microphone and delivered his bitter tirade: "I suppose you are all wondering why I did this. Two reasons: number one, when I broke my neck, did anybody call me, anybody care, anybody send me a card, anybody send me a telegram? One man did, Bill Alfonso. Bill Alfonso called me. What did you guys do, forget about me? What about me? What about Tazz? Reason number two: you want to know why this happened? Because of Sabu. Sabu takes a booking in Japan, and fucks this company? I never fucked this company. And then we bring him back? Paul Heyman sucked his dick in the ring. He never sucked my dick in the ring. Why does Sabu get the royal treatment? Why does Sabu get treated like a god? He fucked this company over. He fucked you people over, and you cheer for him? I am going to keep dogging you people, I am going to keep dogging everybody, until Sabu fights me."

The crowd is going wild, chanting for Sabu, hoping he will come out and give Tazz the beating he deserves. But it won't happen—at least not that night, or the next time or the time after that. "We did that for a whole year, with Tazz calling Sabu out every night, which is unheard of," Heyman declares. "A heel calls out a babyface, and the babyface doesn't accept the challenge, especially a top babyface? That is unheard of in this business. That was historically the biggest moment of the *November to Remember 1995*. We now are literally planning out a year later. We wanted this to be on Pay-Per-View, and were starting to put together our Pay-Per-View matches. Tazz vs. Sabu was going to be on our first Pay-Per-View, there was no doubt about it. We were starting to put things together."

There were other big moments: a Two Out of Three Falls match featuring Rey Mysterio against Psicosis; Steve Austin helping to put Mikey Whipwreck over by losing to him in an ECW heavyweight title bout; Tommy Dreamer and Terry Funk against Cactus Jack and Raven in a tag team match (Cactus Jack wore a T-shirt under his typical black and gold Cactus Jack T-shirt with airbrushed faces of the Faces of Fear from WCW; when Dreamer tore off the shirt to reveal another shirt he had under it—a T-shirt with an image of Eric Bischoff on the front and the words "Forgive me, Uncle Eric" on the back, Dreamer went crazy and pummeled Cactus Jack); Sandman and Too Cold Scorpio beat The Public Enemy for the ECW Tag Team belts. ECW began in part on the strength of The Public Enemy, who had become so big that they were now being courted by both WCW and WWE. Heyman felt they could afford to lose The Public Enemy, because he knew what the other promoters didn't—they were a total creation of his, perhaps more than any other act or gimmick Heyman had come up with in ECW. "If anyone truly understands the business, they'd know that they were terrible. But we made people believe they were great, using the interviews and the vignettes, and we had them doing things no one else was doing, and you couldn't do those things in WCW and WWE. You couldn't bleed all over the fans and use weapons. Outside of the very careful control that I exercised—accentuating your strengths and hiding your weaknesses—no one really knew how to hide their weaknesses. Vince and WCW were both convinced they were the best tag team in the world. No one realized they sucked. Many people today believe if you want to see a testament to the talent of Paul Heyman as a booker, look no further than The Public Enemy. I think the greatest thing I ever did was Tazz. He was the greatest bit of smoke and mirrors I ever pulled off. But a lot of people say The Public Enemy because I convinced people in the business they were great."

After *November to Remember* came *December to Dismember.* On December 9 The Eliminators defeated The Pitbulls; The Public Enemy defeated The Heavenly Bodies; Raven beat Tommy Dreamer again; in a Steel Cage match, The Public Enemy, The Pitbulls & Dreamer defeated

Despite a few well-placed shots by The Pitbulls, The Eliminators won.

The Heavenly Bodies, The Eliminators, Raven & Stevie Richards; Hack Myers beat Bruiser Mastino; Dances with Dudley and Dudley Dudley beat Bad Crew; Tazz beat El Puerto Ricano; and in an ECW Heavyweight Championship Three Way Dance, Sandman won the title by defeating Mikey Whipwreck and Steve Austin, with Austin pinning Whipwreck and Sandman pinning Austin.

Though the year 1995 would end in ECW with *Holiday Hell* on December 29, at Lost Battalion Hall in Queens, New York, it would be another beginning for two more talented performers who would have a big impact on ECW. In that show, Hack Meyers beat J.T. Smith; Tazz defeated Koji Nakagawa; Raven, of course, beat Tommy Dreamer, then lost to the Sandman for the ECW Heavyweight Championship; The Eliminators beat The Pitbulls; Bruiser Mastino defeated El Puerto Ricano; Sabu beat Cactus Jack; The Gangstas defeated The Public Enemy; Mikey Whipwreck beat Too Cold Scorpio for both the ECW TV and half of the tag team title (Scorpio and Sandman were Tag Team Champions); and two recent arrivals faced each other—a new Dudley named Bubba Ray and a strange-looking character named The Blue Meanie.

Mark Lamonica—Bubba Ray Dudley—was born on July 14, 1971, in Massapequa, New York. He was built for mayhem, standing 6-foot-4 and weighing in at 275 pounds. Like many of the New York–born wrestlers, he was trained by Johnny Rodz and also Sonny Blaze. He broke into wrestling in 1991 as a character called Mongo Vyle, and then came to ECW at the end of 1995 as a Dudley, the dancing Dudley brother who also suffered from stuttering until one of his brothers, Big Dick Dudley, supposedly cured him by hitting him with a crutch. He would later be teamed up with his black half brother, D-Von Dudley, to become known as the Dudley Boyz. They became one of the most popular tag teams in wrestling history, known for using weapons and firing up the fans to hate them. They held the ECW Tag Team titles eight times during their tenure in the promotion.

Brian Heffron—The Blue Meanie—came to ECW from a very different path. Born May 8, 1973, in Philadelphia, Meanie, like most wrestlers, got hooked watching the sport on television as a kid growing up in Atlantic City. "The first match I ever saw on TV was World Wrestling Federation. It was Tony Garea and Rick Martel vs. Mr. Fuji and Mr. Saito," Meanie recalls. "After that, I was hooked. I grew up watching guys like Bob Backlund and Hulk Hogan, Ted DiBiase, Ricky Steamboat, and the British Bulldogs."

When he got older, he started looking around for wrestling schools. His quest would bring him good fortune, as he would wind up being taught by Al Snow. "I had been looking in a newsletter, the *Wrestling Observer*, and they had ads for wrestling schools," Meanie says. "I started corresponding with a woman named Phyllis Lee who ran a school in Tampa. We had corresponded for about a year and a half. She told me how much the tuition cost and she told me how much the cost of living was down there in Tampa. I was living in Atlantic City at the time."

At 6-foot-1 and 295 pounds, Meanie was an imposing presence, and after graduating from Atlantic City High School, went to work as a security guard at Trump Plaza, working the graveyard shift. "I spent all night walking around looking for money on the floor and kicking bums out," Meanie remembers. "It helped build character and taught me responsibility. I was able to pay my own way through wrestling school. I had a supportive family that allowed me to save up."

The cost of living in Tampa was too high for Meanie, but he was told about a school in Lima, Ohio, run by a wrestler named Al Snow. So in March 1994, at the age of 20, Meanie began training with Snow. "I went there, and I was really lucky," Meanie declares. "Not only is he an excellent wrestler, but he was an excellent trainer and has been an excellent friend. He was like my big brother. He was very patient and very persistent. If you did not know point A, you would not go to point B until he felt you were ready. If it wasn't for him, I probably would have quit the first month. He helped me along, and I owe a lot to him."

Living in South Jersey, Meanie had become a big ECW fan, and even when he was training in Lima, he would drive once a month to Philadelphia to the ECW Arena for a show. "I started watching ECW when I was a junior in high school," he says. "I attended my first ECW match in September 1993. I was sitting in the front row. There are a lot of shows that if you look at now early on, you can see me in the crowd. I went from being a bleacher bum to being one of the wrestlers."

While he was training with Snow, Meanie—going by the name Brian Rollins—started working on independent shows in Ohio, Michigan, Canada, Chicago, Indiana, and Kentucky, in front of crowds ranging from thirty to three hundred people. He started wearing zebra tights and then changed his name to The Zebra King, the name he would use until he came to ECW—which was his goal in the business.

While he was working the independents, he met Raven on a Pittsburgh show run by Steel City Wrestling. Raven and his lackey, Stevie Richards, were on the show, which ran for two days. They were staying at the promoter's house when Raven, who liked what he saw from this fat kid from New Jersey, came up with a way to use him in ECW.

"Hey, kid, I got this idea for a character for a sidekick for Stevie—a big fat guy who can take a bump," Raven said. "You can take a good bump. You can do some good moves. Would you be up for wearing Daisy Dukes [cutoff denim shorts] and a half shirt?" That was the garb of Stevie Richards, and the goal was for Meanie to be a lackey to the lackey.

Then Raven came up with the idea of calling this character The Blue Meanie. "Hey, kid, I got an idea for you," Raven said. "You ever see the movie *Yellow Submarine?*"

"Yeah, when I was a kid," Meanie answered.

"Maybe you should watch it again," Raven said. "There is a character called the Blue Meanie, and you fit the description perfectly. When you see it, you'll want to paint your whole face blue."

"Well, maybe we can just do the hair," Meanie said.

They rented the movie and went to Raven's house to watch it together. "I hated it, but I went with the character," Meanie recalls. "I said I would give it a try. I had respected Raven so much that I figured he was probably onto something. He had great ring presence and a great feel for ring psychology. He has a great mind for the business. He is very underrated. When it comes to wrestling, what he says and does means so much."

The year would end with a Christmas greeting from Cactus Jack for the ECW TV show *A Hardcore Christmas*. The scene is Cactus Jack's house, with Burl Ives's "Holly Jolly Christmas" playing in the background. Cactus Jack, clean-shaven, sits in front of the Christmas tree with his two-year-old daughter, Noelle, on his lap, with his wife taping as Cactus Jack delivers his good cheer in a wimpy voice:

"Ho, ho, ho—Happy Hardcore Holidays, everybody. This is Cactus Jack, along with the rest of the Foleys here to wish you and your family a Happy Holiday Hardcore season. I took this time out today to try to explain what Christmas means to me, and, by golly, I found out that Christmas can mean a lot of different things. First off, I found out that Christmas can be fun! Ha ha. Why, just the other day there were some Christmas carolers and I snuck up on their little group and, as the door opened and they began to sing, I started chanting, 'ECW, ECW, ECW,' ha, ha, and I'll tell you what . . . I would have gotten away with it too, but all the neighbors heard me yelling as I made my way through the neighborhood. But you know, they didn't care. They just thought, 'There goes that nutty Cactus Jack.' But you know what, they realized it doesn't hurt to have a hardcore person in the neighborhood. Second of all, Christmas is for family. Why just the other day, I was taking gingerbread men out of the oven, and I'll tell you what, I took one look at that cookie sheet and I was wishing that I could, 'Powee!' ha, ha . . . hit someone over the head with it—right in the kisser. Ha, ha, I bet you could get some juice out of that one! Bang bang!

"More important, Christmas is for caring. Now I understand that there is a hardcore balloting going on, and that Tod Gordon is in charge of the voting, but more importantly, Tod is in charge of some very prestigious and worthwhile children's charities and likes to be the first at this special time of the year to write a generous check. Seeing as I don't know the exact names of the charities. I'm just going to make the check out to Tod Gordon himself, and"—winking at the camera—"I think Tod will know what to do with it. Ha, ha. Here, honey, zoom in so they can get a look at all these zeros—ha, ha—not too close so they'll see our address and we're liable to have fifteen hundred hardcore fans on our front lawn chanting, 'He's hardcore, he's hardcore.' Ha, ha. I'll tell you what. I love them, and if it were up to me, I'd have them all in for a cup of hot chocolate. Oh, Santa"—picking up a Santa doll and making a feeble attempt at ventriloquism—"what's the number one wrestling organization? ECW, ho, ho, ECW."

This was the end of a remarkable year of action and stories in ECW, finishing the year with two characters that were prime examples of the characteristics of ECW—mayhem and comedy. There was a lot of mayhem coming up in 1996, but there would be nothing funny about some of it.

chapter six

A Deadly Kiss

The first big event in 1996 took place at the ECW Arena on *House Party 1996,* on January 5. Paul Heyman was adding new stars to the promotion. It was an interesting mix— wrestlers wanting to be part of this new phenomenon in the business, as their colleagues tell them stories about the freedom and excitement of working in ECW. Then the courting by WCW and WWE of the growing stars of ECW, which forced Heyman to try to keep the pump primed with fresh faces.

Rob Van Dam was a fresh face. And he would certainly make an impact.

His real name was Robert Szatkowski, and he was born on December 18, 1970, in Battle Creek, Michigan. A remarkably blessed athlete,

Van Dam was trained by Ed Farhat—the Original Sheik and the uncle of Sabu—and started in the business in 1990 on the independent circuit in and around Michigan. He moved up in 1992, signing with WCW as Robbie V, but left two years later and went back to the independents, also wrestling in Japan. Like so many wrestlers of this era, it was in ECW that the 6-foot, 235-pound Van Dam found his character and the freedom to create his high-flying style. It would be a style that would be the dominant feature in ECW until the end of the promotion. He would hold the ECW TV title for nearly two years until he had to give it up because of a broken leg. Van Dam's nickname in ECW, among others, was "The Whole Fucking Show."

He would make his debut against Axl Rotten, but his style was more suited for an opponent he would face later on that month in another ECW show—Sabu. They would be linked together during their time in ECW, both as bitter rivals because of their similar high-flying styles, and partners as ECW Tag Team title holders, capturing the belts twice.

"Rob Van Dam was great friends with Sabu, and he is another guy who I've seen do things physically that I have never seen another human being do," Tazz says. "He was amazing. Rob Van Dam and Tommy Dreamer, I don't think there was anyone who loved ECW more than those two guys. The passion that Rob and Dreamer had for it were bigger than anyone's passion—maybe even more than Paul's. They loved the company, and I guess that is why those two guys stayed there so long. I think they need to be commended for that."

Also at *House Party*, The Public Enemy defeated The Gangstas; Bad Crew went to a no contest with Tony Stetson & J.T. Smith; Sabu beat Stevie Richards; Bubba Ray Dudley beat Jimmy Del Ray; 911 & Rey Mysterio, Jr., defeated The Eliminators; Tazz beat Hack Myers; Sandman successfully defended his ECW Heavyweight title against Konnan; and Too Cold Scorpio beat Mikey Whipwreck for the ECW TV belt.

Cyberslam 1996 on February 17 at the ECW Arena would include a classic high-flying match between Sabu and Too Cold Scorpio that ended in a thirty-minute time draw, and also the start of one of the most dramatic feuds wrestling had ever seen—Sandman and Raven.

Raven defeated Sandman for the ECW Heavyweight Championship, and their storyline would stun many observers.

ECW's *Big Ass Extreme Bash* on March 9 at the ECW Arena featured the introduction of some new faces and the exit of a very familiar one. Adding to the *lucha libre* style of Rey Mysterio and Psicosis, Heyman brought in Juventud Guerrera, another Mexican wrestler who faced off against Mysterio in a classic Two Out of Three Falls showdown.

He also featured a recently arrived performer, another new and very talented international wrestler, this one from Canada, by the name of Chris Jericho, who would defeat Tazz on this show by disqualification.

Jericho—born Christopher Keith Irvine on November 9, 1970—was part of a generation of Canadian wrestlers who learned the business from the Hart family in Calgary. He made his debut in October 1990 and worked his way around various independent shows and in Japan before coming to ECW.

"I used to watch wrestling when I was a kid growing up in Winnipeg, Canada," Jericho recalls. "When I was about 14 years old, I decided I wanted to be a wrestler. There was this school run by Stu Hart, a famous wrestler and promoter in Canada, the father of Bret and Owen Hart, and I wrote him a letter. They ran an ad on the show about their pro wrestling school. I wrote that I wanted to go to school there. They said you had to be 18 to go to school there. I graduated high school when I was 17, then I went to college and then went to wrestling school in the summer of 1990. I focused my attention on that from the time I decided that was what I wanted to do. I had played hockey and water polo, baseball, soccer. I was always involved in sports.

"After I graduated from wrestling school, I started getting myself booked at independent shows around Calgary and Alberta and western Canada. I eventually started wrestling in Japan, and did some wrestling in Mexico."

He wanted to wrestle in America, though, and had his sights set on ECW. He would have come there a year earlier, if Paul Heyman had answered his messages, Jericho says.

"I had known Mick Foley from shows in Japan," Jericho explains. "He told me to make sure that I called Paul Heyman. I was also friends with Chris Benoit, and he told me the same thing, call Paul Heyman. I started calling Paul in February 1995 and never got a return phone call from him. A few times I spoke to his 'roommate' Dave, who was really Paul but just disguising his voice, pretending that it wasn't him. I kept calling and leaving messages. At one point in the summer of 1994 I got a message saying that if I could make a plane that night, I could be booked on an ECW show. But it was impossible. I couldn't make a plane, it was too late. But that wasn't even Paul who called me. It was Chris Benoit. I kept calling, and finally he returned my call in February 1996. It took me one year to get him on the phone. The first words he said were, 'I've been trying to get ahold of you for the longest time.'

"I had watched ECW because I had a friend who got the MSG network up in Calgary," Jericho continues. "It was developing a cult following, and people were really getting into it. It was so offbeat, the way they did things. But until you actually got there, you really couldn't see how crazy the fans were. I had sort of an international name for myself. I had been a fairly big star in Japan, and these fans were pretty knowledgeable, even though the Internet was fairly new. They learned about other wrestlers through tape trading and newsletters and such. So they heard of me and knew who I was."

Jericho's first ECW bout was in Reading, Pennsylvania, pairing him with Rob Van Dam against The Eliminators. "We were going crazy and having a real Japanese-style match, with 101 moves all over the place," Jericho recalls. "People starting chanting, 'Five star match,' during the match, and that was kind of cool, because that was a real insider term, meaning you're having a great match. So to have that chanted for me my first match was great.

"The next night I was in Queens, and I wrestled Rob Van Dam in a singles match. It was one of those matches where we tried to do too much too quick, and at one point I did something that didn't look too good. I think I missed a little bit with a kick, and then I got one of those 'You fucked up' chants my second night there."

Jericho credited ECW with giving guys like himself—smaller, athletic wrestlers—a shot in the business. "I was part of the second wave of guys that came and then left," Jericho says. "The first wave was Dean, Benoit, and Eddie Guerrero. The second wave was myself and Rey Mysterio and Juventud Guerrera. Ten years ago there were a lot of guys in the business who got international experience and no one had seen them or heard of them before, but they got a lot of different experience because they wrestled all around the world. Today everyone works the same and acts the same. Back then working in Mexico and England and Japan really gave you different styles."

The *Big Ass Bash* also marked Cactus Jack's farewell to ECW, and, appropriately, it was in a match against Mikey Whipwreck. "Fans clapped and cheered for Cactus Jack, despite their brutal reaction to him in recent weeks because of his turn to heel, because they were recognizing his work in ECW and his commitment to hardcore wrestling," Heyman remembers. The match was a brawl, with Mikey Whipwreck taking a beating. The two wrestlers hit each other with chairs and all sorts of weapons, and Cactus Jack ended it with a piledriver. The crowd stood and paid tribute to Cactus Jack, as he picked Mikey Whipwreck up and hugged him before raising his hand. Joey Styles declared, "This is the Cactus Jack that we want to remember. This is the Cactus Jack that we love." Other wrestlers celebrated, and that was the end of Cactus Jack in the ECW.

For Blue Meanie, it was a night to remember. "The most special memory I have of ECW was the night Cactus Jack walked up to me and Stevie Richards and said that we would be a part of his farewell to ECW," Meanie says. "That meant a lot to me. Here I was, barely two years in the business, and someone who I idolized was asking me to be part of something that was special in his career. Me and Stevie looked at each other like, 'Is he for real?' When we did it, I was high it felt so great. I idolized Mick Foley. I still idolize Mick Foley. He was a great wrestler and a great friend. When I think about that night, it still raises the hair on my arms."

While Heyman was bringing in new talent, he was also working on staying ahead of the competition and also expanding the promotion and its television exposure, all with the goal of getting on Pay-Per-View. Those goals were not always compatible.

"Vince is making its product edgier, and it is noticeable," Heyman states. "WCW is picking away at our talent. The obvious need to get on Pay-Per-View is there, but we are still being held back, because of two reasons—UFC [Ultimate Fighting Championship] is having so much trouble getting legalized in so many states, and people are confusing us with mixed martial arts fighting. Bob Guccione's son, Nick, opens up a competing group to Ultimate Fighting Championships called Extreme Fighting. What happens is the media picks up on that word and says, 'All this Extreme and Ultimate fighting is human cock fighting.' So all the state athletic commissions and Pay-Per-View companies say, 'You're Extreme, so you're real.' We say, 'No, that's extreme fighting. We're just like WWE and WCW, we just have an edgier product.' We are having a lot of licensing problems and clearing problems, and we can't get on Pay-Per-View. And this is the time for us to get on Pay-Per-View.

"So I make the decision of getting into the more adult-themed wrestling business, to turn it up a notch," Heyman explains. "I will start doing story lines that are really mature. I don't mean pornographic or in bad taste. I am going to take my wrestling show and make it for college kids and older. Not only more mature story lines, but more intelligent story lines. So with Raven as the champion, I make the decision to do a couple of things. One is to continue the Dreamer feud. Another is that we are going to pull off an angle with Raven and the Sandman that is so outside of the traditional boundaries that wrestling has done, that it is going to be shocking. And number three, I am going to do some stuff that people are going to have to talk about."

The Dreamer-Raven feud took an unprecedented turn when ECW introduced the issue of pregnancy into the story line, claiming Beulah McGillicutty was pregnant. Beulah made this revelation public while arguing with Stevie Richards—Raven's lackey—in the ring.

"That night was amazing," Dreamer recalls. "When Raven heard that she was pregnant, he turned and blasted Stevie Richards, who was always nice to Beulah, and she said, 'It's not him.' And then she pauses and says, 'It's Tommy's.' The place lit up and it was like a soap opera."

When Beulah said the baby was Dreamer's, Raven pushed her into a corner, grabbed her by the hair and started choking her. Of course, Dreamer came into the ring to rescue Beulah and started pounding on Raven. "As I was beating him up, a fan handed me a blueberry pie," Dreamer says. "I took a big bite of it, DDT'd him and laid him out, and left with the girl."

This angle went on for a while, and, since Beulah wasn't really pregnant, at some point they had to find a way out of the pregnancy story line. "Either we are going to have to take her off TV for six months and then come back and say she gave birth, or we are going to have to get out of this," Heyman remembers. "In the meantime, we were going to split Kimona [who once did a striptease on top of the ECW arena to keep the fans happy while the ring was being repaired] away from Raven, because she was becoming a real pain in the ass. We were going to phase her out. We came up with a thing with Shane Douglas, to get him into a three-way feud with Raven and Dreamer."

"I have a match with Raven coming up," Douglas said in a TV promo. "Just so everyone understands, I am not Tommy Dreamer's best friend. I want to fight Tommy Dreamer. And I know a secret about Tommy Dreamer that he doesn't want to hear—that Beulah McGillicutty has been cheating on Tommy Dreamer. And I know the truth about the pregnancy. I am going to tell everybody the truth at the arena before my match with Raven." The last thing you heard on TV before the match was Raven saying, "I just found out what the secret is, and I still love Beulah McGillicutty, and I want her back. No matter what you have done, if Dreamer won't accept you, I'll take you back."

Following that, before Raven and Douglas fought for the ECW Championship at the arena in Philadelphia, Douglas, with Beulah, Dreamer, Raven, and Kimona in the ring with him, grabbed the mike and dropped the bomb.

"I'm going to tell the secret. Beulah McGillicutty is cheating on Tommy Dreamer."

"Who is he?" Dreamer asked.

"Oh, it is not a he, Tommy Dreamer, it is not a he," Douglas said.

Then Kimona ran over to the mike and yelled, "It's me."

The place was in an uproar. Kimona walked over to the corner where Beulah was standing, and Beulah grabbed her and gave her a passionate kiss as they fell to the canvas. They were rolling and kissing on the mat when Dreamer picked them both up, with the fans chanting, "ECW! ECW!"

Dreamer was holding both of them by the hair, one in each hand.

"What do you say, Dreamer?" Douglas asked.

"I'll take them both on, hardcore," Dreamer declared, and he planted kisses on both women, with the fans roaring their approval at this scene.

Little did anyone know that the lesbian kiss nearly proved to be the kiss of death for ECW.

"We built up to that lesbian kiss," Heyman explains. "Just as Beulah comes out, she grabs her by the face, the screen freezes, the show ends, and we put across the screen, 'To Be Continued,' which had never been done in wrestling before. None of the station managers knew where I was heading with this. This was in the days before the Internet, where everything you are going to see on TV winds up on the Internet. It wasn't as widespread. They didn't know what was coming. They aired the cliffhanger of what happens next. They don't realize what happens next. They think one of these girls is going to get hit by a chair or something. That is what ECW is all about, right? So when the next episode arrives at the station, they didn't even really pay attention to it. All of a sudden late Friday night they are airing the show, and someone in the control room says, 'Hey, we got a lesbian kiss going on here.'

"One by one these station managers are calling up and saying, 'We can't air this.' The backlash was devastating. We got thrown off everything. Joe Talnoid, the station manager at MSG television network, had his right-hand man, Paulie Arnold, call Steve Karel and said, 'We are canceling your contract, you are off MSG. You have violated our content standards.' Once MSG threw us off, then nearly everyone followed suit. We got thrown off about 90 percent of our stations.

"We lost everything but Philadelphia, and maybe Wichita, and a few other stations, and everyone else threw us off, no matter how much we were paying," Heyman recalls. "Some stations let us back on pretty fast, but others didn't. MSG didn't let us back on for six months. I had to find other stations. I had to go to TV 31. We had to shop our show around after MSG threw us off. We lost Pittsburgh, Chicago, Buffalo."

Heyman, who was often ahead of the cultural curve, was caught off guard by the reaction to the lesbian kiss. "I didn't see that coming. I knew it would be controversial. I figured it would cost us a couple of stations. I couldn't believe the reaction. This was under the Clinton administration. This wasn't a repressive era. Female homosexuality was not seen on television yet. But we ended up getting it all back."

As Beulah was an integral part of this story line, so were many women in ECW. The promotion made much use of women as sex symbols in various roles, from valets to wrestlers. There was Woman, Beulah, Francine, Kimona, Dawn Marie, Electra, Lita, Missy Hyatt, Tammy Lynn Sytch, and Jazz, among others.

"Being a woman in ECW was probably the one experience that made me tough," says Dawn Marie, one of the most popular females in the promotion. "It made me learn how to protect myself and have confidence in myself. There were no prima donnas in ECW. They groomed us to be tough."

If you thought Heyman learned a lesson from the lesbian angle and the controversial angles surrounding women, and was ready to back off, forget it. He was pedal to the metal, with one shocking angle after another.

"If I had backed off and just presented milquetoast wrestling with flashy production values, I would have been like everybody else," Heyman explains. "What kept me afloat was that I didn't back off. In an environment where two giant multimedia corporations were breathing down our necks, ECW survived for seven years. And the reason we survived was because I believed in what we were doing. We had a different product. The moment we made it the same, there was no reason to watch us. I couldn't violate that."

He violated nearly everything else, though, with another angle—having Sandman's son Tyler turn against him and join up with Raven.

"I had a friend who was going through a bitter custody battle," Heyman says. "My friend worked on Wall Street, and was the most ruthless SOB I had ever seen in that field. He was a killer. Nothing affected him. Nothing was ever personal for him. He was a badass businessman. No emotion. But yet I saw when he was going through the custody fight . . . she moved in with another guy, and she had gotten custody of the child. Their kid was about four years old, and he started calling the other guy Daddy. That crumbled my friend. Just destroyed him. It fucked him up bad. I said, 'Wow, this is something that really preys on human emotions.'

"So we created a scenario where Sandman's ex-wife would return as a disciple of Raven. Sandman did a match at the arena, and Raven came out with Sandman's ex-wife, and Sandman says, 'I don't care how much you fuck my ex-wife. It didn't bother me before, it doesn't bother me now. Try it with her heels on, she likes it better that way.'

"He is having fun at Raven's expense, but then Raven says, 'Well, you may not care about your ex-wife, but you care about your son.'

"So the boy comes out dressed like Raven, with a black T-shirt with Raven's picture on it and a black leather jacket, throws his arms out in a Raven pose, and says into the mike, 'Daddy, you're a drunk. I worship Raven now.' Raven went back to the locker room with Sandman's wife and kid. Sandman was in the ring crying. People were moved by the story. We never depicted or insinuated or made sure there was no way to misconstrue this that Raven was spanking the child or anything like that.

"Raven would do promos where he would say, 'Sandman, I know you are going to challenge me for my title. While you are sitting there thinking about taking my title, think about this. Today I didn't go to the gym. I played catch with your son, and he appreciated it.' Little things like that. There was never a hint of abuse. Yet stations were affected by this. It was a soap opera. They said, 'We can't air this. It's too personal. It's not wrestling.' Right. Wrestling is a soap opera. 'We can't air it. It is about a child.' Why? What am I doing wrong? Why is this so egregious that you can't air it? What are we doing that is so offensive to the audience? I think the audience will want to watch this compelling soap opera."

Here is how that "compelling soap opera" unfolded on the ECW show:

With Raven outside the ring, as Sandman holds a Singapore cane over his head, Sandman's son kneels down next to Raven and declares, "Daddy, you're a drunk. I'm with Raven now."

"He worships me," Raven yells.

Announcer Joey Styles comments, "This has nothing to do with wrestling. We are talking about life here, and you don't mess with the man's family."

Sandman walks back to the dressing room, clutching his Singapore cane, in tears, screaming, "God, don't do this to me."

Then there were the promos.

Raven with Tyler and Lori (Sandman's ex-wife) both dressed in leather jackets like Raven, and Raven is kneeling down, next to Tyler: "Hey, kid, you know your divorce was your daddy's fault."

"I know," Tyler says.

"Hey, Sandman, heh, heh, heh, heh," Raven responds.

Another time Sandman is in the middle of the ring on one knee, with Tyler in front of him. He is dressed just like Sandman.

Joey Styles sets the stage: "We have been waiting to see this."

Tyler hugs Sandman and the crowd roars and cheers. But Raven slides in the ring, as Tyler backs off, and slams Sandman in the back of the head, nearly knocking him out.

Tyler, now sporting a leather jacket and dressed like Raven, strikes the Raven pose, with arms out: "Quote the Raven nevermore." Raven stands next to him, laughing.

"It was the most emotional angle we ever did," Heyman declares.

It was also one of the most painful for some participants. "Me and Stevie became fodder for Sandman's Singapore cane in that feud with Raven," Blue Meanie recalls. "There were plenty of nights where they designed spots for us where Sandman would get a cane and take off on us. There were a few instances where he would hit me right in the forehead, and the Singapore cane would reach over my head and pull a piece of skin off my back, pinching off a piece of skin. This went on for six or seven months.

"It became a contest between me, Stevie, and Nova as to who could loosen up Sandman's Singapore cane. On the cane were these little red strings, and depending on where they were on the stick, if you brought them down a little bit, they loosened up, and if you brought them up to a certain point, it was like a baseball bat. Nova had his cape and while Raven and Sandman were brawling out in the stands, Nova would go over and throw his cape over the Singapore cane, and one of us would get under the cape and loosen up the strings. When it came time for us to get back in the ring for our spot, he would hit me with the cane and I would go to myself, 'Aaahhh, I didn't feel it.' One time they designed a spot where me, Stevie and Nova would take turns caning the Sandman, and we fought over who would cane him first, after getting beat with it for six or seven months. The cane knocked the stuffing out of me and toughened me up."

Not all of the promos were so emotional or controversial. Some were humorous, in particular one created by a trio of Raven's lackeys—Stevie Richards, Blue Meanie, and another addition, Mike "Nova" Bucci—called the Blue World Order, a takeoff on WCW's New World Order.

Nova joined Raven's flock after being discovered using a superhero gimmick on independent shows in New Jersey in late 1995. "I started wrestling in 1992," he says. "There was a guy in New Jersey, Iron Mike Sharpe, who had a school in Bricktown, New Jersey. A buddy of mine used to go to his school. I was going to Ocean County College at the time and working at Wendy's. I was a wrestling fan growing up, and I used to go with my friend to the wrestling school.

"After a few months Mike Sharpe and Tom Rumsby, the Executioner, started talking to me about trying it myself," Nova explains. "I wasn't really athletic. I said I would try it, and I did, and I liked it. Mike had shows at the school every two weeks. It cost $2,000 to go to his school, but you could pay whatever you wanted, whenever you

Blue Meanie and Stevie Richards.

could. I paid like $100 down and $50 a week. Mike was an old-school veteran. I only had intentions of doing the shows at the school every two weeks, and here it is fourteen years later and I am still doing it."

Nova wrestled the independent shows and also served as a jobber from time to time. Whenever WWE came to town, they would call Mike Sharpe and tell him to bring up some extras for the Friday morning tapings. Nova wrestled the Headshrinkers, Adam Bomb, Crush, all those guys. His job was to go in there and get squashed.

Nova, who had come to know Stevie Richards during his independent work, arrived in ECW after Raven saw his act on the undercard of a New Jersey show. "At the time, I was doing a full-blown superhero gimmick," Nova recalls. "I had the cape and makeup. I wrestled on the undercard. During the intermission, Raven pulled me aside and said, 'I love your act. It is like Adam West in Batman. I'm getting something going in ECW with a couple of guys. Your buddy Stevie [Richards] is going to be in it. And there is this kid Brian [Blue Meanie] who will be in it. You would be perfect for the third guy. I am putting together a group of followers, a flock. But they have to be misfits. You guys will be perfect.'"

Nova gave him an 8-by-10 photo that looked like the cover of a comic book, and pessimistically waited for the call to come. "I'd be lying to you if told you I ever thought I would hear from him," he says. "Three days later, when I came home, my mom said a guy named Scotty [Raven] called and wanted to talk to me. I called him, and he said he talked to Tommy Dreamer and Tazz, and showed them my picture. They liked it. I'm sure Tommy and Tazz—it probably never got to Paul—said, 'Scotty, if you like this guy, go right ahead.' We were brought in to get his act over."

So Nova showed up at the ECW arena, nervous and ready to work. "I have been at *WrestleMania* and wrestled all over the world, but going to the ECW arena that night was the scariest night of my life, to go backstage and meet those guys," he says. "I had only done independent shows up to that point, and here I was at someplace that I had really wanted to be. I used to be *in* the audience at ECW shows.

"Tommy Dreamer was the first one to come up and talk to me. He said, 'I saw your picture. The gig ain't going to pay much. If you can get to the shows as much as you can, we will try to hook you up and do some things with Scotty, and we will throw you a couple of bucks whenever we can. But you seem pretty cool, so we will see what we can do for you.'"

Nova's first official match was in Reading, Pennsylvania, against Bubba Ray Dudley. "One of the guys couldn't make it, so I wrestled Bubba in a one-on-one match, and Paul [Heyman] liked it," Nova says. "He told Scotty, 'Okay, Scotty, he's part of your flock.' So we did the Raven's Flock at ringside."

Nova was paid $25 a night. "There wasn't much left after you got a tank of gas and a cheeseburger on the way home," he says. "I was working at Wendy's full-time. I would get done on Friday afternoon, put my wrestling stuff in the car, and I would do the Friday and Saturday shows, stay over somewhere, and come back Sunday and go back to work, clean up the parking lot, and unload the truck Monday mornings."

But Blue Meanie, Richards, and Nova did more than simply serve as Raven's Flock. They came up with one of the more creative angles ECW had seen yet—the Blue World Order.

"Stevie and I started doing a parody, paying tribute to the wrestlers who had come before us, like The Fabulous Ones," Meanie recalls. "Then we started doing teams that were current. WCW had a team called The Bluebloods, which was William Regal and 'Beautiful' Bobby Eaton. Stevie became Lord Stevie, and I became Sir Meanie, the Earl of Eating, because Bob Eaton was the Earl of Eaton. My family crest on the back of my shirt was a plate, with a knife, fork, and spoon. One time Stevie was Baron Von Stevie and I was Colonel DeMeanie."

Eventually, that turned into the three of them forming the Blue World Order. "That was supposed to be a one-night deal, but the crowd reacted so strongly to it, ECW saw a chance to push Stevie and sell a ton of T-shirts," Meanie explains. "They did that. It became a great avenue for Stevie to become a single star. The merchandise woman at the arena told me at one point they were selling two hundred T-shirts a night. It became a big hit and lasted nearly a year."

It started from a parody they did of the rock band KISS at the ECW arena. JT Smith went into the ring to cut a promo, and instead of singing, as was his gimmick, he said his throat was sore and he couldn't sing.

"What I've done is gone out and got the world's greatest rock 'n' roll band here for you tonight," Smith said, and Meanie, Nova, and Richards came out in full KISS makeup.

"We did the bop and the strut, and the place went insane," Nova recalls. "Sandman came out and wound up caning us. I remember in the locker room after that, Bubba Ray Dudley said, 'You guys are never

Nova as the Blue World Order's Hogan.

going to top that. The only thing that would top that would be a parody of the nWo.' Meanie said, 'We should be the bWo, the Blue World Order. We joked around and kidded about it and then we decided to do it. We had to clear it through Raven, and he had to clear it through Paul.

"I made all the signs for the bWo," Nova says. "I remember Meanie saying, 'I'll be like Razor Ramon. I'll be the Blue Guy instead of the Bad Guy.' Stevie said [to me], 'Dude, you have to be Virgil.' Raven says, 'Virgil? He has to be Hogan.' Stevie says, 'He can't be Hogan.' Raven asks, 'Why not?' Stevie said, 'If he is Hogan, everybody is going to think he is the leader of Raven's Flock. Everybody knows Raven's the leader of the Flock.' Raven said, 'Fuck that, he's Hogan.' That is how I got to be Hogan. We had a lot of fun with it.

"It was only supposed to be a one-night thing, but Paul said, 'Keep doing it.' Then we made the shirts, and we sold out a gross of those shirts in one night. Stevie and I said to each other, 'We better get some more paint, because we may be doing this for a while.' We did it for a year. It never got old. We hit the ring throwing the shirts out and posing. It had absolutely nothing to do with wrestling ability or anything like that. But there was a chemistry between the three of us, and the people got it. It was so cool. Raven's lackeys stepping up and doing their own thing. People still remember it. Twenty years from now, people will be walking up to me and saying, 'bWo.'"

They experimented with other parodies not quite as successful as the bWo. "No one ever saw this one," Nova states. "One night in Reading, Pennsylvania, we did the Jackson Five. We had blackface and Afro wigs. It was done tastefully. I was Michael. I didn't have any blackface on. I was white. We only did it once. We were going to do it at the arena, but Paul said, 'No Jacksons. If the wrong people catch wind of this, we're ruined. No Jacksons.'

"ECW shows were like a circus. The strong man. The bearded lady. The high wire act. It was a little bit of everything. So we were an attraction. We were characters—a superhero, a 350-pound guy with blue hair who did moonsaults, and Stevie. We weren't the second coming of the Freebirds."

Another ECW act that made its debut in 1996 might have rivaled that legendary tag team, though, in terms of popularity and surpassed them in intensity—the Dudley Boyz, not as previously constituted, but this version with Bubba and a postal worker from Brooklyn, New York, named Devon Hughes, who would later go by the name of D-Von Dudley.

"My grandmother pretty much raised me," D-Von says. "I remember watching wrestling one night when I was a kid, on Channel 9, WOR, at midnight, and I remember asking my grandmother what that was. She explained to me that it was wrestling. I never dreamed of doing it then."

D-Von and Bubba Dudley.

But as he grew older, he became more interested, to the point where he wanted to be part of it. So he went the route of so many other future ECW stars, and was trained by Johnny Rodz. "I owe a lot to Johnny Rodz," D-Von says. "My grandfather gave me the money for the school. None of my family members believed I could do this. Everybody downed my idea. At the time, I worked for the post office, from a mail carrier to unloading trucks to sorting the mail, but I knew there was more for me ahead than that. But nobody believed in me. Everyone said, 'You have a government job. Stick with it, it has good benefits.' But I couldn't hear that. My grandfather, Richard Davis, was the only one who believed in me. He gave me the money to go to wrestling school."

The 6-foot-2, 240-pound D-Von toiled on the independent circuit, as so many others had, before getting his break in ECW in 1996, calling himself the A-Train. "I put in so much money and time," D-Von says. "There were times when I would drive three hours for a show, and nobody would show up. And if I had a chance to do it all over again, I would do it the same way. I drove all over, and didn't always perform in front of large crowds, but it gave me the experience I needed to go forward and arrive in ECW."

When D-Von first got to ECW there were a number of Dudleyz already there, including Bubba. D-Von would first feud with Bubba before wrestling as a single for a while and then later joining Bubba for their successful tag team. "Bubba was a kind of babyface," D-Von says. "He danced, and when he talked, he stuttered, and people would want to see him dance and make him talk so they could hear him stutter. But my character was supposed to be totally against it. I didn't want it. I didn't want him to try to please the people or encourage him to do it, at one point beating him up in the ring a couple of times for doing it.

"Me and Bubba would have probably never gotten together without Paul," D-Von says. "Nobody knew about us. When we got the chance to work with Paul Heyman, he saw something special in both of us."

What was "special" in the Dudley Boyz was not just how brutal they were or the weapons they used in the ring, of which there were many. It was the buttons they pushed in the crowd, so that many times the fans would lose control, riots would take place, and police would arrive.

"Nobody got the crowd worked up like we did," D-Von recalls. "We would just tell people what they didn't want to hear. We told them they were ugly. We told them they were losers. We told them what we were going to do to their girlfriends or wives or daughters, after the match was over. We told them we were going to beat them up if they didn't shut up. We got in touch with the fans. That was the whole ECW concept. We catered to the fans in a way that we got them involved in the match. We knew how to get under people's skin. Whatever got underneath our skin when we were out in public, we would put that in our act in the ring, and that was how we would incite the fans. It got to the point sometimes where they thought they could whip our ass. They would come in the back, and we would say to them, 'Look. Go home. We're gonna kill you.' And if they didn't listen, then we killed them. Not literally, but they probably thought we had.

"I think just about everywhere we went, it would get out of hand," D-Von says. "The fans would take the storyline to another level. It was as if whatever we were doing in the ring to whomever, they wanted to join in and kick our asses. Every time we went to the ring, we had to watch our backs. We knew that once we realized what we had and what we were doing, we knew we had something special. So just about every night, especially in the last three years of ECW, when we were at our strongest, we knew we had to watch ourselves. It wasn't unheard of, even if they knew they were going to get killed, for some fans to want to jump us, either going to the ring or outside the ring or in the parking lot. Just about every night it was like that. ECW story lines were so emotional and people embraced them so much and the fans let us know that the Dudley Boyz, we hate their guts and we want to see their ass kicked. We made that happen."

The Dudley Boyz would hold the ECW Tag Team titles eight different times. "How Bubba and I took off so quickly and rose so far was unheard of," D-Von says. "We were just on the same page. We wanted to accomplish the same things. There was no jealousy, and that helps make a great tag team and how we stayed together for so long. Arguably, we are considered to be the best tag team in the history of the business, because of the fact that there is no Road Warriors, no Rock 'n' Roll Express, no British Bulldogs, no Hart Foundation—all of those great teams—there are no teams from that era wrestling today. Each generation gets bigger and more competitive. Whether the tag teams of yesterday could be successful today? Some people would say yes. But the Dudley Boyz were no slouches. Whoever was in front of us, we took on. Whether it was hardcore in ECW or with style and attitude in WWE."

What also made the Dudley Boyz so appealing was their versatility and work ethic, according to Ron Buffone. "D-Von and Bubba worked their asses off," Buffone said. "They could go from one week to the next of hardcore matches: being lit on a table, putting someone through a table, with thumb tacks or fire. They were a great tag team."

There was one more Dudley yet to come in 1996, perhaps the most creative character of the bunch, because no one would have ever mistaken 5-foot-8, 170-pound Matthew Hyson for a professional wrestler who would be known as Spike Dudley.

Born on August 13, 1970, in Providence, Rhode Island, Spike grew up watching Saturday-morning wrestling with his three older brothers, who all would engage in their own matches following the TV shows. Spike became a huge wrestling fan, going to local shows whenever he could. But he figured he would always be just a fan, given his size limitations, and didn't make any career plans to go into professional wrestling. He went to college to become a schoolteacher and, at the age of 21, moved to San Francisco to teach third-grade children.

Shortly after he arrived, Spike saw a television commercial for a wrestling school, and considered the possibility that while he might be too small to be a wrestler, he might be able to train to be a referee or a manager, and maybe turn his wrestling obsession into his livelihood. "I called the place, and they said, 'We've trained for everything, so come on down,'" Spike recalls. "So I went down and met them and signed up and started classes. I was training to be a manager at that point, but they throw everybody together in the beginning. Everyone learns to take the bumps and the falls and all that. So I was training with the wrestlers. After about seven weeks, I was the only one among the twelve students left. All the other ones—the big guys—had dropped out. The teacher said, 'Hang around a couple of more weeks, we'll get a few more students and start another class.' A month or two later, they got another ten to twelve guys to sign up, and they started the class all over again. After a month or two, the teacher said, 'Screw this manager stuff, you're fun to watch as a little wrestler. We're going to make a wrestler out of you.' I said, 'Cool, whatever.'"

After about a year of training, Spike started wrestling on the California independent circuit and began honing his craft and putting together some impressive shows over the next two years. He wanted to move up and out, so he made a videotape of his best work. "I had put a little money into it, and it was a nice, professional job with music and editing," Spike explains. "I sent it out to every promotion I could think of—World Wrestling Federation, WCW, Japan, Smoky Mountain, ECW—any promotion that was out there."

Spike had quit teaching at this point and was working for a financial printing firm in downtown San Francisco when he got a call from Tazz. "He said, 'We got your tape and we like your work. What is your deal?' I told him I had this job out in San Francisco. He asked, 'Would you be willing to move to the East Coast?' I said my job has offices all over the country and I said I could probably transfer, so I would be willing to move to the East Coast. He said, 'What we would like to do is see some complete matches, and we'll get back in touch.'"

So Spike sent a tape with four complete matches, and two weeks later got another call from Tazz, who offered him a job if he could get back east. Fortunately, Spike was working for a company that had New York offices, so he got a transfer, packed up his Toyota Tercel, and drove across the country to join ECW.

Tazz had explained the character they wanted. "They were down to just four Dudleyz," Spike says. "They wanted to make a little character out of me, like the cartoon character, 'Hey Spike, Hey Spike,' that sort of thing—a little maniac, being crazy, getting the crap beat out of me and coming back for more. I said fine. I had not seen much ECW. I had seen a couple of clips of Sabu, but that is about it. We didn't have it on television out where I had been. I had no idea what to expect. I just knew it was an up-and-coming promotion that had good TV time, and I was going to get some experience. I said, 'Sure, whatever you want me to do, I'll do.'"

Spike, with spiked hair and a tie-dyed T-shirt, had a memorable debut. "My first match was insane," he says. "At the time Bubba was feuding with D-Von. D-Von was a heel, and he was with Axl Rotten, against Bubba and Big Dick Dudley. It was one of the TV tapings at the ECW Arena, and those guys are fighting all over the place.

"In the middle of the match, Big Dick comes down to the ring with a duffel bag. He dumps it in the middle of the ring, and I pop out of it. The crowd was wondering what the H was going on and who was this little runt. I immediately get destroyed by D-Von. He beats the crap out of me. I disappear, crawling back to the dressing room.

"A few minutes later, those guys are fighting back and forth, and Bubba and D-Von are on the balcony of the arena. The week before, Bubba had dived off that stage from the speaker onto D-Von. Bubba and D-Von had fought their way back to the stage and the buzz was that Bubba was going to jump off again. I had come out and gotten to the stage, so instead he picked me up over his head and threw me off the stage. I landed on D-Von and Axl.

"After the throw, everyone is fighting through the crowd, and it is chaos," Spike remembers. "Bubba is going at it with D-Von. Now, keep in mind, I just met these guys. D-Von had Bubba down and he is beating on him. Now, D-Von is basically my opponent, so I jump on D-Von's back. D-Von doesn't realize it is me. He thinks it is just some fan from the crowd who jumped on his back. So he reaches over, grabs me by the back of the head, and does a judo toss over the shoulder. We are on concrete, and he puts everything he could behind it, because he wanted to lay the guy out, except it is me. I hit the concrete so hard I thought I was dead. D-Von looks down at me and says, 'Oh, shit. Sorry, Spike.'

"I had no idea what I was walking into," Spike says. "For the two or three years I wrestled prior to that, I was with the same twenty or thirty guys, and knew everyone. We didn't have any experience, but we knew each other and everything was familiar. I get to ECW, and first of all, the arena is a shithole. Guys are getting wasted left and right, wrestlers are beating the shit out of each other, without regard to their bodies, without any sort of wrestling training, what I could see. Some of them knew what they were doing, but so many of them were just idiots, going out there so abusive and self-destructive, for the sake of violence. I thought a lot of it was some of the stupidest shit I had seen in my life. I thought to myself, 'I moved from the West Coast for this at $75 a night. What the hell was I doing?' I was terrified. My first initial thoughts were that I hit rock bottom. I thought I was in for a world of hurt. I was petrified.

"But that changed. Paul E. made you feel so special. After my debut at the arena, he came back and gave me a hug and said I did great, and said, 'Kid, we're gonna have some fun with you. Welcome aboard.' It made me feel cool. This was my introduction to big-time players. Then there was the electricity of ECW. It was not like any other atmosphere. My initial reaction to it was that it was stupid. I thought someone was going to get killed. But the more I was exposed to it, and the more I learned about it and saw that guys knew what they were doing, and I was the one who was green. It got better with each match."

Spike moved to Long Island, where he was to continue training at the ECW House of Hardcore school with Tazz, Perry Saturn, Mikey Whipwreck, and Bubba. "Bubba stayed on top of things," Spike says. "If I screwed up, he was right there in my face. 'Why did you do that, what did you do wrong?' All that stuff. He was only doing it for the best of reasons. I was a Dudley now, and he didn't want this green kid to come in and screw up the Dudley angle. He stayed on top of me and made sure I did the right thing. I think he came to respect me and realize that I tried to do the right thing. We traveled together and he sort of became my big brother. D-Von and I always had a great relationship. We had the same type personalities."

It seemed like everything was popping in ECW that year. They took the Tommy Dreamer–Raven scenario to a new level. The Public Enemy was gone. The Gangstas were the hot tag team, and they started to promote The Eliminators as well. They brought together the Dudley Boyz and successfully introduced another new Dudley, Spike, to add a whole different element to the Dudleyz story. And they welcomed Shane Douglas back into the fold.

Douglas had left in June 1995 for WWE and had a disastrous run there. Vince McMahon changed him from "The Franchise" Shane Douglas into a character called Dean Douglas. It was based on Douglas's legitimate past as a schoolteacher. Douglas would do these vignettes by a chalkboard, "I am Dean Douglas, and I will educate you on the art of wrestling." At the end, he would scratch the chalkboard. He was a flop. Douglas asked Heyman if he could get him out of his contract and back to ECW. "Shane knew I could get on the phone with Vince, because I had no problem handing him Austin and all these different guys," Heyman explains. "So I called Bruce Prichard, and I said, 'Bruce,

I need you to conference in Vince.' So he conferences in Vince at home. I said, 'Vince, Shane Douglas is in my locker room, and he wants to quit. He doesn't want to work for you anymore.' Vince said, 'Why the fuck doesn't Shane Douglas tell me he wants to quit? Why does he want to quit?' I said, 'Because he feels that he will never be a star for you.' Vince said, 'Do you want him back?' I said, 'Yes, I could take him back and make a star out of him.' Vince said, 'Fuck, Paul, you didn't stand in my way with Steve Austin, you know Foley is going to come work for me.' I said, 'Yes, Mick just told me that I have about three months to finish him up.' Vince said, 'I figured three months would be good for you.' I said, 'Three months is fine. I have no problem with a guy giving me three months notice.' Vince said, 'If you want Shane Douglas back, you tell him I will have his release to him out by Monday. You have my blessing. Do anything you want with him tonight. He's done.' I walked over to Shane and asked, 'Do you have an interview in your heart?' He said, 'Oh, fuck, do I have an interview in my heart.' I said, 'I don't want you to bitch about Vince. I want you to go up into the ring and say, "For those of you who want to know how 1996 is going to go, you can look forward to the return of 'The Franchise,'" and then just walk out. Just that much of a surprise. Less is more. And that is what he did."

There was a lot to feel good about in ECW. The end of the year brought even more new faces, and some of them were very familiar to wrestling fans. A big man—6-foot-3 and 370 pounds, with a tattoo covering the top of his head—came to ECW.

Scott C. Bigelow—better known as Bam Bam—was born in Asbury Park, New Jersey, on September 1, 1961, and was trained in wrestling by one of the legends of the business, Buddy Rogers, as well as by Larry Sharpe. He began wrestling in 1985 and would bounce around various independent promotions here and in Japan, with a brief stay in WWE before he returned there in 1993 and established himself as a star attraction. At *WrestleMania XI*, he wrestled New York Giants linebacker Lawrence Taylor.

Bam Bam was friends with another newcomer to ECW, one of the most popular wrestlers in the business among his peers—Chris

Candido, who would join up with Bam Bam and Shane Douglas to form the Triple Threat in ECW.

Candido, whose grandfather, "Popeye" Chuck Richards, was a professional wrestler, began wrestling at the age of 16 on the independent circuit. He was trained by Larry Sharpe and made a name for himself in Smoky Mountain Wrestling and had a stay in WWE before coming to ECW at the end of 1996.

Candido would battle personal problems throughout his career, and in 2005, at the age of 33, he died of walking pnuemonia. His presence in ECW was a fond memory for many of his colleagues, and he was a welcome addition to the locker room when he arrived.

"Chris Candido was a terrific human being who did so much for so many people," Al Snow says. "He was self-destructive. He had his demons. But he was so talented and loved the business so much, and when you watched him perform, you could see he came alive. He was happiest when he was wrestling. He had a great sense of humor. We would sit backstage and laugh and joke. You would have the Triple Threat out there, Shane and Bam Bam, with Bam Bam just doing his thing and Shane being all serious, and there is Chris making it all look so effortless, taking a big suplex, falling down, and then doing the Curly spin around the ring, lying on his side and spinning around the center of the ring. Sabu would get so aggravated with him. Sabu would be real serious, and hit him with a punch, and Chris would act like he was cutting himself to get blood, when he didn't even have a blade. The reason he could do that was that he was so good, he could horse around in the middle of the match. He loved what he was doing."

Francine worked with Shane Douglas, and so she was close to the Triple Threat. "Chris Candido, God rest his soul, and Bam Bam Bigelow, we kind of hung out together and traveled together," she says. "Bam Bam was a big teddy bear. Chris Candido was one of the best people I have ever known. He loved life and loved to have a good time out there. He was awesome, a wonderful person."

Lance Storm, who would join ECW the following year, was brought there by Candido.

"Chris was so much fun to work with," Storm said. "He was always about the match and not about himself. There was never, 'Who's going to win?' or, 'How can I get my stuff in?' It was always about the match and how best we could entertain the fans, and sometimes, even more importantly, entertain the boys."

Everybody was pretty entertained, both in the locker room and in the stands, by what went on in ECW in 1996. But not all of it was entertaining. Some of it was so frightening and disturbing that it nearly ended the good times—for good.

chapter seven

Crosses and Chaos

One of the beauties of ECW, for both the fans and the wrestlers, was the freedom the performers had in creating their own gimmicks and matches. Moves and promos were not carefully choreographed, and as word of this spread, talent wanted to come to ECW just for the creative freedom.

"We didn't have writers or creative teams or all that," Tazz says. "Paul just gave us directions, 'Go out, talk about so and so, and just do it.' Paul let you be you."

"Paul E. entrusted us to come up with our story lines and characters and freedom to do whatever we wanted in the ring, no matter how extreme or how violent," Spike Dudley points out. "A lot of promoters, at that time, weren't ready to just cut loose and let anything go."

"You really had control and the freedom to speak your mind as your character," Bubba Ray Dudley notes. "It wasn't rare to sit down and get into an hour-long conversation with Paul E. about a certain aspect of your character or story line and your match."

Heyman says he viewed the wrestlers—and himself—as artists, and if you wanted a masterpiece, you didn't have somebody paint by numbers. "It was an artistic expression," he states. "You can look at this industry any way you want, and if you look down on it and say, 'Come on, it's just wrestling. How the fuck could you consider yourselves artists?' We did. We didn't just want to do the best wrestling TV show, we wanted to do the best TV show. I wanted to have drama as compelling as any daytime soap opera. I didn't want to just do a wrestling show. I wanted to do great television. I wanted to do great arena shows."

Many times, the acts did make for great TV and arena shows. Sometimes, though, when the inmates were running the asylum, disaster struck.

Sandman taking a Singapore cane to Raven.

Raven was a very creative force in ECW and everywhere he went. He had a great grasp of the psychology of wrestling and a flair for dramatic story lines. "He is a genius about the business, and loves wrestling," Mike "Nova" Bucci declares. "He wasn't a great athlete, but he was a master psychologist. The Raven gimmick was one of the top gimmicks of the 1990s, or maybe ever. He was like the Kurt Cobain of wrestling at that point. He went from being Scotty the Body and Scotty Flamingo to that. Raven was more like his true personality. He could look at people and know how to read them. He was very complex, but that is what made him Raven. He was also a lot tougher than people gave him credit for. In the opening of that show, he got a real shampoo job across his head from Dreamer when he was handcuffed to the cage. He would take his bumps and go through tables and was barb-wired a few times and bloodied. He would come in the back and flip his hair back, bloody, and laugh. He was really good at putting matches together."

Raven had an idea for his feud with Sandman and was putting it in motion for the October *High Incident* show. "All week long, Raven and the Sandman had been trying to find an angle," Heyman recalls, "and my way of dealing with these things was very simple. I'd say, 'This Saturday we have to heat up your feud, so we do this angle where Raven sticks a cue tip in your ear, and you bleed from the ear.' And you'd come back, 'I don't know, I don't want to do an injury angle. I want to do something more personal.' So I'd say, 'Come up with something.' I'd throw out ideas, and if someone else had an idea, I'd listen to it."

Raven had been known for, among other things, a pose he would strike in the ring, as if he was being crucified, often standing over his victims after beating them. It was all part of the dark and deep Raven character, and was something that ECW had already played off of, in variations. In previous matches, Raven had handcuffed Tommy Dreamer to the ropes and beaten him with a chair. He did the same thing to Dreamer in a Steel Cage match, cuffing him in a crucifix pose in the cage while beating on him with a chair. The night of the Funk fire, at the end of the show, Raven had Dreamer on top of the eagle's nest, with his arms outstretched, tied to the roof of the building, in crucifix fashion. So Raven wanted to take it one step further.

"Raven and Sandman called me when I was in the studio the week before the show, and they said, 'We have an idea, we know how to heat this up,'" Heyman recalls. "We had done all this stuff with Raven and Sandman's child and everything else. Raven said, 'Sandman needs to be crucified for the sins of his child. So we crucify the Sandman at the arena,' he said, 'and really crucify him.'

"I said okay, because to me crucifying with Raven meant hand-cuffing somebody with his arms outstretched, or like what we did to Dreamer. Sandman calls me and says, 'I'm really going to work on this and make it happen.' I said, 'Go ahead, by all means.' I really didn't understand what they were talking about.

"We got to the arena, and Sandman had the crucifix under the ring, and they went to do it, and it was in pretty bad taste. Two years later, it became the fashion to do it in wrestling, but even I thought it was in bad taste. I was sensitive to it. I'm Jewish. Raven's Jewish. I didn't want anyone thinking I was taking shots at their religion, because I really wasn't."

Sandman was proud of his work. "I made the cross for the crucifixion, cut it up, and brought it to the ring and everything," he says.

But Stevie Richards, who, along with Blue Meanie and Raven, was tying Sandman to the cross laid out on the floor, had a problem with it. "The whole time I am doing it, me and Meanie are there, and Raven is like, 'Tie him up, tie him up, put the cross up,'" Richards remembers. "I'm there going, 'This is fucked up, man.' Meanie said, 'I know,' I was saying, 'This is bullshit.' This was one time at the ECW Arena where the fans weren't saying, 'Go to hell' or screaming. They were just quiet."

Sandman was lifted up and held up on the cross while bleeding from his forehead. Raven stood over the scene in the ring. Sandman would later be carried out on the cross back to the dressing room.

"This is the most horrifying thing I have ever seen in my life," announcer Joey Styles told the TV audience.

Kurt Angle agreed with Joey Styles, and what had been a tasteless moment had now become a controversial moment.

Angle had been a popular and successful amateur wrestler, a two-time NCAA Division I Champion and three-time NCAA Division All-American. He was also 1987 USA Junior Freestyle Champion, two-time USA Senior Freestyle Champion, and 1988 USA FILA Junior World Freestyle Champion. Angle went on to win the gold medal in the 100-kilogram (220-pound) freestyle wrestling competition in the 1996 Olympics in Atlanta.

Angle had emerged from those Olympics as a star, and was trying to find a way to capitalize on his stardom. A short stint in sports broadcasting in his hometown of Pittsburgh failed. He was reluctant to go into professional wrestling, but Heyman was trying to woo him, through a connection with Shane Douglas. "Shane told him it was professional wrestling, but on a whole different level," Heyman recalls. "He said we had a character there who played an Olympic-style/UFC-style wrestler, with a lot of good wrestling moves—Tazz. We would like you to come and comment on the matches. If you think it stinks, say so. If you like it, tell us about it. We bring Kurt to the arena. At the time he had turned down Vince. He thought he was above professional wrestling."

When Angle saw the crucifixion take place, he was outraged. "It offended me so badly that I got up in the middle of the show, went straight to Paul Heyman, and said, 'I am leaving right now. I want you to send me my check, and if I am on TV with that crucifixion . . . if my name or face is seen on TV with that same program, you will be hearing from my attorney,'" Angle remembers. "Paul said he had no idea this was going to happen. I believed him. I figured at ECW there is a little more freelance. Wrestlers do whatever they want to do. Paul Heyman lets them. Then again, I wasn't sure if I should believe him, because Paul Heyman could do that kind of thing. He is very controversial. I just remember leaving that arena so mad and so offended that they would actually do something like that. He told me he didn't know. As a promoter, you are running the show, and if you don't know what is going on, then you're an idiot."

Heyman said he tried to reassure Angle that he had nothing to worry about. "Kurt Angle comes up to me, and he's pissed off. He said,

'Why did that happen?' I said, 'Kurt, I need to talk to my guys about it before I talk to you about it.' He said, 'I'm offended by it. I don't want to be associated with that. I work with church groups. I do endorsements. I better not be on that tape.' I said, 'Kurt, I'm not releasing the tape. We're going to let that footage stay in the vault. I don't want that angle to air.' He said, 'Well, if it does, I'm going to sue you.' I said, 'Okay, sue away, but it is not going to air.' He said, 'I have to leave now.' I said, 'Okay, thank you for coming. We're going to use your commentary on the Tazz match and your appearance at the beginning of the show. I'm sorry that you are offended, and I hope to see you again under better circumstances. Good-bye.' And he left, and that was it."

But the fact that the Olympic gold medalist from the 1996 Olympics walked out of the show made it a pretty big incident.

Heyman told Raven to go back out to the crowd and apologize. Standing in the ring with a microphone in his hand, Raven addressed the fans. "Apparently, Tod Gordon and Paul Heyman—by acting without their knowledge—are offended at my use of religious iconography. And apparently I have offended quite a few people in the audience. Well, you people chose to respect Scott Levy's privacy when I needed the personal time, so I chose to respect your privacy and your religious beliefs, and so for the people who I deeply offended, I apologize."

Heyman said he understood why people might have been offended, and regretted it.

Sandman, though, thought it was an overreaction. "It had backlash because Kurt Angle was in the back, but I don't think the fans gave a damn about that," he says. "I think they liked it. The only backlash was Kurt Angle. If that would have happened a couple of years later, I would have told Kurt to fuck off. But at the time, I didn't have enough power in the business to do something like that. There is no way I would have let Raven go out there and apologize for that. But there was Shane and Kurt, and Shane wanted to bring Kurt into ECW and all this stuff. If it wasn't for Kurt being there that night, Raven would have never gone out and apologized. And if it had happened a couple of years later, I would have said, 'No, you ain't doing it.'"

Angle soon went into professional wrestling and became a star in WWE.

ECW was moving forward. They broke through an important barrier and got Request TV to agree to show the promotion's first Pay-Per-View event, scheduled for March 31, 1997. It would either make or break ECW.

"Hugh Panero, who is now the president of XM Satellite Radio, was head of Request TV at the time," Heyman recalls. "He listened to the fan campaigns. Our fans were bombarding them, just as they had bombarded the TV stations to put us on the air. Our fans waged a campaign—phone, fax, e-mails, petitions—to get us on Pay-Per-View, to both Viewer's Choice and Request TV. Viewer's Choice was still passing. They still thought we were real, and we weren't adhering to a script, but we were, as much as WCW or WWE was, but they thought this wasn't predetermined. They thought this was violence by anarchy. But Request TV decided to put us on the air. As soon as we announced our first Pay-Per-View date, which was Sunday night, March 31, 1997, in Philadelphia, WCW, wanting to come in and blow us away, booked a *Monday Night Nitro* live for the very next day in Philadelphia. We knew we scared people with this Pay-Per-View, even though we were only on Request TV. We are moving forward. We are finally going to do it. We are finally going to see Tazz vs. Sabu, we are finally going to see the Raven-Dreamer blow-off, we are finally going to see all these different things."

Or so they thought. A young man who had dreams of being a star in professional wrestling—a misguided dream for a tragic figure named Eric Kulas—would disrupt those plans and put the entire company in jeopardy.

ECW was doing a tour of the New England area in the fall of 1996, and on November 23 made a stop for a show in Revere, Massachusetts. One of the features of the night was to be a tag team bout between The Gangstas—Mustafa & New Jack—and the team of D-Von Dudley & Axl Rotten. However, Axl could not make the show, so Heyman was faced with the problem of having to cancel one of the prime matches and anger local fans.

Enter 5-foot-10, 350-pound Eric Kulas. He was a fan at the arena that night in Revere, and when word went out that Axl Rotten would be a no-show, Eric and his father made the case to Heyman that he could be a substitute wrestler for the match. He claimed to have been trained by Killer Kowalski and said that he had wrestled on local independent shows. Kulas had obviously been hoping for a shot like this. He said his wrestling name was Mass Transit, and he had a bus driver's suit on hand for his uniform.

Heyman asked for indentification to prove he was of age, and Kulas gave him an ID that turned out to be fake. He was only 17. Heyman said he was also told by a wrestling midget named Tiny the Terrible that he knew Kulas and that he had wrestling experience and was supposedly one of Kowalski's top students. Well, that was phony, too. He was hardly a top student, and his only wrestling experience was a gimmick he did with midget wrestlers like Tiny.

The plan was for Kulas to bleed, so he would have to, as they say in the business, blade himself—meaning cut himself with a blade. According to ECW's version, Kulas said he didn't know how to blade and asked New Jack to do it. That, it turned out, was like leading a lamb to slaughter.

The fans were not particularly happy to see this unknown, fat kid in the ring dressed like Ralph Kramden, instead of Axl Rotten, and being ECW fans, they let him know about it, which resulted in a shouting match between Kulas and the crowd before the action even started. When Kulas was finally in the ring and face-to-face with New Jack, he was in trouble. Out came the weapons. New Jack hit the kid with a crutch several times, then a guitar and a toaster got smashed over his head. As Kulas was laid out on the canvas, New Jack pulled him up into a sitting position and then used his knife to cut into Kulas's forehead—much deeper than a typical cut.

Kulas began screaming as the blood gushed from his forehead and he tried to get away, but New Jack grabbed him and tried to bodyslam him. He couldn't, because Kulas was too heavy. So New Jack put Kulas on a table, went to a corner, climbed to the top rope with a chair, and came crashing down on Kulas's now crimson head.

As paramedics rushed into the ring, New Jack got on the microphone and started talking some brutal trash. "I don't care if the mother-fucker dies," he said. "He's white. I don't like white people. I don't like people from Boston. I'm the wrong nigger to fuck with, bitch."

As they carried Kulas from the ring, his father was screaming at Heyman, demanding an ambulance, yelling at New Jack, and threatening to sue. The incident would eventually grab headlines and create a huge buzz throughout the industry, and would wind up in court. Here is Paul Heyman's version of what happened that night:

"Axl Rotten couldn't make the show. Something happened. Backstage there was a kid who claimed he was trained by Killer Kowalski in Boston. He had a résumé that claimed he was about 21 or 22 years old. One of the referees said he knew the kid. He said he had seen him on independent shows. He was big, about 400 pounds, a fat white kid, about 5-foot-9, a big blubbery guy from Rhode Island. He was dressed up like a bus driver, and he looked like Ralph Kramden. He called himself Mass Transit.

"Well, he had a phony résumé, and he was illegally working some shows in Rhode Island, but the referee never knew it. This kid came in with a midget called Tiny the Terrible, a pretty well-known midget. I asked Tiny, 'You know this guy?' Tiny said, 'Yeah, he is one of Kowalski's top students and has been wrestling for a couple of years. Sure, I will vouch for him.' So I put him out there with D-Von against The Gangstas. Before the match, New Jack says to him, 'Do you want to cut a blade?' The kid says, 'No, can you do it for me?' It wasn't really done that often that you would let somebody else cut you, but it wasn't so out of practice that it was a heinous violation of the wrestlers' code. I myself let someone cut me. Jerry Lawler cut me when I was 21 years old.

"New Jack went too far and he cut the kid too deep, and he gave him a good gash across his forehead—nothing that hasn't been seen before in wrestling, and nothing that some guys haven't done to themselves, to be honest. But the kid panicked and started screaming. The kid's father was at ringside, and the father didn't know he was going to be bleeding. The kid was bleeding pretty bad, but it was from the forehead, which always looks bad but it is not life-threatening. But it does looks bad, and when you are sweating it gives you the crimson mask effect, the blood dripping down your sweaty face. The blood is gushing out of the kid's head. New Jack pins him and says his stuff, he's playing his role. The medics are putting towels on this kid's head and the kid's father is screaming, and the kid is screaming that he wants an ambulance, so we get him an ambulance. But it just didn't seem like that big of a deal. It seemed like a kid got cut too deep and kind of panicked. He was inexperienced, and New Jack shouldn't have cut him that bad, but it happens in this business. The kid is being taken out of the arena, Tommy Dreamer is holding his hand. The kid, playing heel for the audience, gives everyone the finger. Dreamer says, 'What are you doing?' The kid says, 'I'm playing the bad guy. Don't I have heat?' His father came in the back and raised hell. He got into a shouting match with New Jack. I said, 'Send me the bill.' He got fifty or sixty stitches. It happens."

The ramifications went far beyond a hospital bill. Nearly two years later, Kulas's family sued ECW and New Jack for physical and psychological damage. They charged that Kulas did not know he was going to be cut, and that he nearly died in the ring. They also charged that Heyman told a reporter that it was an initiation for him into the ECW family. ECW denied the charges. New Jack said Kulas *did* know what was going to happen and gave his approval to be cut. New Jack also claimed that the father knew what was going to happen from talks backstage. New Jack claimed that you can see Kulas puffing his cheeks, a way to increase the bleeding. Jerome Young, a.k.a. New Jack, claimed that his first two attempts to blade did not work. This is due to the fact that Kulas had never bladed before. When he tried again, he accidentally pushed too deep and that caused the massive bleeding. New Jack's act on the microphone was introduced as evidence, as well as a shoot interview he later did, talking about how he loved to cause pain and violence. But Kulas claimed he suffered scarring from the incident, although there were no visible scars. In fact, Kulas was walking around backstage and talking to other wrestlers before going to the hospital. His conflicting accounts would result in a decision in favor of ECW and New Jack.

Four years later, the story of Eric Kulas came to a tragic end. On May 12, 2002, he died at the age of 22, reportedly of a heart attack.

"New Jack basically beat him up pretty bad," D-Von Dudley said. "It was the scariest thing I have ever seen in the ring. Lawsuits followed. New Jack was acquitted of everything, but it was a scary moment."

John "Pee Wee" Moore, an ECW referee who was in the ring that night, says there was plenty of blame to go around for the incident. "He [Kulas] entrusted himself to another wrestler, which is something that you don't do unless you truly know the person. He wasn't trained properly, and New Jack cut him, got him real good. I wasn't in the ring at the time, but I was there. He was in serious condition. He shouldn't have been in the ring in the first place. The police come and want to charge New Jack with felony assault, but he was gone. That was something I will never forget. Being in the middle of that when the cops are looking for one of us, who they think tried to kill a guy in the wrestling ring. He shouldn't have taken advantage of him like that, but the guy shouldn't have tried out if he wasn't ready. You need to have a mental toughness in the ring and realize that anything can happen, and if it does, you can hold your own with who you are in the ring with. These are tough guys, and guys who aren't tough shouldn't get in the ring."

Heyman would have loved to have the incident slip under the radar, but the wrestling media ran with it, and it became a huge controversy. As a result, ECW's first scheduled Pay-Per-View event—a huge step for the promotion, one that probably meant its very survival—was canceled.

It was a knife in the heart of ECW.

"I was asked by some of the local media there about it and I said I didn't think it was that big of a deal," Heyman recalls. "We were concerned that somebody could make an issue of this, so Steve Karel notified the Pay-Per-View companies. He said, 'We had an incident. We wanted you to know about it. It is probably going to get some publicity. It shouldn't affect our relationship.' We sent them a tape.

"I get a phone call that week from a wrestling publication called the *Pro Wrestling Torch*. A guy named Wade Keller asked me about it, and I made the statement, 'The Pay-Per-View companies have been notified. Tapes have been sent.' Keller decides to verify the story. But when he speaks to Hugh Panero, he says, 'Paul Heyman says that you have viewed the tapes.' That is not what I said, and I had witnesses to prove it. I said, 'We have notified the Pay-Per-View companies, and the tapes have been sent.' I never said 'watched' or 'reviewed' or 'analyzed.' I said '*sent*,' and they were.

"Keller decides to make an issue out of it. He asks, 'Since Heyman says that you watched it, do you condone it?' While this is going on, the kid's family hires a lawyer, and they want to know, 'Why was this kid thrown into a wrestling match when he was only 17 years old?' How the hell did we know? The father said, 'I didn't bring the kid there to wrestle in a match. I brought him there to be a spectator in the matches. He had never wrestled in his life,' which was a lie. He was there to be a spectator. In a Ralph Kramden outfit that he had in a truck that he had to change into? When I met him, he was wearing a sweatsuit.

"They hire a lawyer, issue a press release, and now the Pay-Per-View companies have a controversy on their hands and a reporter breathing down their throats, so they suspend the March 31 date," Heyman explains. "The day I get the phone call that the date has been suspended is Christmas Eve 1996. I get this phone call from Request TV, 'Just so you know, we are going on vacation until the end of the first week in January, and then we can discuss whether or not we can get you on the 1997 schedule, because as of now, your Pay-Per-View has been officially postponed.' So the thing that I have everybody in ECW hanging onto, this dream, the reason why all these people are turning down the other companies—we had already shot our angles and we are heading into the matches on this—this dream of Pay-Per-View has been pulled away on Christmas Eve, with no hope of discussing it for several weeks. It was devastating. It was the worst kick in the balls we could have suffered. Everyone was walking about like deer in headlights."

While this was going on, Heyman was still trying to keep the talent pump primed. In November, he brought former "Thrillseeker" Lance Storm to ECW. Storm was another Canadian wrestler out of the Harts' school. "I got into wrestling as a fan when I was in high school in the 1980s," Storm recalls. "I was probably a fan for about five years before I got into the business. I was going to a university, studying to be an accountant, but I just wasn't enjoying it anymore. I played volleyball at the university. I had a coach I hated. I didn't enjoy university anymore, and didn't want to spend another three years there. So I started looking at other options. I considered wrestling, while I was still young enough to give it a go. So I withdrew from university, and six months later [in 1990] I was in Calgary being trained [by Stu Hart and the Hart family].

"I was working in Japan for a company called WAR," Storm says. "Chris Jericho had left WAR and was working in ECW. So when he went from ECW later to WCW, I was talking to him and realizing that WAR might be on its last legs, from a business standpoint, because it was having money troubles. I talked to Chris and told him I was looking for a job in the States. He said, 'Why don't you call Paul in ECW? He knows your work, and I am sure he would love to hear from you.' So I give him a call and a month or two later, he called me back, and I was in."

Storm says he got a warm reception from the ECW wrestlers when he arrived, but a cool one from the fans. "It was weird. The first time I worked there was at the ECW Arena in Philadelphia. A lot of wrestling companies, when you are there for the first time, you feel like you are the odd man out and not part of the group yet. But ECW, after my first match, I walked back into the locker room area and was greeted with a round of applause and welcome from the owner, and really felt like I was part of the team, even though it was my first time there. I had a few friends there that I had worked with from other companies, which helped, but it was really a welcome group effort by everyone.

"Your first time in, fans are pretty hard on you," Storm notes. "They felt like it was their show, and that you didn't belong, and you really had to earn your stripes, so to speak. But they appreciated and loved the wrestling, as long as you were willing to work hard, they were willing to accept you. It didn't take long for that to happen there, and it was great, a real intimate relationship. They loved the sport as much as we did, and it was fun."

The door was open to both newcomers and well-known veterans, who Heyman welcomed and gave an opportunity to perform however they wanted to, an example being Steve Austin's promos. "Ravishing" Rick Rude was a very popular wrestler, a former WWE Intercontinental Champion who had retired because of a neck injury he suffered in a match against Sting.

But he came back to the ring at the start of 1997 to play a role in ECW. He was a masked interloper who harassed Shane Douglas, and would later hook up with Douglas and the Triple Threat. He became a color commentator, and would be involved in another groundbreaking concept in ECW—cross-promotion promoting.

Heyman was working on some unprecedented cross promotion with World Wrestling Federation. McMahon and Heyman worked together, but with different goals. Vince was battling WCW in the Monday Night Wars, while ECW was battling everyone for attention. So they began talent exchanges, with wrestlers from each promotion showing up at the other's shows.

"Vince's curiosity with ECW started at the *King of the Ring* in Philadelphia, where Mabel was crowned King of the Ring, and the entire arena is chanting 'ECW! ECW!' with great passion and anger at Vince McMahon," Heyman explains. "Vince is coming back to Philadelphia to do *Mind Games,* and obviously we had such momentum at the time, it would behoove his business to acknowledge ECW."

McMahon certainly had become intrigued by the upstart promotion. "I heard about ECW, this other wrestling organization," Vince says. "I kind of dismissed it at first. Then it started making a little more noise. ECW didn't have a lot of distribution, as compared to our product or WCW's product. Nonetheless, when we brought one of their stars into the fold, you would hear a smattering, and sometimes more than a smattering of ECW chants. So there was something there. Why not incorporate it? Why not try to do something with it and see where it goes? I wouldn't have done the same with WCW, but, this was a good way to broaden the business."

They had different reasons for collaborating, but it was seen as a way to help both promotions. "It's not going to help us to be embraced and endorsed by Vince McMahon," Heyman declares. "It's going to help us to rebel against Vince McMahon. So we came up with a way where everybody won."

So ECW wrestlers showed up at September's *In Your House: Mind Games* Pay-Per-View in Philadelphia. During the opening bout on the card—Savio Vega vs. (Justin) Bradshaw in a Strap match—Sandman, Tommy Dreamer, and Paul Heyman were seated at ringside. When Vega fell out of the ring, Sandman stood up and spit beer on him, prompting security to "forcibly remove" the ECW trio from the building. During the live broadcast, Vince McMahon even made reference to this "local outlaw wrestling franchise" that was "creating a disturbance."

"Hey, wait a minute, what is this?" McMahon said on the telecast. "There is a local wrestling organization here in Philadelphia, and obviously trying to make a name for themselves here. . . . These Philadelphia wrestlers wrestle in a bingo hall."

The next night, Tazz interrupted *Monday Night Raw* by jumping over the guardrail at ringside and holding up an ECW sign.

"We were never in the locker room," Tazz states. "Basically we would corral in the parking lot, the ECW guys, and we had ECW guys sprinkled throughout the arena, because we didn't know if Vince's guys were going to try to jump us. We didn't know what the deal was. But I don't think very many people knew, besides Vince McMahon, what was going to happen.

"I remember that night jumping that guardrail and security trying to stop me," Tazz points out. "A guy who was a photographer tried to stop me, saying, 'No man, it's not worth it, it's not worth it.' I was instructed by my boss and a couple of other people, anybody gets in your way, get them out of the way. I just said to the photographer,

Jerry Lawler and Tommy Dreamer.

'You don't want to do this.' I shoved him out of the way and he broke his shoulder."

The collaboration certainly created a buzz for both promotions. "It was good for both," Ron Buffone remembers. "It was good for the talent because they got a chance to showcase their talent. It was good for World Wrestling Federation because they got a chance to show us, and it was good for ECW, because it brought ECW into the mainstream."

The cross promotion took a big step at the February 24, 1997, *Monday Night Raw* at the Manhattan Center in New York. Heyman, Raven, Tazz, Tommy Dreamer, Beulah, the Dudleyz, The Eliminators, Sandman, and the Blue World Order appeared on the show.

Announcer Jerry Lawler confronted Heyman and the ECW wrestlers in the ring that night. "You ought to get down on your hands and knees and thank your lucky stars that you are even getting a chance to plug your stinking Pay-Per-View on *Monday Night Raw,* do you understand that?" he said. "And why Vince McMahon would allow this, I'll never know." Heyman and Tommy Dreamer walked Lawler around the ring, backing him up, and cornered him.

"It was so exciting for us because as the revolution, the ECW revolution, we were finally going to be able to show everybody out there in the world that we were legit," Bubba Ray Dudley recalls. "We really went in there as a team, and as a bunch of guys who believed in ourselves and the company."

Lawler was perplexed by the whole idea and the way the ECW wrestlers acted. "I guess you could attribute it to maybe being arrogant, cocky, self-confident, whatever, but they had an attitude like they were better. I was thinking you guys don't realize how lucky you are to get to be involved and have this worldwide exposure all of a sudden.

"The first thing I remember when I saw these guys were how small they were," Lawler says. "Everybody looked like miniature wrestlers running around, and I remember commenting, after looking at Tazz, to Vince, 'He looked a lot bigger on the Lucky Charms box, you know, McMahon.' This was while Tazz was wrestling in the ring. Then Tazz came over to me and said something to me about that."

Tazz grabbed Lawler, and the two had to be separated. And at one point Heyman had to be held back from going after Lawler.

Heyman, standing in front of the crowd outside of the ring, grabbed a microphone and said, "Does this show suck without ECW or what?" Fans chanted, "ECW! ECW!" while Sandman, with his Singapore cane, and Dreamer led the cheers in the ring. "The whole place was chanting ECW, ECW," Dreamer said. "We did ECW-style matches on *Monday Night Raw.*"

There was one memorable scene involving the giant *Raw* letters at the wrester's entrance from backstage that were a trademark of

the show. "I was wrestling Mikey Whipwreck," Tazz recalls. As Tazz slammed Mikey Whipwreck, Sabu came out and climbed on top of the R and tried to jump off. "He fell off the R onto Team Tazz," Tazz says. "This is live TV, and I had never done live wrestling before. It was an inside joke. We used to make fun of him for it.

"It was a lot of fun, the Invasion stuff. It didn't last long, but it was cool."

"ECW invading *Raw*, to me, started the whole attitude era, where anything could go and anything could happen on *Raw*," Tommy Dreamer says. "Just watch. 'Look, they even brought in guys from another promotion.'"

It brought a different look to *Raw*. "Back then in 1997, they didn't have guys in the ring doing what the guys there do now," Tazz says. "WCW didn't have those types of guys either. The athletes weren't wrestling a fast-paced aggressive style. I feel Paul Heyman created that with ECW. That was the hardcore style, that was the extreme style."

At the same time that Heyman is trying to call attention to ECW, he is also working desperately behind the scenes to calm the fears of the Pay-Per-View company and get ECW's first Pay-Per-View back on the schedule.

"We had to prove to Hugh Panero what I had said to Keller. I had witnesses," Heyman says. "We had a long discussion about the New Jack incident, and assured them that New Jack would not be on the first Pay-Per-View. I told him I would send him a script for the first Pay-Per-View, so he could see what we were going to do, up front, with the promise that they could pull the plug on us any time that we violated the script, and our fans had bombarded Request TV over that time, so they realized this was going to be a money maker. They put us back on the schedule for Sunday night, April 13, 1997, which, by the way, WCW moved their *Nitro* to the night after.

"I never felt in my heart that I wasn't going to get us back on the schedule. I couldn't accept that possibility. The only thing that could happen was us getting back on the schedule. Life doesn't exist without that happening. It was so tough. Everyone thought it was the end. 'What if they don't get us back on for a year or so? How will we last?' I told people we would get back on, and soon. We'll make it. Thank God we did. And the second week of January 1997 it was announced we were back on. Then everyone was pumped up, and the whole dynamic changed. It was like, 'We fucking did it.' The cockiness was there and chests were out, and it was like, 'Motherfuckers, we beat the odds at every turn.' We pulled this off. The warrior came out in everybody."

The "warrior," though, had to agree to some unwarrior-like stipulations before Hugh Panero would move ahead with the Pay-Per-View on Viewer's Choice. First, the Pay-Per-View company had to have approval of a script before the show, and there was not to be any outrageous or excessive blood, gimmick bouts that used blood as the main draw, or any extreme man-on-woman violence. The show would not air until 9 P.M., two hours later than typical wrestling Pay-Per-View shows, and would cost $19.95—$10 less than the other companies sold their shows for at the time. Even with the restrictions, it was a chance for ECW to start raking in the Pay-Per-View revenue and get on the map of that lucrative world.

All Heyman had to do was to keep everyone from going crazy and killing either themselves or each other until *Barely Legal 1997* finally took place. "Going into the Pay-Per-View, the week before, everybody pretty much knew what they were doing," Heyman recalls. "But everybody lost their minds going into this Pay-Per-View. It was the first time that the nerves got to everybody. Nobody knew what life was going to be like on the flip side. Some people had delusions that this was going to make us all millionaires, not realizing that this was just the first step in getting full Pay-Per-View clearance. It was just the next step in our evolution. It was a life-and-death step, but just one step. So many people didn't see that."

Viewer's Choice was trying to wield its considerable power. First, it didn't want Joey Styles to go it alone as the commentator for the show. Typically, in most telecasts, there are two people, a play-by-play person and a color analyst, and the Pay-Per-View company wanted a color analyst for the show. But that was not the way ECW did its telecasts, and Heyman battled them on the issues.

"Joey Styles was frazzled, because the Pay-Per-View company insisted that I have a color commentator on the show, that it was unheard of to do a one-man broadcast on Pay-Per-View," Heyman explains. "But I insisted on it because that was how we were doing our TV show, and I wanted it to be authentic. It was a lot of pressure for Joey, but he shouldn't have felt the pressure. He could do it. That was why I gave him the job."

They also didn't want Ron Buffone to be the producer. "The Pay-Per-View company did not want Ron Buffone," Heyman says. "The week of the show they pulled a fast one on me and said if Ron Buffone is the director, we're not going to do the Pay-Per-View live. I said I am not going to turn my back on the people who have been with me. They backed down. Ron couldn't sleep the entire week, especially since we were doing all these packages and commercials for the Pay-Per-View. Ron was on edge, and we were at each other's throats. He very much appreciated that I had his back, and I did have his back, but we were still at each other's throats."

Buffone did appreciate Heyman's loyalty, both to him and to the product that had gotten them this far. "The battle to get on Pay-Per-View was immense. They didn't want to give us a shot. They thought we were too extreme. And we were an unproven commodity on Pay-Per-View. They didn't want to take a chance. They wanted a minimum guarantee. They had brought in their own people literally to pull the plug on us at any time. It was quite difficult getting on. Even in the process of getting on, they wanted to bring their own people in to produce and direct the Pay-Per-View.

"To Paul Heyman's credit, and I have nothing but the greatest respect for him in this regard, he went not only with the wrestlers but with the production team that got him there," Buffone points out. "Paul believed that these were the people who got me here, these are the people I am using. You don't get to the Pay-Per-View with this production crew and creating a look and a certain type of feel, and then hand over the creative reins to somebody else. Paul believed the look was very important, and to go with something else could destroy the product. If you notice, the promos were always done from one camera perspective, never two where it was cut cleanly in between—all those promos were done one take, straight through, period. That made everyone sharp and on point and creating that intimate feel where you are not cutting away from you. You are literally getting to the wrestler's character, and he draws you in, and you believe what he says."

It wasn't enough that Heyman had to fight these battles with outsiders. He also had to fight the battles among his own people. One of the featured bouts for *Barely Legal 1997* was to finally have Sabu and Tazz face each other, after Tazz spent pretty much an entire year calling Sabu out. Somebody now had to win, and somebody had to lose, and the booker—Heyman—would decide.

"Sabu asked, 'Who is going to win, me or Tazz?'" Heyman recalls.

"I said, 'I am going to have Tazz win, then turn you heel with Rob Van Dam. I'm going to have Fonzie turn on Tazz after the match, saying that Fonzie bet on Sabu, even though Fonzie was Tazz's manager.' Sabu was upset because his uncle, The Sheik, never believed in doing jobs—losing matches. So Sabu said, 'Don't bother turning me heel. I will wrestle the show, but it is my last night. I want you to release me after the show.' I wouldn't do that.

"Everybody was falling apart. Nobody knew what was on the flip side. Some people seemed to be more afraid of the success than actually looking forward to it, and didn't know how to handle it and the anticipation."

Heyman recalls that the night before *Barely Legal*, the promotion held a tribute dinner at the Hilton hotel in Philadelphia for Terry Funk, who was going to wrestle in a three-way for the ECW Heavyweight Championship. "One of the big draws of *Barely Legal* was that the grand old man of hardcore, Terry Funk, would be challenging Raven in the impossible dream, the ECW title. We had captured people's attention with this Funk storyline so much that he was this beloved figure. To make it a complete weekend, we did a Terry Funk banquet. It was more about ECW than about Funk, but it was a chance to say thank you to Terry and get everybody together."

Not everybody. Raven was not there. Heyman didn't want him there because of his role the following night in the Terry Funk title bout. "It was a Three Way Dance, and you didn't know Raven was going to be Funk's opponent," Heyman explains. "It was to be the Sandman, who had the big feud with Raven over Sandman's son; Stevie Richards from the Blue World Order, who broke away from Raven and was no longer Raven's lackey; and Terry Funk. The winner of the Three Way match was to fight Raven for the title. Because Funk and Raven were going to be opponents, I didn't want them up on the podium together, so I didn't have Raven come to the banquet.

"So Raven was pissed off because Sabu, who owed a lot of his career to Funk, was there, and so was Tazz. For Sabu and Tazz to be in the same room at the same time, Raven felt why couldn't he be there? Raven kept saying, 'I should have been there, I should have been there.'"

Finally, the sun came up in Philadelphia on April 13. The day had arrived. All the hype, the hysterics, the triumphs, and the tensions were in the past. There was nothing now for anyone to look forward to or look back on or complain about or criticize. There was only one thing for anyone in and around ECW on this spring day in Philadelphia—make *Barely Legal 1997* a success.

No one wanted to consider any other options.

chapter eight

Pay-Per-View

As traffic went by on Interstate 95 and people went about their everyday lives, just a short distance away, in an industrial section of south Philadelphia, something was about to happen in the lives of a group of people that was hardly everyday.

On April 13, 1997, in a bingo hall that also served as a warehouse for Mummers Day floats and uniforms, lives were about to change, and the tension that surrounded the arena reflected the anxieties about the uncertainties of the day.

Paul Heyman had no time for such uncertainties. He had to keep everyone focused on the task at hand, and put out all the fires that would flare up before and during the company's first Pay-Per-View.

"I knew walking into this day that everybody had to be on the same page," Heyman says. "Everybody got to the arena early."

The ECW Arena has been painted. Additional lighting had been brought in. The big TV production truck was outside, setting up shop. The generator and backup generators are running, and everything is being tested. The Pay-Per-View company supervisors are on the scene, trying to ride herd. The state athletic commission is represented to make sure that *Barely Legal* doesn't somehow become *Very Illegal* and violate state laws.

While all this is going on, a Hollywood filmmaker named Barry Blaustein is there with his camera crew, filming the event and the behind-the-scenes intrigue for a wrestling documentary he is making, called *Beyond the Mat*. Fans have been lining up for hours outside the arena, partying and waiting to get in, going nearly crazy with anticipation of this long-awaited event that they themselves lobbied for with letters and phone calls to the Pay-Per-View company. Backstage is even more crowded than it normally is before the show, with family members on hand to witness the historic occasion.

"We are doing this live, national Pay-Per-View out of a bingo hall on the wrong side of the tracks in south Philadelphia," Heyman says.

Adding to the tension was a rumor circulating that a group of WCW wrestlers, who were in town because Bischoff had changed his *Monday Night Nitro* show to be in Philadelphia the following night to take attention away from the ECW Pay-Per-View, were going to show up and disrupt the show.

That rumor appeared to be one more problem for Heyman, but at the time, it turned out to be just what he needed. "It brought everybody together," he points out. "These motherfuckers are going to try to take down what we built? Fuck them. You saw it sweep the locker room, this group that had been so tight and has become so fragmented and frazzled in the past week, started bonding again. It was tangible."

Heyman went over what was going to happen in everyone's matches. People checked camera angles, lighting, sound. There was a list a mile long of tasks to do. "In some ways, the day seems like a blur, like it happened in five seconds," Heyman says. "In other ways it was like a five-hundred-hour day."

As the hour got closer, the energy from the crowd and the wrestlers was reaching fever pitch. Then, about a half hour before the 9 P.M. live telecast was about to start, the rumor became reality—there were a group of WCW wrestlers at the back gate trying to get into the arena.

"The whole locker room goes back there, like a pack of rabid dogs," Heyman recalls.

But it turned out to be a group of wrestlers who weren't there to create trouble. In fact, they were sympathetic to the ECW style. Still, their presence in the arena would have been a distraction at best, a disaster at worst, particularly with such a volatile fan base that had such a deep hatred for WCW. Heyman had to keep them out. He asked them to leave.

"Guys, this isn't the night to show up," Heyman said to them. "We have to keep this in house. Please be respectful to our needs and our situation. We can't even let friends in tonight from another organization, because we can't trust anybody." The wrestlers left without incident, and everyone went back to the locker room to gather just before the show was about to begin. It was then that Heyman—a legendary motivator—gave a legendary speech that was captured on Blaustein's film.

"I had pulled back on the speeches for a while because I thought they were becoming too commonplace. As much as the reputation was there of being a motivator, I also knew if the speeches became commonplace, you lose the ability to motivate people because it just becomes tonight's pump-up speech: 'Let's go out there and win one for the Gipper.' It has to be something special to talk about."

This was something special to talk about.

Standing on a set of steps, Heyman spoke to his loyal troops: "There are 17 million homes that have availability for this show tonight that will pay $20, hopefully"—Heyman knocks on the wooden bannister—"for the privilege to see you guys do what you have done for three and a half years. Thank Terry Funk for all that he has done for this company, for helping to put us on the map, for being unselfish in selfish times, for taking the young guys and showing them a better way. Tonight we have a chance to say, 'Yeah, you're right, we're too extreme. We're too wild. We're too out of control. We're too full of our own shit.' Or we have a chance to say, 'Hey, fuck you, you're wrong.

Fuck you, we're right.' Because you have all made it to the dance. Believe me, this is the dance. Start the show."

The wrestlers applauded, and then everyone hugged each other before stepping out into the lights, cameras, and live action.

Just before, an incident occurred that illustrates many things about that night and ECW—a technical glitch that shows the chaos of the event and the power that Heyman had over his minions.

Bob Artese was the ring announcer at the ECW Arena. Because this was a live event, he would have to be able to take commands from Heyman and others behind the scenes while he was in the ring—something he had never dealt with before. So he was fitted for an earpiece and told by Heyman to put it in his right ear.

About twenty minutes before the start of the show, Heyman, wearing a headset, started running checks to make sure everyone could communicate with him.

"Everyone can hear me, right? Can the truck hear me?"

"Yes."

"Hard camera, can you hear me?"

"Yes."

"Producer, can you hear me?"

"Yes."

"Bob Artese, can you hear me? Bob, go ahead and announce the dark match. Go, Bob, go."

Artese is standing in the middle of the ring, looking at Heyman and not saying a word.

"Okay, Bob, go. Okay, Bob, go."

Artese is still staring at Heyman, silent.

"Truck, can you hear me? Cameramen, can you hear me?"

"Yes."

"Timekeeper, can you hear me?"

"Yes."

"Okay, Go Bob, go. Dark match. We're a minute behind now. Please Bob, go."

Finally, Heyman takes off the headset and screams at the top of his lungs.

"Godfuckingdammit, Bob, go."

Artese starts. "Good evening, ladies and gentlemen."

Perplexed, Heyman spent the rest of the night communicating with Artese through the timekeeper. "Tell Bob to announce the winner." Or "Tell Bob to announce the next match."

After the show, Heyman pulled Artese aside in a little room under the stairs.

"Bob, can I have your earpiece?"

Artese gives it to Heyman, who puts it in his ear, presses on his headset button, and says, "Hello." It was so loud his ears were ringing.

"Bob, did you have this in your ear?"

"Yeah, like you told me."

"Did it fit okay?"

"Yeah, it fit perfectly."

"Bob, we fit you for this thing, you put it in your ear, you go out to the ring. It works. I tell you to go, and you don't go. Why?"

"I'm deaf in that ear."

"What?"

"I have no hearing in my right ear. I can only hear in my left ear."

"So, Bob, why did you put the earpiece in your right ear?"

"You told me to. Who am I to question you?"

"I understand the logic, but next time maybe it would behoove you to tell me that you are deaf."

Years later, Heyman still laughs at the exchange. "How could you get mad at him?" he says. "He respected me so much he put the earpiece in his deaf ear. I didn't know how to argue with that logic."

The action began in the ring, with The Eliminators facing the Dudley Boyz for the ECW Tag Team titles. "We got our asses handed to us by The Eliminators, but it was a special night because it was our first Pay-Per-View," D-Von Dudley recalls. "Everything was on the line. Like *WrestleMania*, when Vince put everything into it, and if it had failed, who knows what would have happened? It was like that for *Barely Legal*. You had to get over, no matter what. There couldn't be anybody who had an off night, from the opening match to the last match, it had to be a home run, because the company's future and

RVD vs. Lance Storm.

our future was at stake. I remember how intense the locker room was. You could just feel it. People were scared to death. They didn't know what to do. They knew that you couldn't mess up. You had to be on top of your game, no matter what. We made it so good that those people at the arena were on their feet from the time it started until the end. It was unreal."

Rob Van Dam went up against Lance Storm, and won. But he wasn't happy, and, in ECW fashion, he let the fans know about it. "There were a lot of expectations for the first Pay-Per-View," he says. "It was one of those things where I felt a lot of people won't believe it when they see it. ECW was at that stage where there was a lot of talk about it, but we had a lot to live up to.

"I wasn't even booked on it, and I was very upset," Van Dam explains. "I did feel, though, that this was ECW's first chance to show the world what it was and that everything on the show was going to represent what ECW stood for. I felt like I should really be on it. I got thrown on as a last-minute decision, and at the time I was still offended."

His opponent, Lance Storm, knew that Van Dam was angry. "It was sort of a weird position for me because I had just got there, and I was working with this guy on a pretty important show in my career, and he didn't seem to be in the best of spirits starting off," Storm says.

After the match ended, Van Dam let loose. "I had a little extra energy with my match with Lance Storm, and afterwards, I actually verbalized how I was feeling on the microphone, because we had that artistic creativity to do just that, so I did," he says.

Taking the microphone in the middle of the ring, Van Dam spoke to the fans: "You see, I sold out to myself by putting my boots on and getting in the ring tonight, after obviously being chosen as a second-line wrestler to fill in for somebody who was injured." Rob Van Dam is no second-line anything. I swallowed my pride for one reason. It is business, because you see, Lance Storm, by beating you here, Rob Van Dam is worth more money here and Rob Van Dam is now worth more money elsewhere."

In an all-Japanese three-man tag team match, The Great Sasuke, Gran Hamada, and Masato Yakushiji beat Taka Michinoku, Mens Teioh, and Dick Togo. The winners were named the Japanese bWo by the ECW Blue World Order.

"It seemed like that first Pay-Per-View wasn't going to happen," Mike Nova recalls. "Until I saw the trucks there that day, I still didn't believe it was going to happen, and even then, until I got home and watched the tape. I had my brother tape it for me. I still didn't really believe it had actually happened. I still have my press credentials from that day.

"Myself, Meanie, and Stevie, we went out to the ring with Raven that night. Stevie was in a three-way that night with Funk and Raven, and me and Meanie were out there for that. Then we went out for the Japanese wrestlers and made them the Japanese bWo that night, for a six-man they had."

While the fighting was going on in the ring, battles were taking place behind the scenes as well. "We had the Pay-Per-View company there, who didn't want us showing any close-ups of blood or the violence, or of anything really," Ron Buffone remembers. "And then there is me, and I am dying to cut close to the blood and the action and everything. I cut to a close-up, a guy selling an incredible chair shot or some spectacular spot, and the Pay-Per-View guy would say, 'Oh my God, you've got to get off that.' It was a tug-of-war in the truck, everyone trying to inject their own feel for the show.

Raven vs. Terry Funk.

"The close-ups were what the fans wanted to see. The Pay-Per-View company didn't want us to be too extreme, but we always pushed the envelope. Paul would play nice for the first half and then give me the go-ahead to do the show the way we normally would. Then there were times when the guy would be screaming, 'I'll pull you off the air. If you do that again, there will be no next Pay-Per-View. But you have to let the product be the product. That is what the Pay-Per-View companies didn't understand, even during the first Pay-Per-View. After that, it was history."

In the ECW TV title bout, Shane Douglas kept the belt by beating Pitbull #2, but the crowd was nearly as caught up in anticipation of the next match as it was about the match they were watching. After waiting a year for it to happen, Sabu and Tazz would finally square off in the ring.

"For one year, I mocked Sabu, I called out Sabu," Tazz recalls. "I did everything physically possible and mentally possible to taunt Sabu. I beat guys up in the ring and called them Sabu, the whole nine yards. And Sabu wouldn't come out to face me. And then finally when he came out to look me face-to-face—the lights went out, then they went on—and we were in the same ring for the first time in a long time. The fans knew we would face each other at *Barely Legal*. It was a great moment, and we made each other in that match. I'll never forget it."

Ring announcer Bob Ortiz gave it the proper introduction: "Ladies and Gentlemen, Extreme Championship Wrestling presents the grudge match of the century."

Near the end of the bout, Tazz picked up Sabu and slammed him over the guardrail and into the first few rows of seats in the crowd. He then picked Sabu up and slammed him over a table. Then Tazz got Sabu in the ring in the Tazzmission hold, and Sabu finally surrendered.

"The match couldn't live up to the hype, and we had a really good match," Tazz says. "We had better after that, but there was just so much hype and pressure going into that match. We worked hard, and it was a physical match. This was our first Pay-Per-View, and we were the featured match. There was a lot of pressure on us, a lot of

Sandman thinks he has the win over Funk.

pressure on everyone. There was a lot of pressure on Raven, and on Terry Funk, and he was a veteran. I remember being stressed out that day, but I remember having a ton of fun."

After the match, Sabu and Tazz stood together in the ring, acknowledging each other and the fans, with Sabu raising Tazz's hand in victory.

"It was a phenomenal moment for the company, and I was fortunate enough to be part of that promotion and in one of the main events and wrestle my archnemesis, Sabu," Tazz declares. "It was a great moment."

The finale sealed the deal. First there was a three-way match between Sandman, Stevie Richards, and Terry Funk, with the winner getting a chance to go on to wrestle Raven, the ECW Heavyweight Champion, for the title. This night would be a tribute to hardcore and everything that ECW stood for, so it was the icing on the cake to have the veteran legend who helped bring ECW to that point be crowned the champion.

"For me at the time, being 24 years old and living only ten minutes from the arena, to be in the main event with a legend like Terry Funk and a hardcore legend like the Sandman, an ECW icon, was unbelievable," Stevie Richards says.

"Before the match Terry Funk asked, 'How are you feeling, Steve?'" Richards recalls. "I said, 'I don't know what the hell I am doing here, Terry. You have all these amazing athletes who have made a name for themselves, and Paul Heyman picked *me* to be in the main event for this match.' Tommy Dreamer wasn't even wrestling that night. I am thinking, 'What did I ever do to deserve this? This is unbelievable.'"

Dreamer did the commentary for the main event: a match between Funk and Raven for the ECW Heavyweight Championship. Funk pinned Raven, and the night was complete. "It's over. It's over. He did it. He did it," commentator Joey Styles yelled. Fans went wild, celebrating with a bloodied but jubilant Terry Funk.

"What a story," Heyman exclaims. "The impossible dream. This broken-down old man, Terry Funk, comes up against this unstoppable badass young punk Raven. In interviews before this showdown, Raven says to Funk, 'You remind me of my own father, you want to abuse me, you drink, you do this.' Oh my God, it was just so emotional, and for Funk to win it, it was the culmination of all of our dreams, the impossible dream taking place in front of your very eyes. For everything Terry did for us, he deserved it, truly deserved it."

The Pay-Per-View customers nearly didn't see it. First, the show was under a strict time limit by Viewer's Choice. "If we went one minute over that time limit, I think we would lose all the money because they couldn't do the replay or some other issue," Buffone recalls. "They didn't want that to happen. So the media director is in the truck screaming, 'Ron, bring this thing home.' I have Paul saying, 'I'm not cutting this match short. The fans will get the product that they paid for.' And meanwhile, we are getting closer and closer to that time limit. We gave the fans the show they deserved and didn't compromise any matches by making them end early."

For Heyman to do that—stick by his guns—he needed some help from Raven, because there wasn't much time remaining for the final bout against Funk.

"The three-way match went long," Heyman remembers. "I am giving time cues, and Raven, who had become a bundle of nerves, was now the coolest guy in the building. He was standing behind me saying, 'It is cool, I will bring it in. I will do this match in twelve minutes.' Another minute goes by, and he says, 'It's okay, I can do this match in eleven minutes.' He was cool as a cucumber, and he pulled it out."

Then, as if there wasn't enough drama, literally seconds after the match ends and the show goes off the air, there is an explosion, and then the lights go out.

"The transformer, the power supply or whatever, blew up ten seconds after the Pay-Per-View was over, and if that had happened during the Pay-Per-View, it could have been just a big catastrophe," Richards explains. "Our first Pay-Per-View, and people won't even get to see the whole thing. They won't get to see Terry Funk win the ECW world title."

"If the show had run three seconds longer, we would have lost the feed," Tommy Dreamer says. "The building couldn't handle all the power we were pumping out. But we made it there. It was like we won the World Series. We were going nuts, as if the home team finally did it."

"There was this enormous bang, and the TV lights go out," Heyman remembers. "The generator lights stay on, but the TV lights go out. 'What the hell was that, a bomb?' I am asking in the headset, 'What was that?' And I am getting nothing back. I am being handed another pair of headsets. They had switched in the truck to the other headsets. Ron Buffone says, 'The generator blew.' Fifteen seconds after we went off the air, the generator blew. And the backup generator blew with it. The blowout was so bad it got both generators."

It didn't matter, though. ECW had pulled it off—their first Pay-Per-View—and the emotions poured out.

"Everybody back there was so emotional," Richards says. "I cried and kept crying. It was a very emotional time, and a lot of people say things about Paul Heyman. But he put in twenty-four hours a day, seven days a week into this, to get that Pay-Per-View off. It looked as if ECW was about to springboard to another level. I'm sure it was exhausting emotionally, physically, and mentally. He probably cried for a good week."

"We all cried, because we worked so hard to get there," Heyman says. "Terry Funk cried, because even in his fifties, he realized he made this thing happen."

Joey Styles was overcome with emotion. "The first Pay-Per-View was, to this day, the greatest professional night of my life. We had the Pay-Per-View booked, then got run off because of the New Jack incident. But then we got back on Pay-Per-View. It was my first time going live, and if you can't call something live, you're not a real announcer. I prepared long and hard, especially for the Japanese wrestlers who were coming in, and I knew I was making history because I was going to be the first announcer to call a live Pay-Per-View in any sport, without one or two color commentators. I knew everyone in the industry would be watching. It would be the beginning of my career as a wrestling announcer, or the end. There would be no safety net. I would succeed or fail. I would put my performance that night, with no color commentator, up against any performance by any pro wrestling announcer in the history of this business. I think it was as good a job as anyone had ever done.

"I remember feeling such a sense of relief after the show. I walked down from my broadcast position, which was over the front door, and as I came down the steps—my fiancée was there—I broke out in tears. I had never started crying out of happiness in my life."

While everyone was backstage hugging and crying in the dim lighting still available, the fans were still celebrating in the arena and demanding more, yelling for Heyman to come out and make a speech.

"I didn't appear on the Pay-Per-View," Heyman says. "I didn't make any public appearance. I can't do a speech because there is no microphone. I go back into the dressing room and say, 'We are going back out in the ring and take a curtain call. And just so you guys know, they want a speech, but we have no microphone.' We get out to the ring, and the ovation lasted about ten minutes. The whole building is chanting, 'ECW! ECW! Thank you, Paul,' and everyone's name individually. This is picking up momentum, getting louder and louder. It is amazing. I am waiting for it to die down and to get a mike. I held up my hand and hushed the crowd. Everyone got quiet. We talked to them for a couple of minutes and said, 'Thanks.' Nobody slept for a week. Then everybody slept for a whole week.

"When everyone woke up the next weekend, nothing was the same," Heyman says. "Tazz was now *the* star. Raven was no longer the top dog in the promotion. Van Dam, though a heel, was clearly going to be the top guy."

Nothing was indeed the same. It turned out that a week after *Barely Legal,* Raven was talking to WCW and took an offer from them. There would be little time for ECW to rest on its laurels. Now they had to figure out how to keep moving forward with what they had accomplished, and deal with the changes in this volatile business, such as having a talent like Raven leave.

"The mindset that had permeated the company, being the little company that could, dramatically changed," Heyman explains. "Now we knew that we could. Now it became, 'Okay, how do we dip into this money pool?' The business was exploding. How do we get our piece? It was all of us thinking this. In some ways it was a natural evolution, and in some ways a real downfall for the promotion at the time. I was not going to try to hold on to Raven. We had a run with this character that very few could ever duplicate, so I let him go. It was a situation I was faced with two years later with the Dudleyz. As much as they brought to the table, it was time to let them go. I refused to bid for Raven, and wanted to get him out. I didn't want to keep him in my locker room to recruit. That was my biggest concern. When someone was leaving, I wanted to get them out of there, because of the fear of recruiting."

Raven's leaving created some tension inside the promotion. "I remember the time period of just being crazy," Dreamer says. "How could these people, your friends, be doing this? Raven was the first person who called me and he was like, 'You want to come?' We actually got into a fight about this because he thought I told Paul, and I never told anyone."

Heyman, though, used Raven's leaving to squeeze out the climax to the long-running story line of Dreamer and Raven. "We had a tremendous opportunity here," Heyman explains. "We had gone two and a half years with Raven beating Tommy Dreamer every time. Now we had a chance for one of those great moments, where Dreamer would finally get the victory over Raven."

ECW also started to have more story lines with World Wrestling Federation. "I was using the platform to publicize more of our stuff," Heyman says. "Van Dam was getting over so big, so we used him on that, and called him Mr. Monday Night. He is getting over on their TV, a homegrown guy on our shows pretending to be a WWE guy. He is with us, and really getting over as a heel."

ECW began building up their next major show (not Pay-Per-View), Wrestlepalooza 1997, with Dreamer vs. Raven being the main attraction, but there would be a surprise that Heyman was laying the groundwork for. "I discussed an idea with Vince," Heyman says. "What if Jerry Lawler invaded the ECW Arena? What if an outsider formed a faction within ECW? We did what is in many ways one of the fastest paced, one of the wildest rides we ever took, with Wrestlepalooza '97."

The June 6, 1997, show was at the ECW Arena, with Shane Douglas beating Chris Chetti to defend his TV title. Then The Pitbulls defeated Little Guido & Tracy Smothers, the Dudley Boyz bounced Sandman & Balls Mahoney, and Terry Funk successfully defended his ECW Heavyweight crown against Chris Candido.

But there was only one match the fans in the arena that night were waiting for—Dreamer vs. Raven. They would get much more than that.

The match between Dreamer and Raven would end with Dreamer driving Raven into the mat, climbing on top of him, hooking his leg, and then going for the pin. As the fans count one, two, three, Dreamer wins and the arena erupts as Dreamer's hand is raised in victory.

The fans are chanting, "ECW! ECW!" and the lights go out. They come back on, and Sabu is in the ring. He attacks Dreamer. Sabu shoots Dreamer into the ropes. Dreamer ducks underneath and hooks a DDT on

Dreamer tries to get through to Raven.

Sabu. The lights go out again, and when they come back on, it's Rob Van Dam—the outsider, Mr. Monday Night—in the ring. Van Dam and Sabu double-team Dreamer and shoot him into the ropes. Dreamer ducks underneath, turns around, hooks a double DDT on them, and the lights go out. When they come back up, Jerry Lawler is standing in the ring.

Then The Gangstas' music starts playing for the next match, but they are stopped in the aisle. Everybody stops. Bill Alfonso is out there and points to where the announcers are. Shane Douglas and Francine are standing up there.

Alfonso takes the microphone, points to Douglas, and says, "So tell me, Franchise, do you want to defend ECW?"

The crowd roars, "Yes!" But Douglas gets on a microphone up on the stage and says, "This has nothing to do with me. You want to mop the floor with everybody? Be my guest."

So the beating of Dreamer continues. Sabu and Van Dam and Lawler are whipping on everyone. The fans start chanting, "We want Tazz! We want Tazz!"

Tazz, with a towel around his head and Team Tazz following, starts walking slowly toward the ring. All the heels are running from the ring when Tazz gets there, and he clears the ring without raising a hand.

Tazz was scheduled to face Sabu in a rematch from *Barely Legal*. Sabu gets back into the ring, and their match starts. After about twenty minutes, Tazz puts the Tazzmission on Sabu, and Sabu can't escape it. In a desperation move while they are both on the canvas and Sabu is about to be choked out, Sabu kicks his legs up and floats back over Tazz. Sabu is passing out from being choked out, and Tazz, not releasing the hold, has his own shoulders down on the canvas. He is counted out. Sabu beats Tazz, but is choked out in the process. Sabu is unconscious, even though he is the winner.

A very angry Tazz stands in the ring with his hands on his hips. Shane Douglas, who is still on the stage, gets on the mike and says, "Excuse me, but you lost your match. Get the fuck out of my ring."

The fans erupt, because it was unheard of to talk to Tazz that way. Going into *Barely Legal*, Tazz was the heel and Sabu was the babyface. At *Barely Legal*, they both turned. Tazz became the babyface and Sabu became the heel.

"Excuse me?" Tazz says.

"You heard me," Douglas says. "You lost your rematch. You're in my ring. Now get the fuck out of there."

"Maybe you would like to come down here and get me out of this ring," Tazz shot back.

Fans start chanting, "Tazz is gonna kill you, Tazz is gonna kill you."

"Shane, since I just lost, I guess I have to redeem myself," Tazz says. "Let me give these people a memorable moment. Usually I would stand here and say I could choke you out in five minutes. But since you are part of the Triple Threat and have that TV title up there, how about I make you tap out in three?"

"You're on," Shane says.

Douglas comes down and gets in the ring, and he and Tazz go at each other. About two minutes into the match, Tazz hooks the Tazzmission hold. Douglas is trying to hold on, and the clock is ticking down. With about five seconds left, Douglas taps, and Tazz becomes the new TV champion.

Even by ECW standards, this was something that fans at the arena had never seen before.

"When Raven was leaving ECW to go to WCW, that was the night I finally beat him," Dreamer says. "I beat him one, two, three, I raised my hands, the lights went out, the lights go back on, and Jerry Lawler is in the ring. Jerry Lawler"—with his crown on his head and his king's garb—"then beats the crap out of me. The guy from WWE is now beating up the guy who represents ECW, so one feud ended, and one feud started.

"To me, it was like the night Eric Bischoff showed up on *Raw*," Dreamer points out. "How dare Eric Bischoff show up there. Just like how dare Jerry Lawler show up on ECW. And he put a beating on me. Jerry Lawler canes me in my testicles and knocks me out with a cane shot. I was knocked out, and then Jim Cornette woke me up by hitting me with a tennis racket. I had to go to the hospital because they thought I was going to have a rupture, and I had to have a couple of cc's of blood pulled out of my testicles that night. It was another part of being hardcore. Jerry apologized for it later. He bolted after the show because there was that much heat."

At one point, Cornette is in the ring with Lawler, beating on Tommy Dreamer. Lawler takes the mike and yells to the fans, "This hall ought to be built out of toilet paper, because there is nothing in it but shit."

Lawler said it was not the typical heat they generated. "They had seen the ECW guys invade *Raw*, but I could tell by the reaction that they never thought that a WWE wrestler would come to the ECW Arena," Lawler says. "So when I showed up, it was really sheer pandemonium. It was legitimately dangerous. They were that upset. I don't often get scared or in fear for my safety, but that night I was."

"Jerry Lawler had a huge impact, because he stood for everything ECW was against," Dreamer explains. "I stood for everything ECW stood for, and Jerry Lawler stood for everything WWE stood for. It was a clash, the Yankees vs. the Red Sox."

The impact accomplished exactly what Heyman wanted it to. "Nobody remembered that Raven was leaving," he says. "We repositioned everybody. Terry Funk was our champion, but you knew that wasn't going to be forever. Tazz is the TV champion, and that became the focal point. Sabu and Van Dam were now the hottest heels in the universe, and they were affiliated with Jerry Lawler. Tommy Dreamer was now Mr. ECW himself. The Dudleyz and The Eliminators were carrying the tag team division, and everyone was kind of repositioned. June seventh was the big turning point, because now everybody had their sense of purpose again, and everyone was back on course. It was one of the hottest summers we ever had. Before that, the summers weren't as hot. Here it was, June seventh, hot as hell and ever hotter. That was how we recovered from the postpartum depression of *Barely Legal*."

But the next crisis was always around the corner in ECW. This time, it was the rumor that Tod Gordon, the founder of Eastern Championship Wrestling and now a figurehead commissioner for ECW, was suspected of secretly recruiting for WCW. So Heyman fired him.

"Supposedly we had a mole in our locker room," Dreamer says. "We all had to be paranoid, because we had WCW and WWE breathing down our necks to try to take our talent. Everyone was trying to knock us down, and Paul is very paranoid. He broke into Tod Gordon's cell phone and played all the messages of all the guys calling him. Me and Tazz were at Paul's house, and we couldn't believe it was going on. It was Terry Taylor. It was Bill Alfonso. They were just talking, 'Great deal, man, we can bring this all in.' They were going to do an ECW invasion."

About the mole, Heyman says he couldn't be totally sure what the truth was. "I don't know the real story behind it. I have an idea. Other people have a different perspective. But you never really know the truth behind it. You never really know people's motivation for getting on the phone and saying, 'You know what is really happening here?' You don't really know. So you don't really know the truth about situations like this.'"

In a TV interview, looking close-up at the camera, Heyman told the fans that Gordon was fired. "My name is Paul Heyman, and I am executive producer and talent coordinator for Extreme Championship Wrestling. It is a job that was given to me on September 18, 1993, by the founder of this promotion, Tod Gordon. It is therefore my responsibility to inform the public that, with a heavy heart, earlier this week,

ECW accepted the resignation of Tod Gordon as commissioner of Extreme Championship Wrestling. Citing increasing pressures as father of four children and running a family business, Tod could no longer assume the responsibility as ECW's commissioner. We here at Extreme Championship Wrestling wish Tod nothing but the best in all of his future endeavors, and we want to let him know that we intend to make him proud as we carry on his vision of ECW."

Heyman also wanted to fire Bill Alfonso, but Fonzie, as he was called, was very popular with ECW wrestlers. He managed to save his job by putting on a memorable match—man on woman. "We all loved Fonzie and didn't want to see him go," Dreamer says. "He had a great match with Beulah McGillicutty and it saved his job."

The match took place on *As Good As It Gets*, on September 20, 1997, at the ECW Arena, and it was a bloody brawl. At one point, Alfonso's face was bloodied as Beulah beat on him in the corner. Alfonso then beat on Beulah in the corner. Later both of them were outside the ring, and Beulah threw Alfonso over the steel guardrail. Then, with Alfonso lying head down, hung over the ropes in a corner, Beulah took a chair and laid it across Alfonso's face. She ran to the other corner and then ran back and slid feet-first into the chair on Alfonso. The fans went wild, chanting "ECW! ECW!" Later Alfonso tried to bodyslam Beulah, but she took his legs and caught his head, flipping him over on his back. She lay on top of the bloody Alfonso and got the pin and the win.

"Beulah McGillicutty was involved in five of the most intense minutes in ECW when she had that match with Bill Alfonso," Heyman recalls. "They beat the crap out of each other. They had a phenomenal match. Here's Beulah, who was not a wrestler, and here's Bill Alfonso, who was 135 pounds and a former referee, and these guys had an amazing fight, and to this day, if you ask me to name one of the hardest-hitting battles in ECW, it ranks right up there with anything else I have ever seen."

While the action was still intense in the ring, behind the scenes, Heyman was calling on the wrestlers who had been ECW stalwarts to be part of the business operation as well.

"ECW not being a huge company at any point in time, a lot of us participated and had other duties besides being wrestlers," Tazz remembers.

Bubba Ray Dudley welcomed the chance to be part of the business end. "I would do deals with the arenas. I would call up and say, 'This is so and so, and I would like to book a show for ECW.' I got an education in the wrestling business outside of the ring, and what I truly loved about the company is that I was given the opportunity to do that."

"I had two roles," Tazz says. "I designed all of our logos and merchandise. I don't have an art background or anything, but I just had a knack for it, and Paul said, 'Why don't you do this, design our stuff?' I came up with all the sayings on the backs of the T-shirts, all the logos and colors. Merchandise was a huge thing for us. The guys made a lot of money with their T-shirts and stuff.

"I also ran the ECW wrestling school, which was known as the House of Hardcore. We ran a very, very tough, old-school type of dojo. No joke. Out of hundreds of applicants, I think three or four people graduated from ECW House of Hardcore. Paul wanted a school and wanted me to run it, and he did not care if it made money or not. He wanted to just get a couple of guys that respected the industry and knew great fundamentals, and were tough. That was what he wanted, and that is what he got."

Dreamer would move the merchandise. "I would bring all the T-shirts to all the shows," he says. "I would physically drive them. We had a warehouse. Me, D-Von Dudley, and Nunzio would load up the van for the fans to purchase the T-shirts. After the shows we would drive home, and that Monday load all the T-shirts. We would have bandages on our foreheads, and we would carry the T-shirts back into the warehouse.

"I would collect the money from the concessions, and sometimes I would walk out with $20,000 or $30,000 in my pocket. The girls who would work for me were the wrestlers' wives and wrestlers' girl-friends, people who I trusted. Every single wrestler pretty much had a different job."

"We used to answer phone calls, take credit card orders, ticket orders, mail out tickets, field fan calls," Stevie Richards says. "We were like the fan line—answer questions, give out show dates, make mailing lists, all that stuff. It was kind of funny, because people would recognize my voice because I sort of have this distinct voice, and they would say on the phone, 'Man, you sound just like Stevie Richards. What is your name?' I had to make up an ECW office name, and my office name was Lloyd Van Buren."

During this time, ECW starting running a successful series of bi-monthly Pay-Per-View shows, the last one being *Better Than Ever* on December 6 at the ECW Arena. With more than 1,600 in attendance, Chris Candido & Lance Storm defeated Doug Furnas & Phil Lafon and

Dreamer and Van Dam.

Balls Mahoney & Axl Rotten in a Three Way Dance to win the ECW Tag Team titles. The Dudley Boyz beat New Jack & Spike Dudley, and Sabu & Rob Van Dam defeated Tommy Dreamer & Tazz. The promotion had turned the corner in 1997, and was ready to take off in 1998.

"Once we had *Barely Legal,* then we started banging out the Pay-Per-Views, making money," Tazz says.

However, ECW had to struggle to hang on to its talent.

"The wrestling industry in 1998 was like the dot.com industry—inflated—and the pay scale went off the charts," Heyman explains. "Something had to burst. We had guys turning down hundreds of thousands of dollars to go elsewhere and stay with us, and there comes a time when it is just not fiscally responsible to your own family. We had to step up and get advertisers and sponsors and licensing."

What they needed to do was to take the next step up from Pay-Per-View—get on a national television network.

chapter nine

Albatross TV

ECW seemed to be flying as high as a shooting star. It was coming off a banner year, 1997, where it made it onto Pay-Per-View and put on a series of classic story lines, the likes of which the industry had never seen before. It had gained much national attention for a promotion that was operating not out of any corporate headquarters, but out of hotel rooms, basements, and car trunks.

But ECW was still the little kid on the block battling the two big boys, WWE and WCW, and there was no time to stop and enjoy the good times. ECW needed to keep growing, evolving, and also battling to retain what they had already achieved. Everyone was taking notice of this popular promotion. And at least one of the big boys, WCW, seemed determined to put ECW out of business, with constant talent raids. While ECW talent would also leave to join WWE, Heyman still enjoyed a reciprocal relationship with McMahon's company and used it well.

Al Snow returned to ECW in 1998 by way of that reciprocal relationship, and this time his stay would be a historic one for him and ECW as well.

Snow had been with WWE for about two years, and was not pleased with the way he was being used. He was looking to quit, and asked for a release from his contract. McMahon refused, but Snow went to his good friend, Chris Candido, to lobby Heyman to bring Snow back to ECW. Heyman spoke with McMahon, and though Snow was still under contract to WWE, he was now working in ECW.

Snow's angle at the time was trying to convince fans that he had a nervous breakdown over the frustration about his career. "The fans there were very sophisticated and educated in wrestling," Snow says. "They knew me and knew my career and my history, and at that point in my career, I was very frustrated, and figured that, as fans, they would know that. Anybody who had been doing what I had been doing for as long as I had been doing it, and had not had any big success, or as little success as I had, would eventually crack. I started reading books on abnormal psychology and started working on different things in the ring to show that I was having a breakdown, like talking to myself, and nothing was really working."

Then one night at the ECW Arena, while getting some pictures taken for a Japanese wrestling magazine, Snow saw a Styrofoam head lying among the various items in the back of the building, and had what could probably only be described as an epiphany.

"I remembered Mick Foley screwing around in a car one night with Sid Vicious, Bob Holly, and myself, with this Styrofoam head that he carried his Mankind mask on, to keep its shape," Snow says. "He was treating it like his girlfriend. He was making sexual innuendos to it, joking around.

"I remembered a story about a woman who was paranoid and schizophrenic, and she had transferral disorder. She had multiple personalities, but she transferred the sickness onto inanimate ob-

jects. She heard voices coming from them. I thought to myself, 'I'm going to start carrying this head into the ring, talk to it, and treat it like it was a real person.' When I first started talking about coming to ECW, I was talking about maybe shaving the words 'Help me' in my hair. So instead I painted the words 'Help me' backwards, on the head, as a subconcious cry for help."

It changed Snow's career, and has become his signature gimmick— Al Snow with Head—to this day. "I would wrestle a match, totally as a babyface, and at the end of the match, if I lost, I would beat the living shit out of the Styrofoam head," Snow says. "I would piledrive it, and flip out. People started booing me. They were upset I was beating up this Styrofoam head. So I did it more and more. I found a few more heads to use.

"One night in New Britain, Connecticut, fans would bring things to the building for wrestlers like New Jack to use in the ring," Snow recalls. "Somebody brought a beautician's mannequin head for New Jack to use in a match. Spike Dudley and Mikey Whipwreck got it and gave it to me, and that is the head that I have used ever since. Paul E. came to me one night, a few weeks later, in Stamford, Connecticut, on Halloween, and he said, 'You are going to be the next pulp baby-face.' He had plans to put me with Sandman the next night at the arena but in a match with Paul Diamond, and he dislocated my shoulder severely. I was off for six weeks, so I couldn't work the *November to Remember* Pay Per View, and Candido again—boy, do I owe him—during the production meeting proposed that we do a pre-tape in the back with me in the locker room and the head. ECW didn't really do pre-tapes, Paul E. let me do it, and that one promo took off for me from there."

ECW started selling Al Snow "Heads" as merchandise. "One night in Asbury Park, New Jersey, they had 4,000 Styrofoam heads," Snow says. "For my entrance, they would use the strobe light effect when I would come out. When I came out with the lights all shut off and pitch black, with the strobe going, all you saw were these white heads moving up and down. It was an amazing sight.

"Every night a majority of them would come flying back at me in the ring. To this day, I can do anything at all, and all the fans want to see is for me to hit somebody with that head. I was setting up a way for me to work an angle with the head, to get jealous about it, because when I said, 'What does everybody want, what does everybody need, what does everybody love?' Here is a guy who spends his whole career wanting to achieve recognition and success, and he finally does, but what do they really want and need and love? It's not him. It's the Head. That was fine with me. The Head can't cash the checks."

ECW was thriving on creative, offbeat promos like the Head, and also taking the hardcore persona to another level. Tazz carried that hardcore banner, and Rob Van Dam continued to emerge as the ECW's other top attraction, with his high-flying style and his legendary battles with another athletic performer, Jerry Lynn. The two battled each other in an August bout that was considered by many to be ECW match of the year.

But it was one night at Asbury Park that would result in the best moment of 1998, and perhaps the signature moment for ECW—certainly a moment that has been seen over and over again in ECW intros and promotions. It was the *Living Dangerously* show, on March 1, 1998, featuring Tazz against the big man, Bam Bam Bigelow, who was a member of the Triple Threat at the time, for the ECW TV title.

"In ECW I had tons of physical matches," Tazz explains. "A lot with Sabu, Rob Van Dam, and Tommy Dreamer. But this one—against Bam Bam—was right on the top as far as a guy who really dished it out to me. This was probably my second favorite ECW match. It was kind of cool being 5-foot-8 and 240 pounds, and I was the favorite. Bam Bam was the underdog in his own hometown, and he was 350 pounds and about 6-foot-4. That was kind of intriguing. I was a fan favorite at the time in ECW, no matter where we went. I was a New Yorker, and you know people in New Jersey don't like New Yorkers, and we were in Asbury Park, New Jersey, his hometown. He was a big-bad-guy villain at the time, and there were a lot of Bam Bam fans there, which was cool."

As the match was about to begin, announcer Joey Styles set the stage: "Despite the fact that Bam Bam Bigelow is the fan favorite here in his hometown, Tazz wanted it that way. Tazz loves to defy the odds. This matchup is not about a big paycheck, it's not about making a statement on Pay-Per-View, it's not even about the World Television title. This is personal."

It was a brutal match. Early in the bout, Tazz nailed Bigelow, knocking him out of the ring and sending him crashing down on the timekeeper's table and all the way to the floor. Bigelow came back and smashed Tazz into the steel ring post several times, and then, in the ring, powerbombed Tazz. It went back and forth, in and out of the ring. Tazz picked up a fallen Bigelow out of the ring and dropped him into the seats over the steel guardrail. Tazz went down on the floor as well, hitting the back of his head on the steel guardrail.

"It's a small miracle that Bigelow is moving, and that we can't see Tazz's brain," Styles said, marveling at the action.

As the brawl continued, both wrestlers hit each other with tables, chairs, and even a street sign that Bam Bam found under the ring. Then came the classic moment that stunned everyone watching. With both wrestlers in the ring, Bigelow tried to pick Tazz up and slam him, but Tazz grabbed him from behind and locked him up around the neck with the Tazzmission hold. Bigelow was tapping out, but the referee couldn't see it. Bam Bam fell back and both wrestlers fell right through the ring and onto the floor below, as the fans went crazy, in awe of what they just saw. They started chanting, 'ECW! ECW! ECW!' Bigelow climbed out of the hole in the ring and lay on the mat. Tazz started to climb out, but Bigelow pulled him out and covered him. The referee counted to three, and Bigelow was the winner.

"I locked the Tazzmission, and Bam Bam was so strong, he was holding me up on his back like I was nothing." Tazz recalls. "I was choking him out, and he threw his weight back and we both fell

through the ring, and the fans couldn't believe it. Eventually he came out of the hole first, pulled me out, beat me, and became ECW TV Champion. That was a historic moment in ECW, and I was fortunate to be part of it. It was awesome. It was also awesome wrestling Bigelow. I loved wrestling Bam Bam. I learned a lot from him. When he came in, Bam Bam was a big guy from the heyday, a star, and we were still plugging away in ECW. Bam Bam helped some guys out. He helped me out. I respect him a lot."

Tazz wouldn't need the TV title, or the world heavyweight title. He came up with an idea that was probably the epitome of championships for ECW. He called it the FTW title—Fuck The World. "We started it in Queens," Tazz says. "I think I had an old TV championship belt, and painted it orange, and put these stickers that were orange and black over the belt and wrote FTW, and proclaimed it the FTW championship. The ECW called it the "unrecognized" FTW championship. But the title took on a life of its own because people started digging it. The character was anti-establishment, and the belt was anti-establishment. Most people hate their bosses, and I was telling them that I hate my boss, I hate the company, I hate everybody, and fuck the world. This belt said, 'Fuck the world,' and people got behind it. I think it started to get more popular than the real belt, Shane's belt. It was actually the ultimate ECW title, and there were only two people to hold it, and that is Sabu and myself. I miss that. It was a cool part of the Tazz character, the whole FTW thing, and I loved portraying that. There have been attempts to copy it, but it has not been the same.

"The character Tazz couldn't get a shot at the heavyweight title, so I took the attitude that this was a bunch of shit and I was so anti-establishment, before Steve Austin ever was, and Sandman was like that before I was," Tazz explains. "Don't get me wrong, I love Stone Cold, and I don't think there will ever be a superstar bigger than Steve Austin in the industry, but this is what ECW brought to the business. The FTW belt was part of that whole fuck-you mentality. I didn't get a title shot. I don't want your belt. I'll make my own."

The promotion began taking its shows around the country, to

Cobb County, Georgia, Dayton, Ohio, and the University of New Orleans. Meanwhile, the fight went on to keep talent and bring in new faces. ECW scored a victory when they welcomed back a familiar face to the promotion on October 23, 1999—Sandman.

In a tag-team match at the ECW arena between Justin Credible & Lance Storm, with Dawn Marie and Jason Night, against Raven—who had also returned to ECW—& Dreamer, with Francine. The match appeared to be nearing a close, with Storm and Credible going for double pins against Dreamer and Raven, when the lights went out. Suddenly, a spotlight shone on the back of the arena, and the Metallica song began to play, and there was Sandman, standing with his Singapore cane. The crowd went crazy in one of the most emotional nights in ECW history. It was like a step back to the ECW glory days.

As Sandman made his way to the ring, he caned Jason Knight and caused havoc in the ring. The crowd switched between chanting "Welcome back, Sandman" and singing the "Enter the Sandman" Metallica song, then ended up with "ECW! ECW!" Raven did his pose to Sandman before leaving the ring while Dreamer and Francine stayed, and the three of them drank beer together.

Heyman also kept looking for new talent and fought to keep the talent he had developed from leaving. There were a number of Japanese wrestlers who made their appearance in 1998, such as Gran Naniwa, Masato Tanaka, Atsushi Onita, and Gran Hamada. Tanaka's presence would grow, as he would be paired against Mike Awesome for a series of battles. In fact, one year later, in September 1999, at the *Anarchy Rulez* Pay-Per-View in Villa Park, Illinois, Awesome beat Tanaka and Tazz in a Three Way Dance to win the ECW Heavyweight Championship. It would be a decision that would later come back to bite ECW.

Awesome held on to the title until December 13, 1999, when he lost to Tanaka, and ten days later, Awesome won back the championship from Tanaka. Then, three months later, Awesome left ECW for WCW. The problem was that he still held the ECW Heavyweight title. ECW threatened to sue, so Awesome agreed to come back to ECW for a one-time match to lose the belt to whoever they put in front of him.

Who did they put in front of him? Tazz, who had left for WWE but was on loan to ECW. So you had a WCW wrestler defending the ECW title against a WWE wrestler. The incident illustrated the uncertainty that ECW was operating under at the time.

There was a lot of tension over this match. Awesome was not allowed in the arena and stayed in his hotel in Indianapolis with security until just before the match was about to begin. Then he came to the arena to carry out the plan to lose his title. The plan lasted all of three minutes. Tommy Dreamer, the conscience of ECW, came into the ring during the match and delivered a DDT on Awesome, and then Tazz made him tap out with the Tazzmission. Tazz grabbed the microphone and said he came back because when he left he did business "the right way" and that he just showed Awesome the right way by making him tap out.

"There was a big uproar about me leaving, and whether or not I had signed a contract, which I had not," Awesome explains. "I had the belt. Paul was really coming after WCW. I was going to give that belt back to Paul. I didn't want it. But the way it came about was that Paul wanted the belt to change hands in the ring, with me losing. I was willing to do it. It was set up through the attorneys. We had to sign paperwork. I had to sign papers saying exactly what I would do. They were supposed to send over the script and all that stuff. It was just a mess.

"Instead of doing all that, what I wish they had done is said, 'Hey, Mike, we want you to lose this belt to Rhyno.' Because Rhyno was a trusted friend of mine, and I would have gone in there and we would have given them a twenty-five-minute barnburner of a match, and that is the way it should have been. That would have been much better. A clean finish. I would have loved to have done that, instead of the way we did do it, which was strange. I wasn't allowed in the ECW locker room. I had to come in by the front door when they did my ring music. The fans were all standing up and chanting, 'You sold out, you sold out.' I knew I didn't sell out. I did what I did, and knew it wasn't selling out, but I loved it. The fans were so loud. If I am working them, and they are yelling their asses off at me, then I am doing my job."

Tazz then wrestled on *SmackDown!* with the ECW title against Triple H. Tommy Dreamer came running into the ring at the event and tried to save Tazz, but he hit Tazz with a chair, and then Dreamer wound up getting hit by Triple H, too. Tommy then beat Tazz for the belt.

Tazz's departure went much smoother than Awesome's would, and was orchestrated to get the most out of it. But his leaving was still a devastating blow to ECW, and the strongest signal yet that the promotion was in serious trouble. "At the time I was ECW World Heavyweight Champion, and in my prime," Tazz says. "My verbal agreement with Paul Heyman had come to an end. We kept negotiating with each other, but the lawyers got involved and whatever. We more or less came to a verbal agreement, and we were going to have a contract, a written deal. If you ask Paul, he thought I was locked in, and he would probably be right to think that, but I was a little concerned that the company wouldn't be able to swing this deal we had agreed to. I was nervous about that. I had my family to think of. I had an opportunity to talk to WWE, and chose to take that deal. But to Vince's credit, we agreed that I needed to give ample notice to Paul, that I wasn't just going to walk out and screw over the promotion that made me. I wanted to put guys over on the way out the door, the old-school way. We did the right thing, and Paul and I at the time were having some tense moments with each other. He was pissed, and he had a right to be pissed. He thought I was screwing him, and I wasn't screwing him. I believe I wasn't screwing him. I was just concerned because, 'Hey, you cut me a great deal, but I don't know if the promotion can swing it over time.' He said, 'It will, TNN is going to be a success. You will stay the champion.' I said, 'I am just worried about the financial future of the company.' I was a family man and at the time worried about the future. In hindsight, I think I did the right thing. It was very hard for me to leave. Not that the company would go under if I left. I thought the company was going to do well. I just didn't know if they could afford the deal that I agreed to with Paul."

Tazz's departure took place at *Anarchy Rulz 1999* on September 19, in a triple threat between Tazz, Masato Tanaka, and Awesome for ECW's heavyweight title. It was arranged for Tazz to get beat early in the ring, going out the right way. The fans, who were well aware of Tazz's deal with WWE, were not giving him a warm sendoff, yelling during the match, "Fuck you, Tazz," and other cursing chants. But that changed when all the wrestlers who had come out on the stage to watch the match gave Tazz a standing ovation when it was over. Heyman came down and hugged Tazz, who handed the belt over to Awesome in an almost ceremonial passing of the torch. However, the light would not last much longer.

"The last straw was when Tazz left," Kurt Angle says. "After that, all ECW had was Rob Van Dam."

Van Dam was, as he often referred to himself, "The Whole Fucking Show," and on the night Tazz left, gave fans the sort of match that would make him such a beloved ECW wrestler. He held the ECW TV title at the time and engaged in a wild thirty-minute brawl with Balls Mahoney; there were chairs flying and moves using the chairs, such as powerbombs. His high-energy style in the ring, combined with his cool personality, made him a fan favorite. "Rob Van Dam was a cool but brazen personality," Heyman says. "The fans liked the coolness of Rob Van Dam and the laid-back interviews."

ECW was losing the fight to hang on to its talent. But they were fighting on another front as well, caught in a trap that had at first appeared to be the final step to putting the promotion over the top—a national network television contract.

After getting their foot in the door on Pay-Per-View, the next natural step for ECW was to get on television on a regular basis. Up to this point, ECW was seen on syndicated television and network deals they had set up themselves with various regional companies—such as the Sunshine—with ECW often paying for the air time. The promotion needed to get on national television to kick off a series of video games and marketing deals. Heyman needed to expand his income sources to survive the epidemic that was sweeping the industry in 1999—outrageously escalating salaries.

"We crashed as a company in the beginning of 1999," Heyman says. "We couldn't make payroll. Our Pay-Per-View numbers were going up. The Monday Night Wars were dominating the industry. Bischoff started throwing out ridiculous money to entice our guys to jump. Vince had to create a scenario where if guys were going to leave, they could go to him, just to prevent them from going to WCW. The pay scale in the business became like the dot.com stocks. The pay scale was exaggerated and not based on actual income. By the beginning of 1999, WCW started to lose money just based on the enormous payroll it had." At ECW, paychecks began bouncing, and some wrestlers would go for months without being paid.

"We had fallen into a Catch-22. We were popular and our numbers were going up," Heyman says. "Pay-Per-View could foot the bill for the entire promotion, so we had to do more Pay-Per-Views. It's $250,000 up-front costs to do a Pay-Per-View. But you don't see your money for about a year. You get your first payment in four or five months, but you don't see the bulk of it for a year. In Demand was contractually obligated to pay up a year later. Meanwhile, they are falling fifteen, sixteen, seventeen months behind, because they can. What are you going to do, sue them? Then they will just take you off Pay-Per-View."

At the same time, trying to create new revenue, ECW was looking to secure a video game deal. However, to succeed they needed to be on a network. Heyman was working on finalizing a contract for ECW to be on TNN. They reached an agreement, and ECW was scheduled to begin on Friday nights on TNN in August 1999. Heyman said TNN had not revealed all the cards it was holding in those talks—that CBS Cable, which owned TNN, was on the verge of being taken over by

D-Von with the title.

Viacom. "Viacom was going to make a $25 million investment in WWE, and make an offer for Vince to jump from USA to the revamped TNN a year later," Heyman says. "We didn't know any of this. We start talking to TNN. They know something we don't. They needed a guinea pig to see if wrestling would work on the country bumpkin network."

It worked, but not the way Heyman had hoped. The network constantly tried to place all sorts of restrictions on the promotion, its hardcore style and story lines. They also underfunded the shows, while expecting the same sort of production values that were featured in WWE and WCW shows—the very antithesis of ECW. Viacom also barely acknowledged the program in its promotion and advertising. In October 2000, ECW was canceled and replaced on TNN by WWE's *Raw*.

It also didn't help that not only did Tazz leave before the TNN shows started, but ECW also lost one of its other major attractions—the Dudley Boyz. On August 16, the Dudley Boyz won the ECW World Tag Team title from Spike Dudley & Balls Mahoney, on a TNN show, then lost it to Tommy Dreamer & Raven, who had returned to ECW. Then the Dudley Boyz were gone, moving to WWE.

ECW was dealt another blow in March 2000 when Rob Van Dam broke his ankle and was sidelined for a few months.

Relations with the network got so bad that Heyman openly criticized TNN. He used the wrestler Cyrus to play a representative of "The Network," who would come on the show and criticize ECW's violence. Heyman also actually spoke out himself once in a promo on the show. "We hate this network," he said. "We hate their guts for abandoning us. We hate their guts for not supporting us. We hate their guts for not advertising us, and we hate their guts for not having the balls to throw us off the air. And hey, in case you are watching this, network, I dare you to throw us off the air, because I am going to break every rule you put in front of us until you throw me off the air. This, my friends, is a shoot. You better take that $100 million you are going to give to Vince McMahon and spend it on attorneys, because I promise you, network, the war has just begun."

But the war was over.

"TNN said they didn't want any music videos on the show, and felt that our opening theme song was too demonic," Heyman recalls. "They didn't want references to hatred on the show. We can't say, 'I hate you.' Intense dislike is what they preferred. It was horrible when we started on TNN. There was not one mention on the radio, not one press release, not one call to a newspaper. Nothing."

It started off poorly. TNN officials didn't like the opening show, so instead they showed Rob Van Dam vs. Jerry Lynn for the ECW World Television Title from *Hardcore Heaven 1999*, and a history of ECW.

Buffone says the TV deal was a bad one. "We had no commercial time and, basically, no money for the show," he declares. "Yet they expected very high production values, which was a problem in itself because Paul did not want to change the look of the show and the integrity of the product."

It was frustrating for the wrestlers, because they had believed that ECW was on the verge of breaking out when it got on network television, and it soon became apparent that it wasn't going to turn out that way. "It turned out the ECW was nothing more than an experiment," Mike Nova says. "Someone there knew that within a year or so, there would be a much bigger fish in the ocean to catch. They used ECW as a piece of bait. They used ECW to build a case for why they should go for WWE. I never saw a commercial for ECW on TNN, unless I was watching ECW on TNN. I remember seeing advertisements in national magazines for RollerJam and that Rock 'N Bowl thing. These were two shows that weren't doing shit compared to ECW. I'll never forget being down there in Florida once for a RollerJam show, and people were all over us and acted as if those RollerJam guys didn't even exist. When it all went down, and they lost the network, then they did this big campaign to launch WWE, that was lousy. It was over then."

ECW needed the television deal because of a number of other agreements the promotion had made that were tied to the network contract. "I can't afford to lose the network, because the whole video game deal, the deal to do an album, the T-shirt distribution deal, and my home video license are all tied into the fact that I have a network platform," Heyman explains. "All the licenses can be yanked if I lose my network, which I know I am going to do anyway, but I have to stay on long enough to find another network to carry me so I can keep my licenses. So the very network that is cannibalizing me is my lifeblood at the same time. They know I can't leave the network without losing all my licenses, and therefore my ability to survive. What a miserable dilemma to be in."

Heyman thought he had maneuvered a deal to get on USA Network, when, at the last minute, political pressure from conservative groups and others against network violence changed their minds. "I was waiting for the fax for the deal to get on another network when the decision was made not to do it," Heyman says. "I got the phone call 9:01 A.M. Pacific time that the deal was off. At that moment I knew we were dead. Before that moment, I never accepted the premise that ECW would have a mortality. I just thought we would always win. But when I got that phone call, I knew we were dead. I knew the clock was ticking."

The demise was quick after ECW leaving TNN. ECW tried to get on another network but failed. There were more and more missed paychecks, and wrestlers leaving what they perceived to be a sinking ship.

But ECW wasn't the only promotion on its way out. Eric Bischoff and WCW, without Ted Turner's money, was also crumbling. It was now owned by Time Warner, who was looking to get rid of the promotion, which was losing a reported $80 million a year.

In January 2001, Bischoff and Fusient Media announced the acquisition of WCW from Time Warner-AOL. But that deal fell through, and two months later, WWE announced it had acquired WCW, which put Heyman's rival out of business.

This was taking place while ECW was also about to disappear. The last ECW Arena show took place on December 23, 2000, with the final match featuring Steve Corino, the ECW Heavyweight Champion, against Justin Credible and the Sandman in a Three-Way Dance.

On January 7, 2001, ECW put on its final Pay-Per-View, *Guilty as Charged*, at the Hammerstein Ballroom in New York, with an estimated 2,500 on hand. They saw Amish Roadkill and Danny Doring beat the Hot Commodity—EZ Money & Julio Dinero—for the ECW Tag Team belts; in a Three Way Dance, with tables, ladders, chairs, and canes, the Sandman defeated Steve Corino and Justin Credible to win the ECW Heavyweight Championship, only to lose it in a bout against Rhyno, and in a typical twenty-minute masterpiece, Rob Van Dam pinned Jerry Lynn.

Five days later, ECW held its last TV taping in Poplar Bluff, Missouri, and a few weeks later, the last ECW show took place in Pine Bluff, Arkansas. Even at the end, with no prospects for another Pay-Per-View or anything beyond this show, some wrestlers believed Heyman would find a way to save the promotion.

"Everyone assumed it would just be a hiatus, that Paul was getting a new TV deal or something," Mike Nova says. "After the show was over, we were all in the ring, toasting each other with beer. I knew I would never see half of those people again. I had hoped that that would not be the case. But the vibes were there that it was."

The next Pay-Per-View was scheduled for March 11, but it never happened. On April 4, 2001, ECW filed for bankruptcy, and this supernova that had crossed the entertainment sky in the 1990s had flamed out.

There has been much debate about why ECW did flame out.

"I think ECW, unfortunately, got to the point where it was enough of a threat to WCW and WWE to be noticed and worried about," Lance Storm says. "It got to the point where Paul had to offer us enough money to keep us from jumping. Unfortunately, he couldn't afford it. ECW had gotten bigger than an indy, but it wasn't quite the big leagues yet. There was this big void that it had to jump over. You couldn't just bump the pay scale up a little bit. You had to jump all the way, and I think it was too much of a jump. Had he had some degree of immunity, and he could have taken smaller steps, I think he could have taken it all the way to the top. But it was too big a step to make in a short time."

Announcer Joey Styles said he didn't believe it was the TV contract that put ECW in the grave. It was the bidding for talent, and the timing of finally getting on a national stage. "I don't blame the TV contract for the company failing," Styles says. "Financially, everyone was being paid too much money. All of the top ECW guys could have gone to WCW and WWE and made more money, and some of them did. So Paul Heyman was forced to pay close to what they would have been paid to go somewhere else. Paul signed all these contracts, and also assumed that, being on national TV, revenues would grow, as would merchandise sales and DVD sales to cover expenses. But it took too long to get on the national stage. By the time we did, ECW looked like a poor man's version of WWE. The product, at that point, didn't matter anymore. We had lost a lot of our top stars to WWE and WCW. ECW was a shell of what it had been. It had nothing left. It was time for ECW to end. ECW needed to be on national TV five years earlier, and it didn't happen."

Mick Foley also believes that the promotion was past its prime when it did finally emerge as a national presence. "When people think about the glory days of ECW, they usually go back to when Funk was there and I was there," he says. "But at that point we were barely out of Pennsylvania. By the time ECW became popular, they were like yesterday's news. For a few years, they drew really well, but it was almost like it was off the aura and reputation they had already earned. Which isn't to say the guys weren't really working hard and having great matches and giving fans what they wanted. But it seems like their reputation was built up by guys who were scooped up in large part by WCW—and in my case by WWE. But I think the talent raids hurt."

Tazz was one of those wrestlers who left, and he, too, believes it was the talent exodus that killed the promotion. "Talent getting opportunities to leave hurt ECW immensely," he says. "You can't fault other companies. At the time, it was a wrestlers' market. You had three different companies to work for that were doing pretty well. Wrestlers had leverage, and this was a business. Guys like Paul Heyman will let you know that all the time, that it is a business. Some say WCW raided the locker room, but I don't know if they raided the locker room. They just made offers to try to get guys whenever they could, so that WWE couldn't get them."

Bubba Ray Dudley, who had been involved in much of the business side of ECW in the final years, believes two factors contributed to the downfall of ECW. "It was an ultraviolent company that had its niche. Some people wanted to see it, but I don't think ECW would have ever appealed to the masses, because it was too violent. The other thing was that Paulie wasn't the best businessman, beyond the wrestling ring."

Heyman claims while all of those other problems may have been symptoms of what led to ECW's demise, he believes there was one reason why ECW isn't still around today—a dispute between him and In-Demand Pay-Per-View over payments due. "The reason for the death of Extreme Championship Wrestling was because of an executive on the West Coast named Dan York, a senior vice president at In-Demand, who refused to pay well over $1 million to ECW that was back-owed to us over a year," he says. "This was the delay game that In-Demand was doing. What they were doing, and what [boxing promoter] Bob Arum sued them over, was the fact that they promised in their contracts that within one year of your event you will get a final settlement and final estimated settlement, even if they don't get the money. They have to collect it from the local cable companies. What was happening was they were eighteen to twenty-one months behind on their payments. I needed the money to survive. I had lost my network. Dan York said, 'No. You will have to sue us, and if you sue us, we will take you off the air.' At least with that money, we could have kept the door open and regrouped."

As far as the references to his business practices, Heyman says he doubts anyone else could have kept ECW afloat for as long as he did. "When ECW was over, the total indebtedness of the company was $7 million, and $4 million of that was owed to my parents. So the indebtedness of ECW was really $3 million to outside vendors. We never had any money to float. Three million dollars, of which over $1.5 million came back to us in the bankruptcy negotiations with In-Demand. You are looking at a company that in seven years ran up a bill of $4.5 million, of which the majority of that money came in the last 18 months, a direct result of our terrible relationship with TNN. There were other promotions that lost a lot more—WCW lost $85 million—and we never had any financing. We were built from scratch

"Also, in the single most hypercompetitive era in the history of the industry, we survived for seven years. Nobody else could have done that. As for business acumen, nobody would have survived the wars that I got them through, or gotten the right players and the right pieces. Who could see the TNN deal coming? Nobody. Who would have survived all these things? We survived for a year and a half after going on TNN, and that was our death knell. Did I prematurely cause the death of the pop culture phenomenon that I created? No, I think it is a false notion."

Perhaps it it best left to the conscience of ECW, Tommy Dreamer, who may have loved the promotion more than anyone and who stayed until the end, often without getting paid, to summarize the rise and fall of ECW and what it meant to the wrestling industry.

"The bottom line is that ECW changed the face of professional wrestling," Dreamer says. "We didn't get the financial rewards that we should have. We were responsible for the 'Attitude Era.' And we were responsible for anything that could happen on *Raw* when we invaded, when WWE was getting their ass kicked by WCW in the ratings. That whole 'Attitude Era' was all stuff that we were doing and they were just copying it. They were making millions, while we were struggling. ECW, four and a half years *after* it went out of business, people are still clamoring for it. Every time I walked out, people never let me forget ECW. I was probably involved in most of the big moments. I was a fan. I wanted to give, and still do, what the fans want to see. I don't think the business, as a whole, would have boomed without ECW, and we never got the credit we deserved. Chris Benoit, Dean Malenko, Eddie Guerrero would have never had jobs in the industry if it wasn't for ECW. Stone Cold wouldn't have learned how to talk. Rey Mysterio would have never come to the States. It was a lot of guys who gave their hearts and souls to the company. As much as guys wanted to complain about Paul not paying people, most of us stood by him because we loved the product so much. It was our choice to come to work and not get paid. I don't know how many people would do that here [WWE], if Vince couldn't make payroll for one week. I worked for six months without getting paid. I broke my neck and my back and continued working because the show needed me.

"If you go back, and they talk about it here at the first *Wrestle-Mania*, and look at Vince McMahon's face, he put everything on the line on that one Pay-Per-View, and it paid off for him," Dreamer says. "That was me every single day. And Paul. Every show was at that time make-or-break, and it was always for the show.

"We were so close. It was heartbreaking how close we were."

chapter ten

The Passion of ECW

There were so many factors that helped to make ECW rise in the entertainment industry—the right location, the right performers, the right fans, and the right mastermind. Without any of these, ECW may never have had the success it enjoyed. Here, in their own words, are the creators, performers, fans, and others who all contributed to the uniqueness of ECW.

The ECW Arena, Locker Room, and Wrestlers

Joey Styles: "The arena was a second home to me. I had been there so many times. It was a real dive when we worked there, but it was home. There was something about it that you cannot understand if

you weren't there for an ECW event. Nothing can accurately describe or convey the family atmosphere that we were all in on a secret that the world wasn't ready for—a great big wrestling party."

Pee Wee Moore: "Sandman was one of the comedians in the locker room, but everyone kept the place loose. The crowd was loose and everyone knew each other. There were some times when the checks were bouncing when some guys were strung out, but for the most part everyone had fun and joked around with each other. Everyone in the dressing room was cool, because they knew ECW wasn't a place to get rich. It was a place to get noticed so you could get that contract. So there wasn't a lot of backstabbing. I don't recall a lot of tension, other than when the money got tight.

"The ECW Arena was the nucleus of ECW. If you could get over in the building, you could go to Grand Rapids, Michigan, and people would like you. But if you got booed in that building, and went to Grand Rapids, the people would hate you. Philly set the tone, then later the New York crowd got hot, too, and they helped set the tone. But there is no question that the Philly crowd was very intense, and knew their wrestling. The crowd dictated a lot of guys getting jobs."

Tazz: "The ECW Arena was brutal. We didn't have air conditioning. There was no locker room facility, it was like a big storage area. They used to keep stuff from the Mummers Parade there, floats from the parade, and that was our locker room. And in the winter, it got cold as hell, and all we had was this football sideline heater that at times blew fire, and that would heat up the backstage area. It was in the middle of the locker room, and it could burn you. That is what ECW was. It wasn't pretty.

"One of the big things for me about WWE was that you could take a shower after the matches, and there was a real locker room where you could chill out. But as time goes on, I miss those seedy locker rooms and rough conditions, because it was the product in the ring that really mattered, and not how fancy the locker room was. I miss it now. They were great moments, and it was a great place to work. It was blue collar and rough-edged."

Mike Awesome: "The atmosphere in the ECW locker room was the best I have ever experienced in the business. It was like everyone got along, and those that didn't just stayed away from each other. Everyone was hungry, and people were willing to do anything to make it. They would put their bodies on the line and not get paid and get screwed over and still be cheerful and happy about it. That is the way it was."

Tommy Dreamer: "We had incidents where fans would try to cross the line and prove they were tough, but we would beat the fans up. We would have old-school riots. I remember Balls Mahoney fell over the top rope and was leaning against the guardrail. A fan punched him in the face. Balls looked up and he punched him again. By that time, the wrestlers came running out and we had a huge fight with him and his friends. Everyone started fighting. They called in the SWAT police and dogs. There was a time when the locker room would clear and we would lay out everybody. There was one time when a bunch of state troopers who were drunk at a show and pulled guns out and put them in our faces. We were truly the crazed rebels."

Al Snow: "One time we are in a spot show in Pennsylvania, and a good example of the comradery in the locker room, Meanie and Nova and I forget who else, they were doing the bWo, and they were in the ring doing the YMCA routine. I am looking through the curtain, and see that the entire building is doing the YMCA dance. I turn around, and everyone in the locker room is doing it, too. There is Big Dick Dudley, Bubba, D-Von, Shane, everyone but Tazz, of course, all doing the YMCA dance, Balls Mahoney, Axl, singing it along with the crowd, and it cracked me up. You didn't see that anywhere else. The boys were geniune fans of the business and of the company and what we were doing, as the fans were."

Francine: "The best part for me was to work with people who became my extended family. It was never really a job for me. I enjoyed going to work. It was like, 'Hey, I get to perform for fifteen minutes and then hang out with my friends.' There was never a moment where I dreaded going. I knew guys from WCW and WWE and they all say that there has never been a locker room that they heard of like ECW was. I am going on my twelfth year in the business now and have worked a lot of locker rooms, and there will never be a locker room like that one.

"There were a lot of girls that came through that door who quickly walked out. I was there for seven years. You had to love the business and appreciate wrestling. The girls that stuck it out proved themselves. We took the bumps and were dedicated to the sport."

Mick Foley: "It was incredibly hot, and the fans were incredibly passionate, and pretty knowledgeable as far as fans knowing their product. The fans were far more passionate than WCW and what I had been used to. I guess I had a love-hate relationship with the fans there. I loved the fact that they knew their wrestling and that they were so diehard in their love for it. But I hated them in the sense that

they really expected a lot out of the wrestlers, physically and emotionally, and they weren't very forgiving when it came to human error. As a guy who knew how much punishment the human body could take, I felt fans were encouraging guys to push themselves past that limit. But they also, in some cases, could appreciate a well-done scientific match."

Spike Dudley: "I've been in a lot of riots. It wasn't that uncommon that there would be a big fight and the cops would show up. Generally when all-out chaos broke out, I wouldn't go out for them. Generally, our guys in Atlas Security would do just fine. I would not go out unless I heard a wrestler was down or something like that. I was involved in a number of them, and it was scary. I trusted our security guards.

"There was always some idiot taking a cheap shot. I was scared sometimes. I had stuff thrown at me, shots taken at me. But it would be one fucking asshole, out of a group of great fans. I was hit with batteries, golf balls. One time I was going through the crowd, slapping hands with everyone, and one guy just flat-out punched me in the face. I was just doing my entry. But that is not just ECW. That happens in all of wrestling, and always has. They had more opportunities for that in ECW because we were so involved with the crowd."

Mike Bucci: "I remember the huge brawl outside the ECW Arena, when one of those guys from the Mummers Parade took a swing at Sunny and Chris Candido. This is after a show one night. Next thing I know bodies are flying everywhere. It was on."

It was never so "on" as it was one day in Los Angeles in 2000, when ECW was running a Pay-Per-View and clashed with a small wrestling promotion there called XPW—Xtreme Pro Wrestling. A group of XPW Wrestlers threatened to sabotage the ECW event, and showed up at the Pay-Per-View wearing XPW shirts. This was not like WWE invading or some other promotion. This was an unwelcome intrusion. They were seated ringside, and a fight broke out in the arena between XPW and ECW wrestlers. It spilled out into the parking lot, and eventually, the police were called.

Mike "Nova" Bucci: "I was in the back in a sound booth, doing voiceovers, when that went down. I saw Paul, with his hat turned around, throw his headset down and storm out of the arena. When everybody went outside, it was like the OK Corral gunfight. We were on one side of the street. They were on the other side of the street. I don't know who blinked first, but I know who blinked last. Then they went on the Internet and complained about their injuries.

"The XPW thing in Los Angeles was such a defining moment. It rallied the company. We went outside and said, 'You motherfuckers.' Paul Heyman was leading the charge. The company that fought together went out of business together."

Security guard Joe Wilchak: "We were told to watch them at the show to see what they were going to do when they showed up. If they had tickets, we couldn't refuse them the right to come in. They showed up and promised they weren't going to do anything. Everything was going pretty good. But at the start of the main event—they were sitting in the front row—they started doing some stuff, put the shirts on for the company they were with, and we stopped them from doing that because we were waiting for it. The boys in the back emptied out of the locker room, and we thought we were going to have a riot. The ECW guys were serious about not having their work used by another company. We ended up pushing them out into the street in front of the building, and a bunch of the boys came outside and it then did turn into a big fight in the street. Typical of a fight, it lasted about a minute or minute and a half and broke up. Then it erupted again for another minute or two. Then it was all over, and both sides separated.

"What was funny was there were four LAPD officers in the area when this fight was going on. They were just watching. I'm sure they thought it was part of the show. When everyone fought for the second time, at that point they started to realize this was real. It wasn't part of the show. Just as it was breaking up, I was on the end of a line trying to get our guys back into the building. One guy came up next to me with his riot baton out and yelled, 'I want all of you in that building in ten seconds or I am going to call the paddy wagon and you're all going to jail.' He was so wound up and ready for a big confrontation, and I said to him, 'The doors are locked. Can you call somebody inside to unlock the doors, and we are out of here.' He called and the doors opened up and everyone went back inside."

The Fans

The fans were indeed a big part of the ECW experience, almost like interactive wrestling.

Sandman: "The people made the building, the building didn't make the people. Those people were part of the show. I get goose bumps thinking about it."

Tazz: "The fans love ECW. This passion they have for the product and the talent is remarkable. It is like a cult. Those who are narrow-minded think it is limited to Philadelphia and New York. I've done a show in Wichita, Kansas, and gotten out of a rent-a-car about six months ago, at an arena for *SmackDown!*, and there were people chanting for ECW. I've heard it in Canada, London, everywhere. Sure, New York and Philly were probably our strongest fan base, and, hey, if that is true, that's not bad, because they are two of the strongest markets in the country. The fans are so wicked passionate. There is a bond. They are the twelfth man. They are a huge part of the event, and if you don't want them to be, they will make sure that they are. You don't have a choice. They have to be part of it. And it really motivates the wrestlers. When you wrestled at ECW, the pressure was on, because the fans were so tough, especially in Philly and New York.

"But you could not let the crowd control the match. As much as I respected the fans, I think the fans respected the Tazz character, also. Heck, they respected all the guys. Respect was a big thing. The fans wanted you to earn it. We gave them great shows and great moments, but the fans were tough on guys sometimes."

Ron Buffone: "We had a very loyal fan base. Fans loved the product, loved the fact that our wrestlers worked very hard, loved the fact that we never duped them. When a spot got messed up, the fans would chant, 'You fucked up, you fucked up.' We never lied to the fans. Let's say if a guy broke his neck or hurt himself, we would come out and say so. Paul would walk out to the fans and talk to them. When Sabu didn't make a show, Paul came out and told the fans, Sabu chose instead an event in Japan. So fuck Sabu. And that is where the 'Fuck Sabu' chant started. We always dealt with our fans straight, and they respected us for it.

"The fans were as much a part of ECW as anything else. Being at a live ECW event was amazing, to be part of that crowd, with the chants and all that. No fans ever chanted in wrestling before ECW fans did. When we counted down before a show, 5, 4, 3, 2, 1, and the fans then knew right on 2, they started chanting ECW in such a loud, unified voice. You can still hear fans chanting at matches: 'ECW! ECW!'"

Lance Storm: "Your first time in, fans are pretty hard on you. They felt like it was their show, and that you didn't belong, and you really had to earn your stripes, so to speak. But they appreciated and loved the wrestling, as long as you were willing to work hard, they were willing to accept you. It didn't take long for that to happen there, and it was great, a real intimate relationship. They loved the sport as much as we did, and it was fun."

Mike Nova: "I remember full-blown riots, whether it was the Dudleyz with the fans or something happened at the end of the show, and it was audience-interactive, so to speak. The cops would get called in. I remember Tracy Smothers coming out of the shower with soap in his hair and a towel on, with no shoes, and there are cops everywhere, and he nearly started throwing punches at a German shepherd that a cop had on a leash. Tracy was going to fight it.

"I remember the cops in Staten Island came one night because Big Dick Dudley, God rest his soul, supposedly hit someone in the front row of the audience. It was always one of those things where you never knew who hit who first or who did what first. Sometimes a powder keg only needs a small spark, and it was on.

"The single most important part of ECW was the fan base. Without the fans, we would have been a movie with no one to watch. The fans made the impossible possible. If you were never in the ECW Arena for a show, then it is like you were never in the Colosseum in Rome. You'll never know what it was like. That is probably the closest thing to it. You would do anything for that cheer—dive out of the sky, land on the concrete, get beat to death. You thought you were invincible. The chants, 'Where's my pizza,' or, 'You fucked up,' they knew what was going on. These people were outside that arena at two in the afternoon, barbecuing or freezing or whatever. If you could get over in front of those guys, you accomplished something. And they let you know if they liked you or didn't like you. If you worked hard, you won them over."

Blue Meanie: "At the time ECW came along, a lot of wrestling fans were frustrated. WWE was gearing itself more toward children and becoming cartoonish. The characters became so unbelievable, it was hard to take seriously and be proud of something. It was the time of the unknown wrestling fans, when they wanted to put bags on their heads. They watched it, but they wouldn't talk about it in public. Then ECW came along and changed everything. It wasn't just the blood and guts. It was the attitude. Philadelphia had an attitude anyway, throwing snowballs at Santa Claus and all that. Philly fans have that edge, and if something sucks, they'll let you know about it. Fans were looking for an alternative at the time. ECW had an edginess that they could latch on it, and Philly fans took it as their promotion in their town. In many ways it was like fans who went to see *The Rocky Horror Picture Show*. Fans were smart to the business, but they were willing to put some of that aside, to enjoy the story lines and suspend their own disbeliefs."

Al Snow: "One night we had a riot in Plymouth Meeting, Pennsylvania, with about twenty-five cop cars, police dogs, fans fighting with the wrestlers. The Dudleyz had incited it. Bubba would get on the microphone and cuss them out for a half hour, and get the fans so hot that they finally just snapped. There were several times when the fans would go after the Dudleyz, and the Dudleyz would go after them, and the fans would jump in and the wrestlers would come out of the locker room.

"I remember one night at the ECW Arena. Bam Bam Bigelow took Spike Dudley, pressed him over his head, and threw him into the crowd. At a normal wrestling event, the crowd would have just spread out and let him hit the concrete. They caught him and then bodysurfed him around the building."

Spike Dudley: "I had beaten Bam Bam the week before on TV. At this point I was on my own. Bubba had turned on me, and he and D-Von were doing their tag-tag thing. I was the guy who was getting the crap beat out of him. I wasn't getting any wins. I wasn't involved in any angles. Bam Bam Bigelow comes in, and he joins with Shane Douglas and Chris Candido, as the Triple Threat, and without a doubt they are the most powerful force in ECW. So here he comes for your basic TV squash match, and out of the blue Spike Dudley beats Bam Bam Bigelow. The crowd went ballistic. The next week was a Pay-Per-View, and Bam Bam demanded his revenge, and his revenge was that he beat the shit out of me and tossed me into the crowd. Everyone remembers the toss in the crowd, but the story behind it was what made it so great. I wish people would remember the angle as much as they remember the spot. But it was a cool moment. When they surfed me around, that was a pretty cool moment. They were really into it. The fans were such a big part of the show."

Francine: "When Shane Douglas and I were at our peak, during our heel run, the fans would attack us—literally. I couldn't tell you how many times I have been punched, or my dress was torn. It was bad. There would be times going up the aisle where a hand would sneak through. People would grab at my breasts. I got punched in the head one time. I was called names. We were heels. You are supposed to hate us. But when you touch us, that is going over the line. We were there to entertain you. It was disrespectful. We were putting our bodies on the line for them. We were attacked a lot. There were a few times where we had to have people escort us to our cars. It was crazy. There were quite a few times where I was scared to go from the dressing room to the car. Sometimes we would just sprint for our cars and hope that no one would come after us."

Tommy Dreamer: "In the early days of ECW, we used to have Bring Your Own Weapons matches, where fans would bring their own weapons, and no matter what they brought in, we would use it. We used to do this thing where the fans would hold on to their chairs, and I would take the guy's head and keep ramming it and the fans would hold it, and I would be knocking down fans. They were part of the show."

Chris Benoit: "Every show that we did at the arena, you would see just about the same people in the same seats."

Rob Van Dam: "The energy that two thousand people had would fill the arena like twenty thousand people. You looked at the crowd, and almost everybody was wearing a black T-shirt. They looked more like the crowd that would be at a rock 'n' roll concert screaming their heads off. They would be waiting for a wrestler to slip up, so they

could yell, 'You f-ed up, you f-ed up.' The fans actually had their own fans. Fans that sat in the front row at the Philly ECW Arena dressed the same way every time. You would always see Hat Guy, the guy with the straw hat."

There were some fans, like Sign Guy, Hawaiian Shirt Guy, Hat Guy, and Faith No More Guy, who became celebrities themselves. But most of the fans were just young, testosterone-filled men who passionately loved ECW, and took away memories from the promotion that will last a lifetime.

John Pollock: "I'm from Philadelphia, and saw some ECW shows here and there until 1994, and always liked it. Around early 1995 they introduced some new characters and it was going in a different direction, and around January 1995 I started watching every week. I was about 14 then. From 1994 to 1996 I went to a handful of shows, and when I was old enough to drive, from late 1996 until the end of the company, I probably missed only a handful of shows. I was at most every one at that point.

"When I went to my first show live, it was not like anything I had ever seen before. I had grown up a WCW and WWE fan, and it was the smiling babyface guy and the generic heel. It was more of the same. Then you had this new company that was completely changing everything about wrestling. I never knew wrestling could be like that. They had more realistic characters, more realistic story lines, current events used in those stories, and great music. It was so cutting edge and different than anything that was going on.

"I would show ECW to my friends and they would say, 'Oh my God.' It was incredible. As far as wrestling, going to ECW Arena was the best time of my life. I never had as much fun in wrestling than I did at the arena. I'll probably remember those times when I'm 80 years old, if I am still alive.

"The Sabu-Tazz faceoff in *November to Remember 1996* was amazing. They were doing this angle where Tazz was calling out Sabu, and Sabu wasn't answering. This went on for a while. Every match Tazz would get on the mike and call Sabu out, but Tazz and Sabu would never meet each other. In *November to Remember* they did an angle where Tazz beat up Tod Gordon, and Tazz grabbed the mike and was running down Sabu. Then the lights went out. Then they came back on, and Sabu was standing in the ring. The place went nuts. It was unreal.

"The return of the Sandman was a great moment. He had been gone for a year, going to WCW, and came back in a surprise at the end of a show. They turned the lights out, and then turned them back on, and Sandman was up in the rafters. There were people crying at that angle. They were so happy he was back. And this is an arena full of guys you would find in a biker bar. You saw guys with beards and tattoos crying because the Sandman was back.

"I never left an arena show thinking that I didn't get my money's worth. If anything, I felt that I paid too little for a ticket. I would have paid triple what I was paying.

"The wrestlers just seemed more real in ECW, not movie characters. Guys would come out and sign things, hang out with fans before the show. Now the fans were very demanding at times. But it was like a family atmosphere. Every fan there knew they were part of something special, wrestling-wise. There will never be another company like that again. They caught lightning in the bottle for seven years or so. It was the right place, the right city, the right wrestlers, and the right time for it. I don't know if it will ever be duplicated in my lifetime again.

"I was in Club ECW, a special fans list. If you buy tickets in advance for the next four shows, you could get in early through a special entrance. I think they did that in 1998. The shows would start at eight at night. We used to get there at two in the afternoon, and there would already be two hundred people lined up waiting. One time we got in line early, this fat guy, about 300 pounds, takes his shirt off and starts charging people $1 to go up to him and give him a little Ric Flair chop. If somebody did that at a WWE event, one or two might take him up on it and the rest of the people would back off. Well, this guy must have had fifty people waiting in line to take a chop at him.

His chest was beat raw by the time they were done. And it was about 20 degrees outside that day.

"The same people would always be at the shows. There was this one guy we used to call Team Tazz Guy, because he always wore a Tazz shirt. He would show up before the show, and this guy was about 6 feet and maybe 140 pounds, and he would stomp around in the parking lot like he was going to beat somebody up before every show. He was the most animated fan I had ever seen. As soon as we would get there, we would see where this guy was sitting and just watch him for a while, because he was so funny."

Paul Carboni: "I was a diehard wrestling fan growing up. One time I caught ECW on SportsChannel Philadelphia, and went to my first show in December 1994. I think it was the debut of Stevie Richards. He fought JT Smith. Shane Douglas had declared himself ECW World Champion three months earlier. He had started the campaign against Ric Flair. I remember 911 chokeslammed two Japanese guys, dressed in all white with white hats. That was an ECW promo intro video for years. It was at a high school gymnasium. Tazz was doing his Tazmaniac gimmick. And Jason, the sexiest man alive, he was managing the Pitbulls at the time. That was my first ECW live show.

"I remember the television program was so edgy. They did a thing where Shane Douglas piledrove Sensational Sherry, and the pop that he got. He was doing the 'it is cool to be a heel' gimmick two years before Steve Austin was doing it mainstream. Shane Douglas, one time, in the television program, did more or less an hour-long history of wrestling, and he downplayed all of them, Bruno Sammartino, Ric Flair, Hulk Hogan. This was a guy who was just carving his own niche in the industry. It was incredible. It was this long rant, but it was coherent and made a lot of sense, on how the industry was about to change, and he was totally right. I was captivated by the athleticism of Benoit, Jericho, Guerrero, all the international talent they brought in. That made me think this was the next big thing. When you are a 14-year-old kid, and they are bleeping words out, something you wouldn't hear on WCW or WWE, it had such a profound effect.

"I was at the ECW Arena in February 1996 for *Cyberslam*. I was going to get a slice of pizza, and the lights went out. When they came back on, Brian Pillman was standing in the ring. He cut a really wicked promo. He was doing this gimmick where he was the loose cannon, and you were supposed to believe that he was still under contract to WCW—it was called a work shoot, where it was fake, but you were led to believe it was real. He was chased from the arena by Shane Douglas. Later on that night, when the show was over, I saw Pillman in the parking lot, and I was egging him on. I was a 15-year-old fan, and he came after me, and he scared the shit out of me. He probably wouldn't have done anything.

"In August 1999, the Dudley Boyz has just signed their contract with the WWE. This was their last show. The fans had a real bad reputation for being hard on the wrestlers that were leaving, and this was at the point where the Dudleyz had an edgy gimmick where they were egging the fans on. They would curse at you and get really bad.

The fans started throwing things at them. We were ducking down because bottles and cans were flying, and my buddy poked his head up to see what was happening, because it was mayhem, and Bubba Ray Dudley had a bottle of blue Powerade, and threw it back in the crowd. Just as my friend poked his head up, he was hit in the forehead by the bottle of Powerade, and fell off the bleachers. Things like that, the crowd interaction, was surreal.

"Everyone knows the code of the business, that the wrestler can't touch a fan and vice versa. The Dudleyz would come out month after month after month, and say the most vulgar, terrible things into the microphone. They would pick out one or two people from the crowd, and you literally thought they were going to hop the guardrail and take a swing at the fans. As smart as we all were, they made you suspend your disbelief because they were so good at inciting the crowd.

"Terry Funk and Shane Douglas were fighting in a sixty-minute Iron Man match once at the arena. It was the main event. It was fifty minutes into a sixty-minute match. There hadn't been any pinfalls yet. The place was going nuts, and everybody was on their feet. A guy brought his girlfriend to the show, and she just drops. She faints from the heat. Another person looked over at the guy, and said, 'Yo, man, your girlfriend just fell over. I think you better take care of her.' The guy looked at his girlfriend on the ground, lying in a heap, and said, 'Fuck her, this is Shane Douglas and Terry Funk. She'll be all right. Give her ten minutes.' And he watched the rest of his match and didn't help his girlfriend."

Security guard Joe Wilchak: "Before the show, we would see the people in line. Coming into the show, we would check them out, their bags, and check for weapons. We even took the tickets half the time. We got to know people and would talk to them. They get to know who you are. There were times when we had to get pretty physical, and we developed a reputation that you don't mess with the guys with the black suits [Atlas Security].

"It would always amaze me sometimes when we would have problems with people in one show, and we would come back to that area again, and the same guys would say to us, 'Yeah, you whipped my ass the last time you were here.' It was great. They thought it made them part of the show. Even if it got a little rough, people didn't think they were getting beat up. They thought it was part of the show.

"The worst fans encounter was in Harrisburg, Pennsylvania, at the Farm Show Arena. The promoter there had wooden folding chairs. They used to sometimes have different guys help them do the promotions in different areas. On this night, the Dudleyz got everyone riled up, like they always did, and this was a time when everyone was throwing things into the ring—it was acceptable at the time. Well, the wooden chairs started flying. That was really dangerous. People were getting hit with chairs. You just get in the middle, try to see where the main problem is, and break that up, and the rest kind of dissipates on its own. A year later I was at a mall in Harrisburg. That same promoter had an autograph signing with Edge. A kid came up to me and talked to me for about forty minutes. He was waiting in line for an autograph. Finally, he said, 'Can I shake your hand?' I said, 'Sure.' I shook the guy's hand. And he said, 'I had to shake your hand. You really kicked my ass at the Farm Show Arena last year. Remember with the chairs? You whipped the shit out of me. It was great.' That was a typical reaction. I'm sure in their minds it was bigger than it really was, because usually you are just grabbing guys and dragging them out. For some reason, it is some great triumph for them.

"The Dudleyz were the ones who got the crowd riled up the most. Bubba could really incite people when he got on the microphone. They were pretty wild, and they would laugh, and they just liked to see if they could get the crowd going. We had a good relationship with everyone. They would play with us like they did with each other, with the practical jokes and things.

"The worst was in Columbia, South Carolina. It was a building with a stage, and there was grandstand seating. It wasn't very big. The people would get riled up and come down out of the bleachers and up to the rail, trying to push the rail back to get at them, and we used to have to hold them back. And D-Von would be in the ring laughing. But that is what our jobs were.

"The crowds, for the most part, knew how much they could be involved and what they could do. They had their part in the show. The theatrics the fans would do were as much a part of the show as anything. They knew how far they could push it without going over the line and have something happen, except when large amounts of alcohol were involved. But even then, it was a lot of fun.

"Once I hyperextended my elbow. Spike Dudley was getting thrown out of the ring and into the crowd. We were supposed to be in the area to make sure nothing happened. I reached over the rail as Spike came down into the crowd and he landed on my elbow, and I hyperextended it. But that was a dumb move by me. I didn't know Spike would be doing stuff like that for the next five years. He knew what he was doing. I didn't.

"The Dudleyz came in for the main event, and I am trying to hold the crowd off with one arm. Then Big Dick Dudley got arrested. I think someone threw something in the ring and hit one of them, and Big Dick caught the guy in the door as he was going out, and Big Dick wound up getting arrested. It was at the Sportsplex in Staten Island."

ECW fans had their own familiar chants they would use for certain situations or specific wrestlers. Here are the ones most often heard:

"E-C-W"—when fans felt an extreme or hardcore move was used that warranted recognition.

"Oh my God"—a tribute to announcer Joey Styles's signature call during a big moment in a bout.

"Sit the fuck down"—used when fans would be standing up when the rest of the crowd would be sitting down.

"Shut the fuck up"—chanted when a heel wrestler talked too much against a babyface wrestler or against ECW during a promo or shoot interview.

"Sweep it up, asshole, sweep it up"—chanted when someone swept up debris from the ring.

"This match rules" or "This is awesome"—yelled when fans are really entertained by a match.

"Philly sucks"—New York fans would shout this against Philadelphia fans in their competition as to who was more hardcore.

"Fuck New York"—the Philadelphia fans' defense against the attacks by New York fans in their feud over which group was more hardcore.

"This is brutal"—yelled when there were a lot of weapons used and blood spilled in a match.

"Holy shit"—fans would chant this when a wrestler used a move that could have seriously hurt them.

"The Whole Fucking Show"—a tribute to and nickname for Rob Van Dam.

"Tazz is gonna kill you"—the chant for opponents of Tazz.

"What's your name?"—fans would yell this at Bubba Ray Dudley, who supposedly suffered from a stuttering problem.

"She's a crack whore"—yelled at female valets.

"You fucked up"—chanted when a wrestler messed up a move and the fans recognized it.

"You sold out"—used to rip ECW wrestlers who were leaving the company.

"He/She's hardcore"—praise for a performer after a particularly violent act.

Paul Heyman

Al Snow: "Paul E. was a masterful manager of human relations. He would have his speeches before every show. You just felt like you were part of something. That is what the manager of a company is supposed to do, make you feel that it is as important to you as the company is to him. We all knew that a lot of the time Paul E. was lying, but we felt so good about it and how he made us feel about it. I never got totally swept up in the Kool-Aid speeches, but I would marvel at how good he was at getting everyone involved and swept up in it."

Bubba Ray Dudley: "Paul E. to me was the David Koresh of pro wrestling. He could talk his way into making you believe that great things were going to happen, and great things did happen. But Paul E. always made the grass seem greener. He brainwashed a lot of guys, but as a boss and as a businessman, he did what he had to do in order to get his wrestlers to perform on a certain level and carry out his story."

Pee Wee Moore: "I referreed at ECW for eight years, and saw everybody come and go. The thing that ECW did was they played to a hardcore audience, and they responded. WWE and WCW was all corporate. But ECW played to a different audience. ECW and Paul E. gave the fans exactly what they wanted. He knew exactly what they wanted to see, and that is why even when he lost wrestlers, he could still give the fans what they wanted. He was very good at what he did. I learned more from him than anybody. I used to watch him. He knew just what he wanted his people to do and what they had to do. I don't think any wrestling booker maybe in the history of wrestling knew the crowd better than Paul E."

D-Von Dudley: "Paul E. is a genius. A mastermind. A terrible businessman, but a genius and a mastermind in running a wrestling organization. If you could take ECW back then, when it was at its peak, and just give the creative part to Paul E., and give the financial part of it to WWE, the ECW would still be around. It was too much for one man to handle. It is the old Steve Austin saying, 'Don't trust anybody.' It's always been that way in this business. When you are running a company that was rising the way ECW was, it was hard to trust anybody with getting things done, getting things out. Paul E. had that attitude, that he wanted to do it on his own. It was a small company when Paul first took it over, and he was able to do it all. But as it started to grow, at that point he should have trusted other people to take some of the load off him. I think it burnt him out. Then came the bounced checks. But, a man took a no-name company and made it the third largest company in the business, and you can't put him down. If it wasn't for ECW and Paul Heyman, WWE attitude probably would not have existed."

Chris Jericho: "Paul is the master Machiavellian manipulator, and I say that with the utmost love in my heart for him. It is impossible to be mad at this guy. He is such a great motivator and such a positive guy. Behind the scenes at shows, he would have meetings and pump the guys up. There were guys in that locker room who would have killed for Paul, I'm sure. They almost killed themselves for him. He was also 100 percent full of shit, and if you knew that about him, it was easy to get along with him. As a booker and a story-line master, he could be one of the best I ever worked for. As far as organization for a promotion, I think he was in over his head.

"One time I got my ticket, and I was going with another Calgary wrestler named Johnny Smith. I called to change my seat, and the airline said, 'We got your seat, and we are very sorry about your brother-in-law.' I said, 'Excuse me?' They said, 'We're very sorry about your brother-in-law passing away.' I said, 'My brother-in-law, what are you talking about?' They said, 'Your bereavement fare. We're sorry your brother-in-law, Chris Benoit, passed away.' I said, 'Oh, my brother-in-law. I'm sorry, I've been so distraught over this whole thing, and I apologize.' This jackass waited so long to do this he bought a bereavement fare for me. So me and Johnny Smith were trying to figure out how we were related, if he was both of our brother-in-law. When I got to the arena, I told Paul E., 'Look, if you are going to book me on these kinds of fares, let me know about it first.' He said, 'Don't worry about it,' and he pulls out this big pad of hospital papers. He writes down, 'Thank you for allowing this fare to go,' and blah, blah, blah, and signed it Paul Heyman, M.D. Sometimes the airlines want to see a doctor's note for bereavement fares. So I had my signed Paul E. doctor's note just in case.

"But then you would show up for the match, and it would be the best time ever, and it was all worthwhile.

"The thing is, on the independent scene, which we all were at the time, if another promoter tried to pull that crap, you would say, 'Forget it, I'm not going, I don't need that hassle.' But with Paul E., it was just part of the deal. It gave you the right to work in ECW. That is how important it was to be there. That is how addictive and fun . . . That is how to describe ECW in one word—fun."

Spike Dudley: "It was a family. We weren't making the most money. Things were tight. When we traveled, we would have four or five guys in a rental car, and in a hotel room. We partied together, hung together. There was no office or headquarters. The office was Paulie. Most people would say it was the happiest time they had in wrestling, even when checks were bouncing. As long as we had a show, man, we were happy. It was a very special time and place."

What Was ECW?

Lance Storm: "I think a lot of people misunderstand what ECW was. They think it was just the blood and guts. What the difference was in ECW . . . I always looked at wrestling as art, and in ECW you were allowed to paint whatever picture you wanted, and if it would sell, you would succeed. In WCW and WWE, you were an artist for hire and you had to paint the pictures they were telling you to. That is why everyone loved ECW so much. As an artist, you were allowed to paint whatever picture you wanted. The fans appreciated it because they got to see everything. You had the Chris Benoits in there, and he just wrestled, that was what he did. You got to see the best wrestlers wrestle. Then you had the guys who wanted to throw a stick and land in barbed wire and bleed, and since that was what they wanted to do and were passionate about it, fans got to see that. They got to see an art gallery that had the best painters painting the pictures they wanted, instead of seeing artists for hire painting the pictures they were told to."

Al Snow: "Professional wrestling is an art form. It is not a science. The reason that *Mona Lisa* is in the Louvre is because it was painted with passion, an artistic expression. Paint-by-number pictures are not. In a lot of cases, nowadays, people are trying to control performances, but it has to be an expression. Paul E. would come to you and say, 'This is what I want.' Then it was up to you to do it, however you felt you needed to do it to get what you wanted, or to get yourself over. The other thing about ECW was the true, absolute comradery that we all had. It was amazing. At that point WWE was cutthroat. Morale was down. Business was bad. To go to ECW and watch everyone support each other and cheer on the other guy was great. You would do something good or get over really good, and then go back to the dressing room behind the curtain, and they would all be clapping. Everybody would appreciate what you just did. That was like night and day. This is the way it should be. Everybody there was trying to get everyone over, to put on a show that we all cared about. The guys were trying to put on the best show we could, from top to bottom. We wanted those people leaving saying, 'Damn, what a great show.'"

Joey Styles: "The one thing that we had in ECW was the us-against-them attitude. We always felt that WCW and WWE were constantly trying to put us out of business. So it was us against them, so you saw a lot less of the backbiting and the political maneuvering and the every-man-for-himself attitude that you see elsewhere in the sports entertainment industry. It was us against them, and we all put the company first."

Tazz: "ECW was built on an ethic. The word 'hardcore' is just a gimmick word. Hardcore wrestling wasn't violence and tables and blood. Hardcore wrestling was a work ethic. No matter if there were a hundred people in the seats or a thousand, you busted your ass. You worked hard, and that is what hardcore meant. To me, hardcore was a work ethic, our attitude. We were the little engine that could, and we did."

Paul Heyman: "In the 1980s there were thirty-seven full-time wrestling territories, and they all got wiped out by the McMahon expansion. The Memphis territory survived because they could always find someone to put up a few hundred grand, and then pay their wrestlers $25 a night. They would run shows with thirty people and make money because they wouldn't pay anybody and bilk investors. The Von Erichs went out of business, and that was a huge company. Bill Watts sold out to Jim Crockett. Jim Crockett sold out to Ted Turner. Verne Gagne went out of business. Stu Hart went out of business. All these territories went out of business. All that was left was Vince and Turner. The only way to compete with these giant companies was to be a giant company, and we weren't. We were a company that was strictly based on Paul Heyman's bookings. There was no budget, no advertising, no big pay scale, comparatively. The fan interaction was the story, and to this day still is. It was the most interactive form of sports entertainment that has ever happened.

"My two greatest inspirations for ECW can be boiled down to two instances in my life. I saw a lot of concerts when I was a kid. I saw a Led Zeppelin concert, and the audience would sing all the songs with them. Once I saw them when Jimmy Page was so high, I think he gave Keith Richards a run for his money. I don't think Jim Morrison was ever this high. He would do a guitar solo intro before every song. He took you on this mystical journey and no one would know what song they were doing until they were about two minutes into it. It was really crazy. There came a moment when they took down all the lights and put the spotlight right on Page. He looked out at the audience, and he never really spoke much to the audience—Plant usually did all the talking—he came up to the microphone and stood right next to Plant and said, 'Let me feel the room, man.' He put his hand up in the air. It was very staged, but you couldn't tell watching it. He takes his hand, puts it on the guitar, and right before he hits the first chord, he smiles at the audience and says, 'I feel it.' Then he perfectly hit the first few chords of 'Stairway to Heaven.' The place exploded. It was this magical moment. And he stopped playing, and smiled, and he soaked it in. And he kept doing this. The wave of the emotion was amazing.

"I thought, 'This is control, like nothing I have ever seen. He owns these people.' It was a religious experience.

"He got the moment. I wanted the whole ECW show to be that way. That whole thing with the Sandman's entrance, that is the Jimmy Page moment.

"The other inspiration is *The Rocky Horror Picture Show*. The way the audience interacted with the film creating its own good time.

"You take those two things and put them into wrestling, and you've got a hell of a show, even if your show sucks. I'm going to put on a show, and even if it sucks, people are going to think they had a great time. How could I go wrong? Not a lot of our shows sucked, but even if they did, no one ever walked away saying they had a horrible time."